GANDH
ASSASSIN

ADVANCE PRAISE FOR THE BOOK

'In *Gandhi's Assassin*, Dhirendra K. Jha has anatomized, with calm resourcefulness, the politics and psychology of a fanatic. He has also written a secret and sinister history of modern India—the one we need to understand our ruinous present'—Pankaj Mishra, author

'This book goes beyond the plot that resulted in Mahatma Gandhi's assassination, which the author meticulously analyses. It is indeed highly revealing of the omnipresence of the RSS on the Indian political scene in the 1940s. If the organization did not fight British colonialism and did not contest elections, it was intimately related to Savarkar's Hindu Mahasabha, the first Hindutva party, and, more importantly, organically linked to the Hindu Rashtra Dal, a militant body co-founded by Nathuram Godse—a man who, as Dhirendra K. Jha shows, never left the RSS'—Christophe Jaffrelot, research director, CERI, Sciences Po and CNRS, and Avantha Professor of Indian Politics and Society, King's India Institute

'Dhirendra Jha's book is not just a very readable and credible account of the plot and the people behind Gandhi's murder, including a psychological analysis of his assassin, but a comprehensive study of the wider politics of the Hindu Mahasabha, the RSS and their leaders, including Savarkar, which makes it a must-read and highly relevant in today's context'—Mridula Mukherjee, Professor, Modern Indian History (retired), Centre for Historical Studies, Jawaharlal Nehru University

GANDHI'S ASSASSIN

THE MAKING OF NATHURAM GODSE AND HIS IDEA OF INDIA

DHIRENDRA K. JHA

London • New York

First published in the UK and US by Verso 2023

1 3 5 7 9 10 8 6 4 2

Verso
UK: 6 Meard Street, London W1F 0EG
US: 388 Atlantic Avenue, Brooklyn, NY 11217
versobooks.com

Verso is the imprint of New Left Books

ISBN-13: 978-1-80429-297-6
ISBN-13: 978-1-80429-298-3 (UK EBK)
ISBN-13: 978-1-80429-299-0 (US EBK)

British Library Cataloguing in Publication Data
A catalogue record for this book is available from the British Library

Library of Congress Cataloging-in-Publication Data
A catalog record for this book is available from the Library of Congress

Contents

Preface

Nathuram Godse, the man who killed Mahatma Gandhi, came to notoriety out of nowhere. The Indian state and the people at large knew remarkably little about him when the murder shook the world on 30 January 1948. Within the network of Hindu communal politics to which he belonged, he hardly occupied a place of great significance. Yet by wielding the gun on Gandhi he, previously a small-time hothead, became a historical figure representing the antithesis of the Mahatma.

After the murder, it became a commonplace to trace the sources of Godse's motivation to the communal politics that swept through much of the country during the 1940s and peaked after Partition in August 1947 in the year of independence. The period began with immense anxieties about the impending division and culminated in the communal frenzy and massacre that accompanied the creation of two independent states—Muslim-majority Pakistan and Hindu-majority India.

This period, of course, was a crucial influence on Godse. But the plot to kill Gandhi was a manifestation of something else as well. More deeply rooted and enduring than anything arising from the specific circumstances of the times, it was a manifestation of—and a desperate attempt to resolve—what might be described as a battle for the soul of India, an anxious and long-standing struggle to define the emerging nation state.

For almost a quarter of a century, one side saw the other as a bitter enemy. Hindu supremacists treasured the subcontinent as a site of a unique religious ethos. They therefore sought to impose Hindu principles over a nation that, under the stewardship of nationalists pursuing the agenda of self-rule and Indian independence, was being steered towards secular democracy. These conflicting ideas of national identity, along with Godse's own desire to represent fully the forces to which he belonged, constitute an extraordinary background to his life through the last quarter of British rule in India.

The story is compelling even where it does not touch upon Godse at all. Discourses generated and emotions provoked outside his limited area of operation—often by exponents of the ideology of Hindu Rashtra (or state)—had profound consequences not only for Godse but for the entire political spectrum.

Godse's worldview owed much to his upbringing in a traditional elite-caste Hindu family, and it was rooted, too, in the desire of a section of Maharashtrian Brahmins to revive their political dominion. The generation to which he belonged grew up just when this revivalist leadership was getting inspired by European dictatorships. The influence of Italy and Germany stoked in Godse, as in many other Maharashtrian Brahmin youths, a transforming vision of Hindu communal ambition and a religious faith in its eventual victory.

In fact, at the time Godse became a young adult, he found himself caught by two contrasting and conflicting ideas—liberal ideas about modern, secular national identity and Brahmin ideas about faith-based political identity. For a while he oscillated and then settled for the latter, influenced at every critical juncture by men belonging to his own caste. These men, in fact, were so important in his life that there was hardly any room for women in it. Godse's world was one of a man obsessed with his desires to constantly prove his masculinity and virility in his overall quest to uphold Hindu majoritarianism in the struggle to define India's national identity.

Godse's point of operation was, therefore, the point of convergence for varied anxieties and resentments caused by an agonizing identity crisis among those who held rigid aspirations, vivid yearnings and who, in a traditional agrarian economy shaped over centuries by British colonial demands, came of age to limited opportunity. The Godse saga also provides a particularly consequential insight into the geography of Hindu revivalism. It emerged in the Marathi linguistic region of central India, where it is still headquartered, and as the pace of India's independence accelerated during the 1940s, the belt grew to include the uncertain states ruled by Hindu rajas. These leaders stood to lose customary privileges in the event of the British withdrawal and saw their association with the Hindu Right as some kind of security for the future.

From there the march of communal instability progressed through the west to the north and the east, and through diasporic communities overseas.

The course of Gandhi's life reveals that by the time he was killed he had comprehensively countered the project of Hindu Rashtra and the virulent idea fuelling it, forcing its proponent organizations—Rashtriya Swayamsevak Sangh (RSS) and Hindu Mahasabha—to the margins of Indian politics. It was largely due to Gandhi's own immense moral power and his all-out efforts as the supreme leader of the anti-British struggle that, in a short span after Independence, the validity of the vision of a secular and democratic nation seemed beyond question. It rose above the turmoil of the time and became the unifying principle of the post-Independence India.

The assassination of Gandhi was an act that sought to derail the secular project of Independent India. The putative resolution posited by Godse can now be seen as benighted and even self-defeating in light of the popular outrage and enduring disgust at Gandhi's murder. But the disputants that engendered the assassination remained at large. Furthermore, the dispute continued and, if anything, became even more acute over the coming decades.

The assassination of Gandhi was followed by a massive government crackdown on the RSS. It was banned for a year and a half, and thousands of its leaders and cadres were arrested. For long after the ban was lifted in July 1949, the movement remained cautious while working under severe constraints. Jawaharlal Nehru, the prime minister who had been the most trusted lieutenant of Gandhi, now assumed his mentor's unofficial mantle as the guardian of secularism. During the remaining one and a half decades of his life, Nehru, with his resolve to confront Hindu communalists now stiffened by the assassination, repeatedly invoked the ideal of a nation dedicated not to Hindu majoritarianism but to culture and the spirit of modern democracy and representation-based secularism.

'Remarkable changes in our political structure have taken place in the six months that have gone,' Nehru wrote to heads of provincial governments on 20 February 1948, three weeks after the assassination. 'The Hindu Mahasabha, as a political organisation, has liquidated itself. The RSS has been banned and the reaction to this throughout the country has been good. These events have, of course, been precipitated by the assassination of Gandhiji, but they indicate wholly healthy development in our political life. They are necessary steps to the creation of what we have been ceaselessly trying to achieve viz. a democratic secular State in India.'[1]

One and a half years later, when the ban on the RSS was lifted, Nehru inveighed against the Hindu Right in another such letter to the heads of state governments. 'As you know the ban on the RSS has been removed,' he wrote on 20 July 1949. 'This does not mean that we are convinced about the bona fides of the RSS movement, although they have promised to behave in future. All it means is that we feel that we must gradually relax the abnormal measures we have taken in restricting the normal liberties of the individual and the group whatever that might be. We do not propose to relax in the slightest our vigilance and we shall take instant action whenever necessary.'[2]

For many years, the RSS's aspirations remained tempered due to the presence of Nehru. His insurmountable legitimacy across the communities, including Hindus, seemed to make the RSS deeply unsettled about its cherished goal. After Nehru's death in 1964, a series of prime ministers who succeeded him, despite their individual follies and shortcomings, continued to regard secularism as the dominant norm of the Indian political system.

Yet, the dreams of a Hindu majoritarian alternative persisted. Behind the scenes, the RSS retained its affection for its vision of Hindu Rashtra and hostility to India's secular democracy. For long on the surface, it seemed to remain as a ragtag unit of volunteers that might be of little importance. But in reality, it never lost sight of its dream of redefining India. Quietly—sometimes even secretly—the RSS kept growing along with its hydra-like structure of affiliates.

The situation started changing around the mid-1980s when, after having gathered enough self-confidence, the RSS launched the most pivotal of its Hindu majoritarian campaigns for capturing the political centre stage—the movement to construct a new temple on the site of a sixteenth-century mosque in Ayodhya. The issue had been a subject of a localized legal battle since 1949, when a band of Hindu supremacists, claiming that the site was the Hindu deity Rama's birthplace, surreptitiously planted an idol in the mosque and practically converted it into a temple. Once picked up by the RSS, the issue was brought to national attention and quickly turned into the focal point of religious tensions between Hindus and Muslims.

Keeping the Bharatiya Janata Party (BJP), its electoral outfit, and Vishwa Hindu Parishad (VHP), its affiliate responsible for mobilizing sadhus, in the forefront, the RSS set out to win the support of Hindus and Hindu religious groups through a series of mass ritual actions, use of religious imageries, and conclaves of Hindu religious leaders backing the campaign. The BJP president at the time, L. K. Advani, then rode a *rath*—a Toyota pick-up modified into a chariot—around the country to rally Hindus to the cause. His journey—*yatra*—began on 25 September 1990 at Somnath in Gujarat, where a temple had been destroyed by a Central Asian Muslim invader, Mahmud Ghazni, in the eleventh century. The yatra was planned to go through hundreds of villages and cities in the states of Gujarat, Maharashtra, Karnataka, Andhra Pradesh, Madhya Pradesh, Rajasthan, Haryana, Bihar and Uttar Pradesh before reaching Ayodhya. Though Advani was arrested before he could enter Uttar Pradesh, his yatra, by bringing militant Hindu sentiments to the fore and provoking communal riots along its route, transformed the BJP into a major political force in the country.

A series of events thereafter, carried out by the RSS and its affiliates, culminated in the demolition of Babri Masjid on 6 December 1992. The demolition shook the soul of the nation. It revealed how India could still be pushed into a collective identity crisis, still be forced in the quest for self-definition and therefore still be made most vulnerable. The offering of a ready-made and prefabricated Hindu majoritarian identity for the nation, the one that India had wrestled against in the past and which Gandhi had fought relentlessly until his death, set the ground for the BJP's growth at the centre.

When the BJP formed a government in 2014, the original fault line resurfaced. The world's largest democracy is once again in the throes of a collective identity crisis, once again confronting a political project that seeks to promote Hindu authoritarianism along the lines of Nazi anti-Semitism. The project is premised on the same old idea that India is a Hindu state and minorities must subscribe to Hindu primacy. This is a position that threatens the very foundation of its democracy in which all citizens of every faith and all Hindus of every caste have equal standing.

As in the past, Hindu supremacists today belong to the RSS and its large family of affiliates as well as to organizations that have mushroomed in the last couple of years under the rightist ideological umbrella. They are jingoistic and full of contempt for minority communities. They look to Narendra Modi, a long-time member of the RSS, as the deliverer of Hindu Rashtra.

In their vision of the ideal state, Godse acts as a forerunner, one who removed the main obstacle in their way. Godse's influence stems from their understanding that his killing Gandhi was not a crime but a step in the right direction. They, therefore, do not call this assassination a *hatya* or murder, but a *vadh*, a term used to describe the slaying of the forces of evil.

The recent period has witnessed massive efforts to steer the national discourse to treat Muslims as the 'other' by way of speeches from the mouths of cabinet ministers and media. Social media is used to portray Muslims as anti-nationals and, on the streets, violent attacks are perpetrated on them in the name of cow protection or against beef-eating, and there is talk of the 'love jihad'. This is described by Hindu Right as a ploy contrived by Muslim men to lure young Hindu women into marriage and conversion into Islam, this being projected as an internationalist conspiracy against the Indian nation state. All the while, this is in conjunction with the BJP government's efforts to push forward its Hindu majoritarian agenda, including a 2019 citizenship law seen to directly discriminate against Muslims by fast-tracking citizenship for immigrants of six faiths other than Islam. Combined, these actions have started to erode and subjugate Gandhi's vision of amity in a secular India with equal rights for all religions.

As the hatred came out of the margins and occupied the mainstream, Godse started to emerge as a new icon. In the past, Gandhi's assassin was rarely talked of in public by RSS men (and they can only be men in the RSS), in spite of their being intoxicated by his heroism. But with the BJP's electoral victory in 2014, followed by its even bigger landslide in the 2019 general elections, the shyness vanished. In fact, hardly ever in the past was Godse so openly extolled by those seeking to give him a place in the national memory as has been the case since 2014.

The most jarring aspect of this shift has been the aggressive applause for Godse from a group of high-profile MPs of the ruling party, trying to blur the national memory. The sentiment was expressed most explicitly by the BJP's Pragya Singh Thakur, an MP currently facing criminal proceedings for alleged involvement in a lethal anti-Muslim terror plot.

The growing cult of Gandhi's assassin seems rooted in the same resentment against Muslims and nostalgia for a Hindu

Rashtra that inspired Godse to shoot the Father of the Nation. Whether in the attempts to build shrines to Godse in Meerut and Sitapur in Uttar Pradesh and Gwalior in Madhya Pradesh, or in MP Pragya Singh Thakur's pronouncing him a 'patriot', by glorifying Godse the ruling dispensation is sending out a clear message that Gandhi's ideas are anathema to them.

The process has, unsurprisingly, coincided with open resentment towards Gandhi, who had refused to grant Hindus primacy over followers of other faiths. In Meerut, a leader of the Hindu Mahasabha captured media headlines on 30 January 2019 when she re-enacted the murder of Gandhi by shooting his effigy with an air pistol after garlanding the picture of Godse.

But the resentment is not always symbolic. On the 150th anniversary of his birth on 2 October 2019, the Gandhi memorial centre at Rewa in Madhya Pradesh was found vandalized and the word 'traitor' scrawled on a picture of the Mahatma. Similarly, in February 2022, a life-sized statue of Gandhi was found broken and thrown a few metres from its location in a park in the East Champaran district of Bihar.

Hindu authoritarianism is also being pushed out into the West, where it has gathered support from diaspora communities. One of the most grotesque examples of this was witnessed on 27 January 2021, when a statue of Mahatma Gandhi was found vandalized, broken and ripped from its base in a park in California. 'The 6-ft tall, 650-pound (294 kg) bronze statue of Gandhiji, in the Central Park of the City of Davis in Northern California, appeared to have been sawed off at the ankles and half its face was severed and missing,' said a report published in a local daily.

Later that year, American universities and academics witnessed a swift and shocking backlash when a group of US-based researchers announced an online conference to discuss the rise of the Hindu Right in India. 'Nearly a million emails were sent out in protest to universities, the event website went offline for two days after a false complaint, and an email account associated with the event was attacked with thousands of spam messages,' the *Washington Post* reported on 3 October 2021. 'By the time the event unfolded Sept. 10, its organizers and speakers had received death and rape threats, prompting some to withdraw,' it added. The mass emails to universities, as per the news report, were organized by advocacy groups such as the Hindu American Foundation and the Coalition of Hindus of North America.

For years, the RSS has cultivated a relationship with diaspora communities in the US, Britain and many other countries. It has used these communities to raise funds and shut down any criticism of India's Hindu Right. A large number of Hindus who reside in countries like the US and UK travelled to India to campaign for Modi when he ran for re-election in 2019. The RSS-linked advocacy groups—such as the Hindu American Foundation—have also been routinely lobbying US Congress for causes aligned with the Modi government, including its contentious decision of August 2019 to strip India's only Muslim-majority state Jammu and Kashmir of its autonomy, split it into two centrally governed territories and lock it down for weeks.

Even a group of European parliamentarians were mobilized to back the Modi government's Kashmir decision and become part of what was described in India as a PR stunt. In October 2019, while the local politicians were not allowed to enter Kashmir, these largely right-wing European parliamentarians were given a tightly controlled tour of Srinagar, the state's capital city, that included a boat ride on the picturesque Dal Lake. 'The delegation initially comprised twenty-seven members from countries including the UK, Spain, Germany, France, Italy and Poland—although four decided not to visit what has been India's only Muslim majority state and returned to their home countries,' said a report published on the BBC website on 30 October 2019.

In the UK, the RSS has been drawing extensively upon Hindu groups such as Overseas Friends of BJP (OFBJP) and the Hindu Forum of Britain for moral and material support for its project of establishing India as a Hindu Rashtra. The OFBJP, in particular, has become a key tool in Modi's diaspora diplomacy. After Modi became prime minister, it helped organize his visit to London in 2015 when around 60,000 British Indians attended a rally at Wembley Stadium in his honour. During the 2019 elections in UK, it also sought to forge strong links with the Conservative Party, claiming that many of its politicians had a track record of championing 'Hindu' concerns. 'Last week, a UK support group for the BJP, India's ruling Hindu nationalist party, said it was campaigning for the Tories in 48 marginal seats. It also emerged that WhatsApp messages were circulating among British Hindus urging them to vote against Labour, accusing it of being "anti-India", raising fears that tensions are being stoked ahead of the election,' the *Guardian* reported on 11 November 2019.

Not only in the West but also in India, the Hindu Right has been extensively using social media platforms such as WhatsApp and Twitter to steer the discourse in its favour. Globally, the anniversary of Mahatma Gandhi's birth is celebrated as the International Day of Non-Violence, but in India, after Modi became prime minister, it routinely becomes the day when hashtags #GodseAmarRahe (May Godse be immortal) and #NathuramGodseZindabad (Long live Nathuram Godse) go viral on twitter. Given the massive presence of organized

Hindu supremacists on Twitter, one can assume that it is not a spontaneous trend but is pushed through carefully orchestrated campaigns.

Shocking as they are, these incidents seem to raise only one question: has India as a nation crossed a boundary, beyond which Godse is a national hero and Gandhi a traitor?

September 2022
New Delhi

Section I: Ploy

1

Nathu

Nathuram Godse's head ached but his eyes remained fixed on the entrance to the lawn of Birla House. A wing of this grand New Delhi mansion served as the living apartment for Mahatma Gandhi. Blending into the crowd gathered in the lawn, Godse waited stealthily about ten paces from the main gate, positioning himself right along the way Mohandas Karamchand Gandhi would take to reach the wooden podium from which he led his evening prayer meetings. From his reconnaissance of the prayer ground, Godse knew that Gandhi could appear at any moment. It was quarter past five in the evening on Friday, 30 January 1948. The air was cool on his face, and above him the sky had turned grey, almost ready to be enveloped in darkness.

The assemblage stirred. Godse saw Gandhi emerge at the entrance, flanked by two young women, his grand-nieces. Manu was on his right and Abha to his left. Gandhi stopped for a moment. His face lit up with a smile. Letting go of the shoulders of his grand-nieces, he brought his palms together in a namaskar to greet the assembled crowd.[1]

Godse reached for the pistol in his pocket and released the safety.[2] He waited. There was no panic, just a vague disquiet. Gandhi then walked quickly towards the podium, the crowd opening to enable him to pass through. As he came close, Godse pushed his way roughly past Manu as if to touch his feet, a practice Gandhi disliked. Manu tried to stop Godse, saying that they were already late. Scarcely had she spoken when he violently jerked her away. She stumbled backwards, Gandhi's rosary, the case for his glasses, his spittoon, and her pen and notebook—articles she always carried to the prayer meeting—falling from her hands.[3]

Then, in one furious movement, Godse stepped in front of Gandhi, his hands folded over his pistol. 'Now I stood at a distance of one and a half feet from Gandhi,' Godse recounted, 'I said namaste Gandhiji, and then I pointed at his chest and fired.'[4] A total of three shots were fired in quick succession at almost point-blank range. One bullet hit Gandhi in the chest and two in the abdomen.[5] At the first shot, Gandhi's foot, which was in motion, faltered, but he still stood, his palms still joined in a namaskar. When the second and third shots rang out, he collapsed, uttering his last cry: 'Hey Ram!'[6] It was seventeen minutes past five.

The horrified crowd, nearly 200 in number, looked stunned. Herbert Reiner Jr, a young official of the US Embassy in Delhi, who stood nearby, was the first to realize what had happened. 'People were standing as though paralysed,' he said in his statement to the *New York Herald Tribune*, 'I moved around them, grasped his [Godse's] shoulder and spun him around, then took a firmer grip on his shoulders.'[7]

The 32-year-old American, who was in India as disbursing and financial officer for the US State Department, had visited Gandhi's prayer meeting on the advice of his mother, who had written to him that 'he might not have many chances to do so'.[8] He was joined in his short and savage struggle with Godse by Raghunath Naik, the gardener at Birla House, who hit the assailant on the head with his *khurpi*, a garden trowel. Amarnath, an assistant sub-inspector who stood at a distance of about 2 metres from Gandhi when the shots were fired, rushed forward and took Godse into custody.[9]

Godse was whisked away by the police. He was first kept in a room on the ground floor of Birla House and then shifted to the Tughlak Road police station, about 1.5 kilometres away, in central Delhi.

A reporter, who saw Godse soon after he was brought to the Tughlak Road police station, described him as 'very calm'. Godse was handcuffed and sat on a wooden bench when the reporter saw him in 'a dark, unlighted' lock-up—a 10-foot by 10-foot enclosure with cemented floor and concrete walls. The room's iron-barred gate opened into a veranda, where several armed guards were stationed to prevent any attempt to rescue the assassin. Godse was wearing a white shirt, blue pullover, grey trousers and khaki jacket. Blood was pouring down his forehead over the left side of his face. The police told the reporter that this was due to 'the blows which the spectators' had heaped upon him; the rumour that the assassin had tried to shoot himself was baseless.[10]

Godse got up from his seat when the reporter approached him. The journalist threw questions at him and Godse answered them all. He revealed his true name and the place he belonged to, but seemed sensitive about his age; he evidently didn't want the journalist to know that he was no longer a young man. According to the news report that was published on the front page of the *Hindustan Times* the next day, Godse revealed that he was twenty-five. But the journalist did not buy the lie.

He noted in his dispatch: 'He gave his age as 25, but he looked considerably older'.[11]

~

The reporter was right in his observation—Godse was not twenty-five, but thirty-eight. There was something striking about this exchange between the two. Godse's attempt to conceal his real age fit in with the traits that had emerged in his childhood and developed deep roots in him. His craving for a virile image meant that he resented anyone making a note of the fact that he had passed his youth and was nearly middle-aged.

This desire of a masculine image had shaped the style and actions of his past life, and it seemed to be a prominent force even after he killed Gandhi. The artifice dominated Godse's thinking from his formative years.

Godse was born on 19 May 1910 in Baramati, a small town in Poona district of the Bombay Presidency. His father, Vinayakrao Godse, was a petty government official who worked in the postal department and his mother, Lakshmi, a devoted housewife. They belonged to the Brahmin community, an elite social group that is said by legend to have emerged from the brain of Lord Brahma, the mythical creator of the universe. Brahmins see themselves as the upholders of Hinduism, a religious system which rests on a belief in supernatural powers embodied in idols, stars, planets, rivers, trees, sacred animals, and divine men and women. It stresses on castes, that is, birth-based hierarchical arrangement of endogamous social groups. Theologically, Brahmins occupy the apex of Hinduism's social pyramid, enjoying a complex set of privileges and observing a baffling combination of restraints. Originally, they were, as per Hindu mythology, mendicants and philosophers living apart from the material world and its temptations, but through centuries they were transformed into a priestly class.

This was a society where social roles were rigid and preordained, and public and intellectual life was dominated by religious texts, rituals and caste identities. Superstitions and legends controlled their vitals so deeply and revealingly that by the time of Godse's birth, his parents—as also a significant section of Brahmins—remained ambivalent towards the changing social environment that resulted from the spread of modern scientific education and liberal tendencies in late nineteenth- and early twentieth-century India.

Godse was the fourth son in the family. Three older sons, born in 1901, 1904 and 1907, had all died in infancy. Only Mathura, a daughter born in 1898, the first offspring of Vinayakrao and Lakshmi, had survived. There was, therefore, a deep sense of anxiety in the family when Lakshmi gave birth to her fourth son. With some medical help, they might have worked themselves out of the difficult situation and the subsequent history of their family—and of India—might have turned out quite differently. But the world of Godse's forefathers, filled with superstitions, meant much to his parents, who saw in the terrifying deaths of their infant sons the role of a divine curse which allowed only their female child to remain alive.

So, when Godse was born, his parents decided not to take any chances. To trick fate, the newborn son was brought up as a female. His nose was pierced and he was made to wear a *nath* or nose ring.[12] This, they thought, would exorcise the dark spirit, propitiate their family deities—Hareshwar, a manifestation of Lord Shiva, and Yogeshwari, his consort—and allow the newborn to survive. It was thus that the child came to acquire the name 'Nathu' or the one with a pierced nose, and then Nathuram, even though his official name was Ramachandra Vinayak Godse.

Godse survived. A few years later, his mother gave birth to another son, Dattatreya. Thereafter, they had a daughter Shanta, followed by two more sons, Gopal and Govind. They believed that Godse had rid the family of the curse.

But Godse appeared to have been discomfited by notions of virile masculinity. He played with girls of his age and remained huddled up close to his older sister and mother while at home.[13] His parents promoted it by allowing him to dress in female clothes. The conflicted feelings that emerged from this effeminizing in his childhood seem to have affected Godse for the rest of his life.[14]

As his early years were entangled in superstition, the heightened religiosity that they bequeathed to him may have overwhelmed him even after he gave up the female attire and began going to school. All available testimony about Godse's childhood suggests that he was not particularly social and at times had trouble communicating and became an ardent devotee of the family deities early on. As a preadolescent boy, he also claimed to have acquired the ability to occasionally go into a trance and speak as an oracle. In an orthodox Brahmin family, this was talked of with pride, filling the child with a strong sense of being among the chosen few.

He became the touchstone of oracular abilities for his family when he was said to have cured Mathura of a mysterious ailment through 'divine healing'. That was when Mathura returned from her marital home when her ailment persisted despite a long treatment. Godse undertook to perform a 'rare' form of worship to heal his sister. 'And lo! She was cured,' wrote Gopal Godse, his younger brother.[15] The feat, it seems, was treated as a miracle by the family, who looked upon Godse with unequivocal admiration as a psychic in their clan. The praise must have added to his taste for mysticism, for he continued with the worship even after Mathura was 'cured'.

The worship he revelled in at this juncture required elaborate preparations. Fresh cow dung was applied on a portion of the floor near a wall in the room. After this, soot was mixed with oil and the resulting paste was spread to form a circle the size of a palm on a platter, which was then kept leaning against the wall in front of a lit lamp. Godse would first perform puja and then, squatting in front of the platter, look intently at the soot. 'He was then asked anxious questions by those around and the answers that came from the mouth of that worshipper were taken to be those given by the goddess,' wrote Gopal. 'The worshipper could sometimes see in the soot-black portion of the platter the image of the goddess or some figure or some letters. In reply to the questions put to him he would describe what he saw there. Oftentimes what he told was not the direct answer to the question put to him. So the answers were taken to be symbolic and inferences were drawn with various conjectures. The whole thing went on for about an hour or so.'[16]

In later years, Godse's oracular religiosity faded away, but his longing to be accepted in his idea of a masculine world would define his persona, forming the basis for crucial decisions. In his later life, he showed a reluctance to discuss his childhood in public, referring to these memories only obliquely. Even while narrating his life history to the investigators after assassinating Mahatma Gandhi, he cut the experiences of his childhood so short that they would fill merely three of ninety-two handwritten sheets of paper; his descriptions incorporated details only from the time he crossed adolescence.[17]

~

Godse's religiosity and oracular performances had made his home the biggest part of his small world. Even when his schooling began, he could indulge in his oracular practices freely. His father had a transferable job and was posted mostly in semi-urban localities of the Bombay province. Godse studied till the third standard in a Marathi-medium school at his birthplace, Baramati. 'My father was then transferred to places like Khed and Lonavala in Poona district where I completed my primary school education,' he later said.[18]

As there was no provision of English education in the places Vinayakrao was posted in, Godse was sent to a secondary school in Poona. Here, he lived with his aunt's family and clearly felt the abrupt change in his environment. Evidence available on his schooling at Poona is fragmented. It seems that in the new milieu he missed the comforts of his home as well as the attention he used to get from his family because of his oracular performances. For long, therefore, he was a loner. He felt restricted at his aunt's place and left no opportunity to visit home during vacations.[19]

'Even after he was sent to Poona for his English education, he used [to] perform this Puja, whenever he came home during the vacations,' wrote Gopal. But as his education progressed, Godse's 'oracular abilities' declined. By the age of sixteen, he lost his concentration and ceased to perform as the medium between the deities and the family.[20]

After Godse withdrew from mysticism, he seemed to have spent most of his time among friends rather than on studies. Sometime towards the end of 1928, months before he was to appear for his matriculation examination, he left his aunt's place and moved into a rented room. Despite domestic hardship, Vinayakrao managed to spare money for his son's rent and other expenses, hoping that Godse would get a job after completing his matriculation and share the financial burden of the household.

Godse, however, failed to meet his expectations. It seems that, for him, the shift away from his aunt's place was merely the fulfilment of his desire for freedom. If anything, it marked his liberation from the stringent rules of his aunt's household and gave him an opportunity to live for leisure and other inclinations. Rather than concentrating on his studies, Godse's life in the rented room rolled along noisily with his friends. One activity that consumed most of his time was swimming. 'Swimming was my special hobby,' he said later, 'In quiet waters, I could swim for two miles without break.'[21]

Time passed and the exams approached. In the absence of adequate preparation, Godse failed the matriculation examination held in early 1929. His marks in English were so poor that he could not get the matriculation certificate. One consequence of this failure, Godse later explained, was that he gave up school forever out of disgust and capriciousness. The failure once again left him on uncertain turf, just as he had found himself early in his childhood when he was raised like a girl.

Devoid of any sense of direction, Godse moved back with his family, which at that time lived in Karjat, a suburban locality between Poona and Bombay. Within months, in 1929, his father was transferred to Ratnagiri with a promotion and the family moved with him. An ancient town overlooking the Arabian Sea and situated in the dramatic Western Ghats of the Bombay Presidency, Ratnagiri was the last place Vinayakrao's job took him to. It was also the first district headquarters in which he had ever been posted.

Everyone in the family found Ratnagiri splendid, never imagining that in this old, beautiful town lurked a horrific, ruinous shift of their fate.

~

Gandhi was in his mid-forties when he returned to India in January 1915. At the time, he did not appear to be the sort of man who would shake the British Empire. Instead, he seemed tentative and cautious, and kept a low profile even though he was welcomed as a hero and someone who had upheld the dignity of India in South Africa. Born in a middle-class Hindu family in an obscure princely state of Gujarat on 2 October 1869, Gandhi had passed the Bar in London in 1891 and spent over two decades in South Africa. It was in South Africa that he had first experienced the full force of colonial racism and experimented with his non-violent methods to fight it.

For some time after his return, Gandhi travelled around the country, meeting people, gaining experience and trying to understand India. He found what he wanted in the indigo fields of Champaran, a northern district in the province of Bihar, in the beginning of 1917. The successful Champaran Satyagraha—the rebellion of indigo farmers under Gandhi's leadership against British plantation owners—set in motion a chain of events that culminated in the launch of a nationwide Non-Cooperation Movement in 1920.

The movement, which involved complete boycott of the government and promised to deliver Swaraj or self-rule within a year, was the first of its kind. The response was massive and it came from all quarters of Indian society, crossing boundaries of wealth, age, caste and religion. Everyone seemed to be expecting a victory but just when the movement reached a crescendo in February 1922, Gandhi called it off, declaring that some of his followers had sinned against god. His reason was the mob violence that occurred in the small town of Chauri Chaura in Gorakhpur district of the United Provinces.

Gandhi's sudden withdrawal of the movement sent a wave of shock and anger among his followers. 'The drastic reversal of practically the whole of the aggressive programme may be politically unsound and unwise,' he told them, 'but there is no doubt that it is religiously sound.'[22] His arguments did not convince the freedom fighters. Leaders of the Indian National Congress, the main vehicle of the freedom struggle, were dismayed and the masses disappointed. With Gandhi no longer in command of a powerful movement, the government decided to arrest him. He was kept in Yerwada jail in Poona for two years, from March 1922 to February 1924. For the next four years, he mostly toured villages, fought against untouchability and superstitious beliefs, and tried to reconcile differences between India's two largest communities—the Hindus and the Muslims.

In 1929, however, Gandhi started working intensely to prepare the nation for the next round of the non-violent mass movement. Jawaharlal Nehru, the son of the then Congress president Motilal Nehru, now emerged as one of Gandhi's closest political aides. Nehru had left the practice of law to join the Non-Cooperation Movement but had been devastated after its sudden withdrawal. Exhilarated though he had been by Gandhi's entry into Indian politics, Nehru differed from him on treating non-violent means as religion. Many years later, he argued in his autobiography that 'the non-violent method was not, and could not be, a religion or an unchallengeable creed or dogma. It could only be a policy and a method promising certain results, and by those results it would have to be finally judged'.[23]

Having travelled extensively in Europe during the period of despondency after the abrupt suspension of the Non-Cooperation Movement, Nehru's stature had grown abroad as well as in India, especially among the youth. He had been the working secretary of the party and Gandhi looked to him to build bridges with the younger generation. The split between

Gandhi and Nehru had ended. Gandhi took the nation by storm as he came out of his self-imposed exile and returned to the active politics of open rebellion against British rule. The demoralization that had set in within the Congress following the collapse of the Non-Cooperation Movement gave way to new hope. The division among party leaders vanished as a new possibility appeared on the horizon.

In September 1929, Gandhi undertook a long tour of the United Provinces. He spent nearly two and a half months in major cities and small towns of the province, addressing public meetings, and urging students, women and the masses in general to wear khadi and join the Congress. With Gandhi coming out of seclusion and travelling in the United Provinces, Congress leaders throughout British India, including Ratnagiri, became active, holding regular public meetings in their respective areas and preparing the masses for an impending showdown with the colonial regime.

The change in atmosphere provoked a vigorous and open debate about political freedom. India started experiencing a great upheaval. A more radical movement—the Civil Disobedience Movement—was about to erupt with the objective to achieve 'purna swaraj', or complete independence.

~

For Godse, it was the kind of environment he had never experienced before. At the time of the Non-Cooperation Movement, he was too young to respond to it or even understand it. Now, with plenty of time at his disposal and no work to do or studies to pursue, he set his sights on what was happening around him.

He had long believed that he had no wish other than to pursue his spiritual quest—something that had earned him a sense of being unique in his household. Given the background of his family and his own upbringing in an atmosphere of heightened religiosity, he could not have been expected to know much about colonial exploitation and the growing unrest against it. But as events were shortly to show, it didn't take long for him to get drawn into the political whirlpool which was building up in the country. So removed had the British now become from Indians and so arrogantly did they behave, dismissing even the basic demands of their subjects, that barring small groups that directly depended on the colonial regime or expected to benefit from it, they had lost the trust of all.

More specifically, as far as Godse was concerned, the communal formations that would later try to hold back sections of Indians from joining in the nationalist struggle were still in the nebulous stage and had not yet reached him. Thus, despite the acute sense of his own worth in the family, Godse, like most youth in Ratnagiri, started taking a keen interest in the rapidly developing political situation right from the time his father was transferred to the coastal town.

'I began to take part in protest meetings and processions which were being organized against the British government,' he recalled.[24] 'When the call was given to students to boycott their schools and colleges, I dropped the idea of reappearing for matriculation exam.'[25]

Godse's involvement with the Gandhian movement was not only restricted to boycotting his formal studies. He occasionally tried his hand at addressing protest meetings and playing a leading role in localized processions too. 'In the beginning, I didn't know how to speak from the dais,' he recounted. 'But after speaking in two or three meetings and carefully listening to comments of people, the level of my confidence increased and I learnt how to give speeches. Thereafter, I became a regular speaker in protest meetings organized by Congress in my locality.'[26] Godse was even rounded up 'along with around fifty other protesters' by the police 'once or twice' but let off after being detained in the police station for an hour or two.[27]

But all this was not to the liking of the man with whom Godse had started meeting frequently around the beginning of 1930—the time when Godse's involvement with the freedom movement led by Gandhi had started deepening.[28] It seems safe to assume that in his heart, even as he made the first serious attempt to define his identity, Godse was still in search of guidance.

Godse was about to find the father figure who would transform his life: Vinayak Damodar Savarkar.

2

Savarkar vs Gandhi

Savarkar or Tatyarao had stylized his persona with a care verging on pedantry. In the past, he had been staunchly anti-British. But by the time Godse met him, he had long surrendered his nationalistic fervour to focus completely on mobilizing Hindus against Muslims, though without giving up his patriotic allure. It is hard to find another freedom fighter who made as strong an effort to cover his tracks, glorify his own personality and reap dividends even on sacrifices he had never made.[1]

For all his hidden contradictions, he led an austere lifestyle. He maintained an acute culture of decorum all the time and hid his private life and interpersonal relations behind it. Biographical accounts on him as well as his own autobiographical writings only cursorily mention his wife, Yamuna, or his family life, and seek to impose adult Savarkar's perspective on his childhood experiences.[2]

Born on 28 May 1883 in a Brahmin family in Bhagur, a village near Nasik town in the Bombay province, Savarkar was a voracious reader from an early age and had an excellent memory. He completed his schooling in Nasik and received his college education in Poona. In 1906, Bal Gangadhar Tilak—the militant chieftain of Indian nationalism before Gandhi turned the movement to non-violence—secured for Savarkar a scholarship that enabled him to proceed for an advanced law degree to Britain. Here, operating from India House, a student residence and the den of Indian revolutionaries in London, Savarkar's life seemed to take a definite anti-British course.

He gathered around him a group of raw young men and imparted to them a passionate love for the nation and intense hatred for British rule in India. He led the group to produce a manual on bomb-making and sent copies to India.[3] In 1907, to commemorate the fiftieth anniversary of the revolt of 1857 against British rule, Savarkar completed his well-known tract, *The First Indian War of Independence—1857*. He also led his followers in celebrating Martyrs' Day on 10 May 1907, the day on which the 1857 uprising had begun.

However, for all this evidence of patriotic feeling, what is borne out by his life's story is Savarkar's tendency to dodge personal risk. Rather, he conducted himself as a behind-the-scenes operator, issuing directives from a safe distance and grooming protégés to carry out the actual acts of militancy. This trait first became evident in the wake of the murder of Curzon Wyllie, a British official attached to the secretary of state for India, in July 1909.

Madan Lal Dhingra, a young man who belonged to a rich family of Punjab, had arrived in England for higher studies in 1906. Though not a resident of India House, he fell under Savarkar's spell, who worked on him assiduously, preparing him for the day that he would become a martyr to the cause of the nation. Like other members of the group, Savarkar had administered to Dhingra an oath of complete loyalty to his 'revolutionary programme', which essentially meant absolute surrender and obedience to him in whatever he planned.[4]

According to Savarkar's official biographer, Dhananjay Keer, Lord Curzon, the former viceroy of India, was Dhingra's first target, but he failed in his attempt.[5] Wyllie was the next target. 'So on the last day of June 1909, Madanlal Dhingra came to Savarkar in the Students' Hostel kept at the residence of B.C. Pal in Sinclair Road, where Savarkar had been staying since April 3, 1909,' Keer wrote. 'There they had a talk. Then Savarkar and Niranjan Pal [a follower of Savarkar] accompanied Dhingra to Notting Hill Gate Station. Savarkar gave him a nickle-plated [sic] revolver and while bidding him farewell he said, "Don't show me your face if you fail this time".'

Despite the warning, Savarkar evidently was not confident that Dhingra would be able to complete the task on his own. By Keer's account, Savarkar dispatched two of his trusted aides the next day to ensure Dhingra did not falter:

> Next day, 1 July, Savarkar sent H.K. Korgaonkar and G.C. Varma [two of his aides] to the Imperial Institute where a meeting was to be held to celebrate the annual function of the National Indian Association. The two deputies were to keep Dhingra to the resolve. Night fell. The function was celebrated. And at the conclusion of the meeting Dhingra sprang upon Curzon Wyllie with the fierceness of a tiger and shot dead the man who was the eye and the brain of the India Office [British government department set up to oversee the administration of India].[6]

Keer did not reveal this crucial piece of information while Savarkar was alive. Thus, there is no mention of it in the first edition of the biography, which was published in 1950. He did so only in the revised edition published in December 1966, ten months after Savarkar's death. Dhingra, on his part, displayed complete and total commitment to Savarkar, and preferred to pass through the trial alone. He was executed on 17 August 1909.

In the absence of any evidence, the connection between Savarkar and the murder was particularly difficult for the British investigators to assess, even though they suspected his complicity in the crime. Nevertheless, after the murder, Savarkar lived in constant fear of getting arrested, taking shelter in obscure places in London, Brighton and Wales, staying only a few days in each place before moving on to the next. All the while, he was being closely watched by the police.

Later that year, on 21 December 1909, A.M.T. Jackson, district magistrate and collector of Nasik, was shot dead. The assassin, Anant Kanhere, was arrested, tried and later hanged. Keer holds that the murder of Jackson was committed to avenge the 'dreadful transportation' of Savarkar's elder brother, Ganesh Damodar Savarkar.[7] On 8 June, Ganesh, popularly called Babarao, had been sentenced to transportation for life to the Cellular Jail in the Andaman and Nicobar Islands for his role in anti-British activities in the Bombay province. Though the connection is not entirely clear, Jackson is said to have been instrumental in the arrest of Babarao.

During the investigation of the Jackson murder case, it was discovered that Savarkar had secretly dispatched from London some Browning pistols to India a while back and that one of these weapons had been used for the assassination.[8] But before the pistol was traced to him, Savarkar went underground, a manoeuvre he had evidently planned in advance. He slipped into Paris in the beginning of January 1910. Then, quite inexplicably, he returned to London two months later, apparently convinced that there would be no arrest warrant against him, that he would be protected by Britain's laws and would in no case be deported to India.[9] Whatever Savarkar's calculations, they were to prove utterly misplaced. He was arrested the moment he alighted from the train in London on 13 March and soon deported to India.

On the way, he tried to escape from the British ship when it reached the French coastal town of Marseilles. He even made his way through the porthole window on the ship to the quay but was quickly overpowered and dragged back. Once in India, he was tried, found guilty and transported to the Cellular Jail for double life imprisonment, meaning fifty years in total.

~

The Cellular Jail, where Savarkar was kept in a cell 7.5-foot wide and 13.5-foot long, was one of the most dreaded prisons in the world. Like other prisoners, he had to wear a wooden tablet around his neck, mentioning his year of release—in his case, 1960. This jail was different from other prisons in that sadism was part of everyday life and all possible torture techniques, including solitary confinement and clamping of fetters to prevent the bending of knees, were used frequently. Pounding coir and pressing oil were part of the daily chores and the prisoners were beaten, even flogged, if they did not complete their quota of work.

It is possible to imagine that torture of the extreme kind—as well as the prospect of spending fifty years in that jail—might just have proved too much for Savarkar to withstand. Within two months he was on his knees, writing mercy petitions to the British authorities, making abject appeals, and promising loyalty, obedience and good behaviour in return for clemency. He was brought to the Cellular Jail on 4 July 1911, and he filed his first mercy petition on 30 August.[10]

Though the text of this petition is not available, it is referred to in his mercy petition of 24 November 1913. The latter was his third petition, in which he said,

> I am ready to serve the Government in any capacity they like, for as my conversion is conscientious so I hope my future conduct would be. By keeping me in jail nothing can be got in what would be otherwise. The mighty alone can afford to be merciful and therefore where else can the prodigal son return but to parental doors of the Government?[11]

The British government's refusal to respond to his mercy petitions did not stop him from writing them at regular intervals. Simultaneously, he also sought to ingratiate himself with the jail authorities. Thus, by the time Bengal's militant nationalist Trailokya Nath Chakraborty was taken to the Cellular Jail in 1916, Savarkar and Babarao 'were found favourites of the Jailor or Superintendent'.[12]

When most of the political prisoners decided to launch a movement against their barbaric treatment and inhuman conditions in the jail, the Savarkar brothers refused to take part in it. 'They were not prepared to forego [sic] those concessions and join us in the proposed movement,' wrote Chakraborty.[13] The Bengali revolutionary was also baffled to see how much Savarkar and his brother were guided by the instinct of personal safety while trying to retain the allure of patriotism. 'The Savarkar brothers used to encourage us secretly but when we asked them to join us openly, they refrained,' Chakraborty noted.[14]

Savarkar's petitions and 'good behaviour' in the Andamans paid dividends, and he, along with his brother, was shifted to jails in the Bombay Presidency in May 1921. While Babarao was released unconditionally in September 1922, Savarkar was discharged in January 1924 on the condition that he would not participate in politics and not go outside Ratnagiri district without the permission of the authorities. The Government of Bombay's order for Savarkar's release from jail on 5 January 1924 stated:

> He [Savarkar] has also, though it was explained to him that it was in no way made condition of his release, submitted the following statement: 'I hereby acknowledge that I had a fair trial and just sentence. I heartily abhor methods of violence resorted to in days gone by, and I feel myself duty-bound to uphold Law and the constitution to the best of my powers and am willing to make the Reform a success in so far as I may be allowed to do in future'.[15]

Savarkar's admirers claim that his mercy petitions were a mere ploy so that he could come out of jail and take part in the anti-imperialist struggle.[16] It is true that some degree of cunning was part of Savarkar's persona, but it is also true that once released from jail, Savarkar was never seen even on the sidelines of the freedom struggle. On the contrary, he now openly started looking upon the colonial regime as a boon and an opportunity to cleanse India of Muslims.[17]

The circumstances surrounding Savarkar's political transformation—from being anti-British to a Muslim hater—remain somewhat unclear. By Keer's account, Savarkar, while in primary school, had proudly vandalized a local mosque along with his Hindu friends and then got into a brawl with angry Muslim boys.[18] However, accounts from the later period of his life suggest that Savarkar's childhood communal instincts did not survive for long and he went off the deep end as an adult. He started public life as a reasonably secular, non-sectarian and fiercely anti-British political leader. One may trace some elements of Hindu chauvinism in his past thinking too but there is no evidence to suggest that it distorted his political ideas in a significant way.[19] One indicator is his well-known tract, *The First Indian War of Independence—1857*, which projected the idea of a unified Indian resistance to colonialism and argued that Hindus and Muslims must come together to oust the British.

But when he came out of prison, he was no longer the same old Savarkar—he was now a tight-lipped, fanatical man who had developed a crude, often xenophobic view of Muslims. How did this happen? There can be no certainty or pat explanations. His followers and he himself suggest that his experiences in jail sharpened his antipathy towards Muslims. In his autobiographical writing, *The Story of My Transportation for Life*, the original Marathi version of which was first published in 1927, Savarkar talks bitterly of the ill-treatment by, and proselytizing activities of, Muslim warders—those who were drawn from among the jail inmates to implement the prison authorities' diktats.[20] Keer also stresses much on Savarkar's sufferings at the hands of Muslim warders.[21]

To be sure, the story of his political transformation, as told by Savarkar and his followers, is unique in every sense. No other prisoner in the Andamans ever complained of or wrote of Muslim warders proselytizing or ill-treating Hindu inmates, nor is there a record of the conversion of any other nationalist to communalism because of experiences in the Cellular Jail.[22] The story, therefore, is most likely untrue in many or all its publicized details.

The best evidence suggests that Savarkar's hatred for Muslims was genuine, of course, but he seemed to have mustered it cunningly to ingratiate himself with the British government—his theory of uniting Hindus against the so-called internal enemies, the Muslims, did not only promise to hold back a section of his co-religionists from joining the anti-colonial nationalist struggles, but also helped the British implement its divide and rule policy in India.

In 1923, about a year before he was released from prison, he penned a monograph, *Hindutva: Who is a Hindu?*. In this text, he claimed the whole of India for Hindus, asserting that they alone, and not Muslims or Christians, considered its territory sacred. 'All Hindus claim to have in their veins the blood of the mighty race incorporated with and descended from the Vedic fathers, the Sindhus,' he wrote.[23] 'We [Hindus] are one because we are a nation, a race and own a common Sanskriti.'[24]

To Savarkar, the term 'Hindutva'—literally meaning Hinduness—represented a politically conscious Hinduism that sought to organize Hindus as a nationality. India's Muslims and Christians did not constitute a part of this vision of the nation. His text was designed to identify the etymology of Hindus which, to him, meant the followers of the faith of 'Vedic fathers', a faith known generally as Hinduism. It also conspicuously echoed his call for action against enemies of the faith, particularly Muslims, for he specified that 'a conflict of life and death' ensued 'after Mohammad of Gazni crossed the Indus'.[25] Savarkar wrote: 'In this prolonged furious conflict our people became intensely conscious of ourselves as Hindus and were welded into a nation to an extent unknown in our history.'[26] The text, therefore, intended to carry Hindus into a state of opposition towards Muslims. In this sense, Hindutva was more of a prejudice than an ideology—it made no demands on the state and did not require it to significantly change in the way that an ideology, socialism or capitalism or any other ideology, might require.[27]

Savarkar's monograph thus sought to channel the dominant anti-British sentiment of Hindus into anti-Muslim action. It was the first explicit assertion that Hindus constituted a separate nationality—a theory that was embraced by Mohammad Ali Jinnah's Muslim League seventeen years later in 1940 when it adopted a resolution saying Hindus and Muslims were two distinctive nations and demanded the division of India.

At his residence in Ratnagiri, Savarkar spent most of his time with his loyal disciples, explaining the scope of his doctrine of Hindutva and discussing ways to unite Hindus not against the British but against a section of fellow Indians, the Muslims.

A wide gulf separated this group from those who were fighting to free India from British rule. While the world outside saw enormous turmoil fuelled by the demand for complete independence, Savarkar's group remained busy with its anti-Muslim agenda.

~

There is no specific record about what led Godse to visit Savarkar, nor about who arranged the introductory meeting. According to Godse's brother Gopal, a silent link seemed to have developed between the Godses and Savarkar the moment they moved to Ratnagiri in 1929. 'Quite unknowingly it so happened that the place where we had now gone to reside was the very place where Savarkar had stayed when he first came to Ratnagiri. Thereafter he shifted to another house at the other end of the same lane,' Gopal recounted.[28] Savarkar was a distant figure during Godse's early adulthood but apparently an inspirational one, for he paid his first visit to Savarkar just three days after his family shifted to Ratnagiri.[29] Yet, most of the reliable evidence about Godse's transformation into a fully recognized follower of Savarkar dates to the early months of 1930.

Godse was nineteen when he first met Savarkar. He was thin but looked healthier than Savarkar, who was a notch taller than him. Restrained in his demeanour, Godse remained quiet and deferential, apparently mesmerized by Savarkar's stature as a revolutionary who had returned after a decade spent in the Andamans. Godse's political beliefs were vague at best, if they could be said to exist at all. Though he had started taking part in Congress-led processions and protest meetings against the colonial regime, and had even addressed some of them, he was essentially an outsider who had still not made up his mind regarding his own future. Yet, he loved the rush of adrenaline from these political activities and seemed set to throw himself into the freedom movement.

Godse's conversion into a follower of Savarkar and an enthusiastic cheerleader of Hindutva was not smooth. His own observations testify that initially he was not very responsive to the commands of the eccentric exponent of Hindu communal philosophy. 'He [Savarkar] seemed annoyed when I informed him about my decision not to re-appear for the matriculation examination in response to Gandhi's call to boycott schools and colleges,' Godse said later. 'Twice or thrice he tried to persuade me to change my decision, saying how important it was to continue my studies.'[30]

Savarkar's suggestion could seem like a bit of well-meaning advice by an elder but it may hardly have been so, given his eagerness to keep his flock away from the great upheaval India was experiencing at the time. As it happened, Godse refused to back off from his decision, thus foiling Savarkar's first overt bid to extricate Godse from the camp of anti-British agitators.[31]

Godse's initial resistance suggests that he was self-conscious about his conversion experience in the beginning, but this broke soon enough. Perhaps he was thrilled to be close to someone who was seen by many—especially Chitpawan Brahmins—as the authentic continuation of the line of the Peshwas, former Brahmin rulers of Maharashtra. Like Savarkar, Godse too came from this elite subgroup of Brahmins who considered themselves the heirs of the Peshwas. It seems that the caste bond he shared with them gave him, in his own eyes, a certain sense of superiority over other Hindus.

Chitpawans are one of the rare Brahmin communities in India who claim to have a long history of valour on the battlefield, apart from the usual priestly privileges that Brahmins traditionally enjoy. As rulers during the later medieval times, they also had a long history of struggle against Mughal and Pathan rulers in India. This fact now led them to reinterpret their history in terms of the needs of Hindu nationalism; they presented themselves as the upholders of a tradition of Hindu resistance against Muslim occupation.[32]

In any case, Godse might have been no stranger to the sense of pride that Savarkar provoked in enthusiasts of Hindu revival. Being ancestrally connected to Poona, Godse would have known—even if vaguely—something of this sentiment. Poona was seen by traditional Chitpawans as the staging area of Hindu national revivalists. It was in the hills beyond Poona that Shivaji was born, where he lived and launched his guerrilla campaign against the forces of Mughal emperor Aurangzeb. Shivaji was a Maratha of the warrior caste but his heirs, the prime ministers or the Peshwas, were Chitpawan Brahmins. Poona served as their nerve centre as, after Shivaji, the Peshwas fended off the Mughals, the Pathans and the British until succumbing, finally, to the last in 1818. Poona's Chitpawans had produced a stream of men opposed to the British rule like Tilak, the militant Congress leader, and the Chapekar brothers—Damodar Hari Chapekar, Balkrishna Hari Chapekar and Vasudeo Hari Chapekar—the Indian revolutionaries involved in the assassination of W.C. Rand, the British plague commissioner of Poona, in 1897.

Though Godse belonged to a lower middle-class family, his known ancestors, by virtue of belonging to the Chitpawan Brahmin caste, were of the priestly class at Uksan village near Poona. The family's genealogy holds that towards the end of the seventeenth century, they had moved to this village from Harihareshwar, the land of the rocky beach in the sheltered creek formed by Savitri river on the Arabian Sea coast in Raigad district of Maharashtra. *Godse Kulvritant*—a compilation of the genealogies of all Chitpawan Brahmins belonging to the Godse clan—puts Vinayakrao, Godse's father, at the eighth ladder of his known ancestors, starting from Ramchandra Godse, who lived towards the end of the seventeenth century.[33] Little is known about the intervening generations, except that the descendants of Ramchandra Godse, like other Chitpawan families, came into prominence and received land grants in Uksan village during the reign of the Peshwas in the eighteenth century. As agricultural land got divided through generations, Vinayakrao's father, Vamanrao, inherited a meagre estate.

Like his forefathers, Vamanrao lived by mixing the profession of priesthood with agriculture, but he was keen on his son getting modern education. He, therefore, set up a parallel establishment in Poona as soon as his son finished his primary education.[34] Vinayakrao was the first member of the family to complete his matriculation. Thereafter, he secured a government job in the postal department. As his job was transferrable, Vinayakrao almost abandoned his ancestral village, although he still owned a small patch of agricultural land and a spacious house there.

~

Godse's background was enough to make him interpret his conversion or recruitment into Savarkar's clique at that age as a natural passage of a true Chitpawan. Whatever his ideas about his past and his caste, it seems that Godse, for some time as a young adult, moved freely through the two worlds, oscillating between a radical anti-British sentiment advocated by Gandhi and a conciliatory attitude to the colonial regime preached by Savarkar in the name of preparing Hindus to fight the so-called internal enemies, the Muslims.

Eventually, the latter prevailed. And Godse, in his own way, started finding more comfort among his caste brethren and was integrated into their revivalist project. They were an eclectic group—some religious, some irreligious—tied together by their caste loyalties as well as their dependency on Savarkar's leadership. It seems Godse's shift away from the freedom movement was also rooted—as he claimed years later—in the apprehensions of his father, who as a government servant didn't want his son to annoy the authorities. 'My father feared that my activities might jeopardize his job, and so he asked me not to take part in any movement that sought to break laws,' he recounted.[35] There is no known record about which of the two factors—Savarkar's persuasion or his family's pressure—had a greater bearing on Godse's decision to give up his association with the nationalist agitators. It seems certain that while his father might have expressed his apprehensions ever since Godse began to take part in Congress-led protest meetings, he always ignored them until Savarkar took him on a different course.

Savarkar's way, however, was cautious. He spoke with force but always flinched from revealing his mind, indulging instead in demagoguery carefully crafted to hide his conciliatory sentiment towards the British. 'Barrister Savarkar rarely discussed politics as he had pledged not to do so during his restricted confinement,' recounted Godse.[36] Perhaps he could not have known then that the demagogic rhetoric represented substantially strong politics of a certain kind.

Anxieties caused by Gandhi were the hallmark of this politics. Gandhi was presenting himself as if he was neither conservative nor progressive and was merely working to bring together the common essence of the two. But the social changes he suggested and the political activism he demanded from the people were highly subversive of orthodox Hinduism.[37] By taking the fight against British rule to India's villages and framing the low-status, non-Brahminic and peasant cultures as genuine Hinduism, Gandhi was threatening those Hindu elites who dreamed of reviving their past supremacy. Even his bid to fight colonialism by fighting patriarchy and trying to bring women on an equal footing with men, was being watched with deep anxiety by such Hindus. What must have multiplied their sense of insecurity was the fact that Gandhi, despite seeking to subvert Brahminical hegemony, was not ready to call himself a social reformer; he was convinced that he was a sanatani, an orthodox Hindu.

Ripping up this vision of Gandhi was an important part of Savarkar's politics. For only then could he have thought of making his politics succeed. Savarkar had some advantages. The vision he espoused was easy to convey to those who shared his obsession with Brahmin ascendency in politics—projecting

Muslims as enemies of their faith-based nationalism to unite various castes of Hindus without altering the hegemony of the traditional social elite. It was precisely this possibility that Gandhi threatened with his constant emphasis on Hindu–Muslim unity and his attempts to politically redefine Hinduism by dislodging Brahmins from the centre of society. For the section of Chitpawan Brahmins, particularly those who couldn't reconcile with the gap between their traditionally privileged position and their actual status in the contemporary sociopolitical setting, anxiety was a permanent emotion of the time. As they longed to redeem their lost glory, the charisma of Gandhi did not appeal to them.

There was also a parochial and casteist flavour to this aversion. Gandhi was a Bania, a caste of traders and moneylenders, and belonged to Gujarat, a sociocultural zone in the Bombay Presidency distinct from Maharashtra, the region traditionally dominated by Brahmins. A section of Maharashtrians always had reservations about Gujaratis, and many Brahmins considered Banias as scheming.[38]

~

At least twice in the past, Savarkar had met Gandhi. They met in London in the busy autumn of 1909, long before Savarkar gave up his anti-British life. Though Gandhi had not yet formally entered the struggle for independence in India, his fight for the rights of Indian migrants in South Africa had started capturing the imagination of freedom fighters back home. On 24 October, the Indian diaspora in the United Kingdom invited Gandhi—who was already in London to press for changes in discriminatory laws in South Africa—to preside over an event on Vijaya Dashami, the last day of Dussehra festival marking the victory on the battlefield of Lord Ram over demon king Ravan. Savarkar, of course, as part of the militant nationalist circle at London, was the main speaker at the event.

Though the organizers had told them not to make political speeches, both Gandhi and Savarkar succeeded in conveying their political ideas to the audience of about seventy-odd people. Savarkar agreed with Gandhi that it was perfectly possible for Muslims and Hindus to live together peacefully.[39] But while Gandhi talked about Lord Ram as a selfless and conciliatory figure always ready to sacrifice for the sake of others, Savarkar focused on the 'nine days' preceding Dussehra, when Hindu gods vanquished the demon king with the force of arms, implying thereby that the same methods should be used to deal with British conquerors in India.[40]

Eighteen years later, when the two met again, they had changed beyond recognition. While Gandhi had progressed to become the supreme leader of the Indian national movement, Savarkar had developed a scurrilous kind of anti-Muslim sentiment and had left behind all his anti-British fervour. The meeting was clearly an effort by Gandhi to win cooperation from Savarkar for the nationalist cause. But the latter seemed to regard Gandhi with some suspicion; certainly, he was wary of Gandhi's penchant for fighting against the British regime and supporting Hindu–Muslim unity. Still, in his efforts to outflank Gandhi through his appeals to Maharashtrian Brahmins, Savarkar seemed to find the meeting an opportunity to understand his opponent.

This meeting took place in Savarkar's Ratnagiri residence on 1 March 1927. Savarkar asked Gandhi to clarify his views on untouchability, a typical Hindu practice of ostracizing lower castes who were branded impure, and shuddhi, the religious conversion of minorities, especially Muslims, to Hinduism through ritual purification.[41] Gandhi did provide an outline of his thoughts on these issues. Though the exact wording of what he told Savarkar was not recorded, it is safe to assume that his explanations would have been the same as what he had been advocating and practising over the years: that the custom of untouchability must end along with Brahminical dominance, and that religious conversion or reconversion was not the solution to any problem.

To be in Savarkar's good graces, Gandhi concluded by saying: 'We cannot have long talk today, but you know my regard for you as a lover of truth and as one who would lay down his life for the sake of truth. Besides, our goal is ultimately one and I would like you to correspond with me as regards all points of difference between us. And more. I know that you cannot go out of Ratnagiri and I would not mind finding out two or three days to come and stay with you if necessary to discuss these things to our satisfaction.'[42] Savarkar's response was short and tentative. 'I thank you, but you are free and I am bound, and I don't want to put you in the same case as I,' he said. 'But I will correspond with you.'[43]

The meeting must have been frustrating for Gandhi. Given Savarkar's obsession with the Hindu–Muslim relationship, Gandhi could not win even limited cooperation from the Hindutva ideologue. The two would never meet again, but much of Savarkar's life would be defined by his antipathy towards Gandhi.

~

By 1929, when Godse moved to Ratnagiri, Savarkar had freed himself from much of the strain and awkwardness that had accompanied his transformation from an anti-British to an anti-Muslim figure. But for a youth already flirting with the freedom struggle led by Gandhi, the new politics of Savarkar had to be injected slowly and with extreme care. Through his past support for gun culture and his stories of sacrifices in the Cellular Jail, Savarkar seems to have postured as a dissenter, rather than a collaborator, of the British regime when he first met Godse. In his confused state of mind, which was yet to embrace Gandhian nationalist feeling, Godse might well have seen in Savarkar's nuanced views a different and more aggressive kind of nationalism.

Once the conversion began, Godse was led step by step into a new world; he started having regular sessions with Savarkar, debating one subject or another. Between sessions, Godse would read books and articles written by the Hindutva ideologue and copy them in his own handwriting.[44] 'Once he brought a copy of Savarkar's *War of Independence of 1857* and used to read it at night. When Nathuram could not understand anything our father explained,' wrote Gopal.[45] Savarkar also guided Godse on the kind of literature he should be reading, thus developing in him a taste for books.[46] This made Godse share the liberals' desire for acquiring more knowledge, but his strict adherence to Savarkar's ideology clouded his mind so much so that he seems to have gained limited perspective from what he read.

Such was the change that by the time Gandhi launched the Civil Disobedience Movement, Godse had become Savarkar's fellow traveller. When Gandhi entered the sea at Dandi village in Gujarat on 6 April 1930 and broke the salt laws by picking up lumps of natural salt lying in a small pit, the whole nation watched him attentively. Similar peaceful breaches of law started taking place in other parts of the country and soon became a massive anti-British upsurge. In particular, the stretch on the west coast from Cambay to Ratnagiri—the region known for natural saltworks—became the focal point of the Salt Satyagraha.

The reverberations of these momentous developments did not affect Godse in his new world. His acquaintanceship with Savarkar had deepened, and the clique he had joined seemed oblivious to all that was happening outside. The distance between him and those making sacrifices for the freedom of India had widened and he did not find the upheaval at all appealing.

Savarkar had won. The pattern of Godse's life had begun to form.

3

The Brahmins of Bombay

Under Savarkar's tutelage, Godse had started to disassociate himself from the freedom movement but it had done little to change the withdrawn strain in his nature. He remained a low-spirited young man who gazed out upon an incomprehensible world with a mixture of bitterness and longing. The personal and political views he acquired in the new company consisted of an assortment of prejudices which could hardly provide him a plan of action with a defined role for himself. By and large, therefore, Godse, under the spell of Savarkar, remained in a state of total inactivity. This, along with the friendlessness that marked his years in the coastal town, explains why he was not confronted with any choice at all until a chance to explore a new life came to him in the summer of 1932.

Earlier that year, his elder sister Mathura had come from Itarsi, a city with one of the biggest railway stations in central India. Her husband, P.T. Marathe, a railway employee, was posted there. 'When she returned, I accompanied her and started living with her family,' Godse recounted.[1] Two months later, Mathura's husband was transferred to a railway station close to Nasik. Her family shifted to the new destination, but Godse did not leave Itarsi. He seemed bent on finding his livelihood there and, to achieve this, tried his hand at several things. 'I started selling khadi clothes and doing fretwork,' he said.[2] He was quick to learn Hindi, the language of north and central India, and was often seen performing kirtans in the new language.[3] He also claimed that during this period he began to read a great deal, impatiently and haphazardly, as though he wished to absorb the entire library near Itarsi railway station within a short period.

However, he soon became edgy, exhausted from the vagaries of business, and started looking for new ways of sustenance that could interest him. He found his escape in the job of an errand boy for a provision shop near Itarsi railway station. In particular, he was attracted by the perks that the new job offered—a second-class train pass and expenses for travelling. 'During the leisure time, after procuring goods for the shop, I used my pass to travel to places like Lucknow, Allahabad, Jabalpur, Bhopal and Jhansi,' he later said.[4]

How much of all this is true is impossible to say now, but it is certain that for two years, from 1932 to 1934, Godse managed to support himself at Itarsi. In a concentrated and obstinate manner, he lived there only for himself, until he was called back by his father. 'Some time in 1934 I received a letter from my father asking me to return home and share the burden of the family as he had retired and fallen ill,' Godse said.[5]

Vinayakrao had retired around the middle of 1933. With his retirement also went his monthly salary, as well as the free government accommodation in Ratnagiri. A small retirement stipend was not enough to meet household expenses, especially since the family now had to shift to a rented accommodation.

Being a man of modest leanings in all manners, he decided to move to a place where the cost of living was cheaper and rent lower than in the expensive coastal town, and where he would have acquaintances and relatives for support. Poona was not an option as it was costlier than Ratnagiri. In the ensuing months, while Godse was still in Itarsi, the family, facing financial strain, shifted to Sangli, a small princely state about 175 km into the mainland from the coastal city.

Godse responded to his father's summons instantly. He left the job in Itarsi, collected all his belongings and headed straight for Sangli. There is no evidence that he made any contacts with political parties or individuals connected with the Hindutva ideology during the first few months of his stay in Sangli. Rather, it seems as if he spent his initial months in virtually a hollow space, showing no interest in finding his way to those who shared his communal notions and remaining ideologically solitary. The same friendlessness that had marked Godse's years in Ratnagiri and Itarsi continued in Sangli during this period as a sense of responsibility towards his family seems to have prevailed upon him. He tried hard to integrate himself with his family, throwing himself actively into his father's efforts to increase the household income. The family at that time was in total disarray. The financial strain suffered at the time of the marriage of Godse's younger sister, Shanta, about a year back was still palpable. His younger brothers—Dattatreya, Gopal and Govind—had not completed their education, and his father's meagre pension was not enough to run the household.

Without a matriculation certificate Godse was ill-qualified for a respectable job. He, therefore, started learning the craft of tailoring at a school run by a Christian mission at Sangli. Tailoring, which Hindu men generally considered as the craft of women or the trade of Muslims, was suggested by a relative who ran a shop of tailoring equipment and was aware of its prospects. In any case, with much hope, Godse started a tailoring shop, named it Charitartha Udyog, and spent hours every day to ensure his business succeeded. Soon, profits started trickling in but were not enough to meet the needs of the family—a realization that led him to simultaneously open a kiosk to sell fruit near his tailoring shop.

Generally, Godse was never extravagant and put in enough labour too, but he lacked the kind of endurance needed for the success of any start-up. His enthusiasm for business was overlaid by an obvious unstable temperament marked by a propensity for impulsive decisions. The contradiction began to show up sooner rather than later—when the earnings did not match his bloated expectations, his interest in his first serious initiative at business plummeted.

And with that began his fresh search for new stimuli. This would lead him into the lap of the Rashtriya Swayamsevak Sangh (RSS), a paramilitary outfit of Hindu men who vowed to implement the vision put forth by Godse's mentor Savarkar.

The pattern that had started to form under the influence of Savarkar in Ratnagiri now started to repeat itself.

~

The RSS had arisen in Nagpur—the capital of the Central Provinces and Berar—from within the town's Brahmin community in 1925 and had gained considerable ground in Sangli by the time Godse started looking for new stimuli and new goals. All its founders—Keshav Baliram Hedgewar, B.S. Moonje, L.V. Paranjpe, B.B. Tholkar and Ganesh Savarkar (Savarkar's elder brother Babarao)—belonged to the Brahmin caste. So were most of its members. Started as purely a local affair, the RSS gradually emerged as a communal private army of Hindu men who hated Gandhi and his idea of Hindu–Muslim unity and kept themselves away from the freedom struggle. Its leaders claimed to train its members for an eventual fight against the so-called internal enemies—the Muslims—whom Hedgewar, the first sarsanghchalak or the chief of the RSS, called 'snakes'.[6]

In 1926, the RSS adopted for its volunteers a uniform based on that of the colonial police force—khaki shorts and khaki shirt—and added to it a black cap a few years later. The same year, it also instituted a daily routine of military drills and marches, physical exercises, weapons training and ideological classes as well as the elaborate paraphernalia of a flag, an oath, and a prayer in Marathi and Hindi. Later, in 1939, as the RSS spread its activities to new areas, the prayer was in a mix of Sanskrit and Hindi and the colour of the shirt changed from khaki to white.

Shaped without a constitution, the RSS did not openly define its aims and objects. Yet it was widely perceived as an organization through which the Maharashtrian Brahmins dreamt of establishing in India the Peshwa rule—a euphemism for the rule of Brahmins—after the withdrawal of the British. The RSS's adoption of the bhagwa (saffron) flag of erstwhile Peshwas as its own flag was seen as an indication of its secret desire. The non-Brahmin Maharashtrians, therefore, had no sympathy for it.

The RSS flitted evasively through the fault lines of the Hindu caste system, presenting itself as against caste-based discrimination while all the while working for Brahminical hegemony. Displacing the wrath of non-Brahmins from their real oppressors, the Brahmins, onto imaginary enemies, Muslims, remained the hallmark of its strategy. It used religious identity and loyalty to attract youth and train them against so-called internal enemies and tried to make them believe not in Indian nationalism but in what they referred to as Hindu nationalism—an idea that had been expounded in *Hindutva: Who is a Hindu?* by Savarkar.

There was a noticeable difference between the RSS's presence in violence against the Muslim community and the convoluted nature of its involvement, or lack of it, in the national movement.[7] When Gandhi launched the Salt Satyagraha and the Civil Disobedience Movement in 1930, the RSS felt the rumblings within its ranks. Many of its ordinary members were in favour of joining the movement. To stymie the rumblings without revealing the organization's desperate bid to remain in the good books of the British, Hedgewar wrote to RSS branches stating that members could join the Satyagraha in an individual capacity and that the RSS as an organization 'had not resolved' to participate in the movement.[8] Also, since his own lack of participation would have dented his reputation in the eyes of his cadres, as this could have been interpreted as flinching from the national cause, he joined the Satyagraha. But before that, he resigned as sarsanghchalak since this would have formally associated the RSS with the anti-British upsurge.[9]

The explicit reason given by the RSS for Hedgewar's participation in the Satyagraha, which led to his imprisonment for nine months, was that this gave him 'an opportunity to get acquainted with the patriotic youth from many places who would throng prisons; and he could expound to them the need for the positive work of building up a disciplined nation-wide organization. That would greatly help in expanding Sangh [RSS] activities in future.'[10] Whatever the reason, this was the only time when Hedgewar and a small section of the RSS—all acting in their individual capacities—came close to the anti-British struggle. On all other occasions, the RSS stayed away from it and even tried to stop Hindus from joining it.

In contrast, the organizational presence of the RSS in violence against Muslims—which constituted the core of the style of functioning of an organization that suffered a persecution complex—was quite frequent. The British government first took note of the RSS's violent communal tendencies in 1929, when its spies discovered a plot by Babarao to kill 'some prominent Muhammadan leader'. An intelligence report sent from Calcutta to Kavasji J. Petigara, the Bombay Presidency's deputy commissioner of police (special branch), on 13 September 1929 stated:

> I have just received reliable information that Ganesh Damodar Savarkar is implicated in a plot to murder some prominent Muhammadan leader either at Delhi or Bombay in retaliation for the assassinations of the Hindu leaders Sardhanand and Rajpal by Muhammadan fanatics. I am sorry that we have no further information about this proposed plot.[11]

Babarao had visited Calcutta to procure arms for the purpose, the report revealed, adding that he could not succeed in obtaining 'revolver or explosives' during the trip.[12] On 17 September, four days after the British spy's report from Calcutta, a secret note was issued from the Intelligence Bureau's Simla headquarters to Delhi's Additional Superintendent of Police (CID) A.C. Fryer, giving him a list of Babarao's 'intended victim' and asking him to keep a close watch on the entire issue. 'It is possible that [Savarkar's] intended victim may be Muhd. Ali, Dr. Ansari, Abul Kalam Azad and Mufti Kifayatullah, but you are in the best position to know which particular Muhammedan leader has recently come in for odium for his extreme separatist pro-Muhammedan or anti-Hindu activities in Delhi,' the note said.[13] Though intelligence reports of the time do not give more details about the plot and why it failed, it is indeed curious that all the 'intended' targets were well-known nationalist leaders belonging to the Indian National Congress.

Babarao, who, unlike his brother, had been released from prison unconditionally in 1922, played the role of a catalyst and worked with ever-increasing vigour to transform the nascent RSS into a force in Marathi linguistic regions of the Bombay Presidency. During the early 1930s he merged his youth organizations—the Tarun Hindu Sabha and the Mukteshwar Dal—with the RSS and accompanied Hedgewar on tours of western Maharashtra, introducing him to Hindu fundamentalist leaders. It was primarily because of Babarao's efforts that Poona became the second stronghold of the RSS after Nagpur.

The young men responded to the curriculum of physical training and exercise with enthusiasm and bravado, getting carried away by mistaken notions of manliness and virility. For a man like Godse, who longed to be accepted as a model of Brahminical masculinity, the RSS was an ideal organization.

~

At the centre of the RSS activities in Sangli was Kashinath Bhaskar Limaye, a tall and handsome Chitpawan Brahmin who had a passion for physical fitness and for the possession of a hard, strong body. He got up early, performed a variety of exercises and then, after an elaborate worship, rushed to attend an RSS shakha, where swayamsevaks (volunteer members) would assemble in rows for a military-style drill at six in the morning.[14] He was forty-one when Godse met him late in 1934, but Limaye's energy was still indefatigable. Restless, impatient and vibrant, he seemed to never tire and never relax. Only months before, he had been made the sanghchalak of the Maharashtra division of the RSS. Though Poona acted as the headquarters of the organization's activities in this division, he operated mostly from Sangli, where he had gathered around him a band of highly motivated disciples who imitated him in his contempt for Muslims and glorification of Brahminism.[15]

Like Godse, the evidence available about Limaye's education is also fragmentary. He seems to have received some of his primary schooling in Urun Islampur village close to Sangli town and attended high school in Kolhapur, a neighbouring princely state.[16] After completing his matriculation, he got himself enrolled for the Intermediate of Arts at Poona's elite Fergusson College but because of financial constraints, he could not continue his studies.[17]

In 1916, shortly after his return from Poona, Limaye joined as a teacher at a high school run by the princely court of Sangli state.[18] Two years later, acting under the influence of Tilak, who was a Chitpawan Brahmin like him, Limaye left his job, started working for the Congress and formed a private firm, Deccan Commercial Company, which was an agency to sell swadeshi goods. In Sangli, however, he continued to be known as 'Limaye Master'.[19] Tilak's sudden death in 1920 and the replacement of the old guard in the Congress by a new group led by Gandhi, who promoted the creed of non-violence and emphasized unity between Hindus and Muslims, alienated Limaye and made him inactive in the Congress.[20]

He travelled widely in Hyderabad, Karnataka and Maharashtra to sell swadeshi goods. Around the mid-1920s he met Savarkar. Soon, Limaye was a frequent visitor at Savarkar's

Ratnagiri duplex, where he listened to his sermons and repeated them to his own friends back in Sangli. Limaye also got in touch with Babarao and in the course of time became so close to the brothers that he himself began to be seen as a member of the Savarkar family.[21] The years that followed were for Limaye more of the same: promoting Deccan Commercial Company's business, denouncing Gandhi's anti-British movement and discussing means to fight internal enemies, the Muslims.

At some point during 1932, when Hedgewar started his tours of Maharashtra, particularly the Marathi linguistic regions of Bombay province, to expand the RSS's activities, Limaye met him. At that time, the RSS was a highly localized organization active only in Nagpur and the neighbouring areas of the Central Provinces and Berar. Available evidence credits Babarao as the man who facilitated its expansion in Maharashtra. 'In 1932, Ganesh Damodar Savarkar brought Hedgewar to meet Limaye at Sangli,' claims Limaye's biographer D.S. Harshe. 'For four days[,] the trio remained closeted in Limaye's house, discussing the ideological issues, the concept of Hindu Rashtra, a disciplined military-like organization and sustained and continuous organizational work.'[22] It was then that Limaye took the oath of the RSS, accepted the post of the sanghchalak of Sangli and started the organization's first shakha in the town.[23]

Perhaps because Limaye was new to the RSS and unaware of its elaborate paraphernalia, including uniform, military drill and prayer in front of the bhagwa flag, a trained worker was sent from Nagpur to Sangli. This man, mentioned as Yalkundwar in Limaye's biography, stayed with Limaye for some time and instructed the new recruits of the RSS in Sangli regarding the organizational principles and shakha operation.[24] Limaye used to be present in the shakha every day, listening attentively to Yalkundwar's instructions and demanding military-like discipline from the boys he had gathered for the RSS activities.

Limaye also used his frequent business sojourns in different parts of Maharashtra to convince youth to join the RSS. His views and outlook might have been disappointing for the nationalists, but they were shared by a section of Maharashtrian Brahmins who, like him, dreamt of reviving Peshwa rule in the country. Limaye's hard work yielded results and the RSS base expanded in Maharashtra beyond Hedgewar's imagination. The RSS chief's letter to Limaye dated 10 December 1932 summed up the pivotal role the latter had played in the expansion of the RSS in Maharashtra: 'The Sangh activities in Maharashtra rest solely on you—I have told this to you in the past as well. I am confident that you have got the ability to succeed if you continue to work like this.'[25] The letter also showed that Hedgewar immensely valued his friendship with Limaye. 'I wanted you to be with us at Nagpur during Vijaya Dashami celebrations [of the RSS]. You couldn't come that time, but do come, if it is convenient to you, at the time of Christmas camp [of the RSS],' he wrote.[26]

Limaye was not immediately appointed as the Maharashtra sanghchalak of the RSS. The crown fell on him two years later. 'In May 1934, Doctor [Hedgewar] came to attend Sangh's first summer camp at Poona,' recounted Limaye's RSS colleague N.G. Abhyankar. 'On that occasion he [Hedgewar] held a meeting with K.B. Limaye, Bhaurao Deshmukh, Vinayak Rao Apte and me. He suggested that Poona be made the headquarters of the RSS activities in Maharashtra. [. . .] In the meeting Limaye was made prant sanghchalak, I was made Poona vibhag sanghchalak, Deshmukh was made [Poona] zilla sanghchalak and Apte, Poona city sanghchalak.'[27]

Bapusaheb Pujari, a Sangli resident who started attending the RSS shakha in 1933, remembers Limaye as 'a father figure who knew every swayamsevak in Maharashtra by name' and who believed that 'India must be changed quickly and in all its parts in order to make it a Hindu rashtra'.[28] That belief of Limaye had developed much before he actually joined the RSS and was so deeply ingrained in him that within a few months of his rise to the position of the RSS's Maharashtra chief, he became one of the most prominent lieutenants of Hedgewar.

~

Years later, after he had assassinated Gandhi, Godse told his interrogators that 'the RSS was new to Maharashtra' when he joined it and that he 'joined the organization because its aim was to achieve freedom for Hindu society'.[29] It would seem that his decision to seek new stimuli in the RSS—and not in some other outfit or activities—was largely because the credo of the organization fit in with the Hindutva lessons he had received from Savarkar at Ratnagiri. It must also have been influenced to some extent by Godse's constant search for a truly potent life. The charged atmosphere of the RSS shakha, given to masculine physical culture, seemed to have served Godse as a means for self-hypnosis, while he found in its conspiratorial ideology and outlandish goals the necessary ingredients to satisfy his own muddled reactionary impulses.

At a time when India was passing through the most crucial phase of its modern history, the RSS shakhas swarmed with votaries of Hindu chauvinism, who played games, performed calisthenics, did military drills, prayed before a bhagwa flag of erstwhile Peshwas and fostered the notion of sacrificing one's life in order to establish a Hindu rashtra. While the Lezim, a drill using wooden idiophones fitted with metal discs, had an important place in the training programme of young swayamsevaks, for boys up to the age of fifteen, swinging of lathis through intricate patterns regulated by a shrill sound emanating at regular intervals from the shakha chief's whistle was at the core of preparing the adult members to take part in future combat operations.[30] Military-style bands performed martial tunes and the bivouac, under a nimbus of militant patriotism, was transformed into a site of brutish soldiery. The thrill of the uniform and the exclusivity conferred by the oath ceremony were titillations supplemented by the decidedly communal temper that prevailed in the shakhas. Swayamsevaks attending them flaunted their religious identity and felt themselves part of a Hindu opposition directed chiefly at the so-called conspiracies of Muslims to prevent India from becoming a Hindu rashtra.

Perhaps the bravado displayed in RSS shakhas made Godse draw the conclusion that he had the laws of history on his side. For it was from his kind of background that the cadres most often came. The RSS in those days was chiefly an organization of Brahmins looking forward to a return to Peshwa raj after the withdrawal of the British Crown. They dreamed of a feudal structure dominated by Hindu social elites.[31] Their argument was simple—the Peshwas had been the last among Indian rulers to be conquered by the British and therefore, after the termination of British rule, Hindus, as descendants of Peshwas, should be vested with political powers.[32]

Non-Brahmins both in the Bombay Presidency and the Central Provinces—the two states where the RSS was primarily active—despised them and sometimes even attacked them. S.H. Deshpande, an active member of the RSS in Poona between 1938 and 1946, initially found it awkward as he had no prior experience of the non-Brahmins' hostility towards the RSS. Unlike other men of his shakha who resided in the Brahmin-dominated western part of Poona, S.H. Deshpande, though a Brahmin, lived in the city's eastern part, which was populated mainly by non-Brahmins. 'In the evenings as we returned home from the shakha we were often shouted at derisively by the boys who had their homes in the eastern part; or a man might glare at us threateningly. I remember, a boy once hit me with a stick and then disappeared in the rapidly deepening twilight,' he recounted. 'These stray incidents brought home to me, albeit slowly, the realization that these "easterners" looked upon the RSS as a "Brahmin Club".'[33]

In fact, the RSS at the time was not just a Brahmin club but a club of those young Brahmin men who, for one reason or the other, felt insecure in their surroundings and craved the protective umbrella of a group. Their social awkwardness, sometimes even caused by their inability to compete in the modern education system, reflected in their distorted relationship with society. They found themselves deprived of the privileged position once enjoyed by members of their caste and saw in the success of the Hindutva project a scope for rising socially and attaining leadership positions. Daily contact with the office-bearers of the RSS in shakhas, held either in the evening or in the morning, the respectful manner of mutual address, fiery assertions of violent intensions during meetings, etc., provided self-confidence and appealed to the Brahmin youth, who nourished a painful sense of insecurity and of being left out.

This explains why Godse, despite his decision to concentrate on the tailoring business and help his father meet family expenses, almost rushed into the RSS fold the moment he got bored with his business venture and looked for new impetus. He was twenty-four and seemed a desperate loner who, in a concentrated and obstinate manner, lived only for himself. Aside from Limaye, who admired him and guided him enthusiastically, not another human soul occupied a large space during the most important years of Godse's early adulthood. The duo could forge a bond because they had compatible values and work habits—both belonged to the same caste, both were dedicated disciples of Savarkar and both ran their respective businesses. While Limaye seems to have successfully merged his business responsibilities with RSS work, Godse visibly retreated into the Hindu militant world after he failed to meet the challenge created by his small tailoring occupation.

Limaye trusted Godse and seemed to have found him suited for the organization's publicity work.[34] For Godse was attracted neither to the freedom struggle nor to girls. And yet, he was always enthusiastic to prove himself—a quality that must have been noticed by Limaye when he decided to give him the responsibility to supervise the propaganda work of the RSS in Sangli and nearby areas. Soon, Godse became a dedicated swayamsevak. He lived with his parents, but the RSS had become his new home. Barring his addiction to coffee, he stayed away from all pleasures—he did not smoke, never drank and would not cast his eyes even in passing on women. All his energies and the drive of his growing ambition were thrown into the RSS work.

One consequence of all this, Godse later explained, was that he stopped paying adequate attention to his tailoring business, which declined further. The impact was felt by the family, which could barely make ends meet. 'One day, therefore, my father asked me to withdraw from my public life and concentrate on earning money,' he said, 'but by that time my public work had expanded so much in Sangli that leaving it completely and focusing back on my business seemed impossible.'[35]

Godse's connection to the RSS ran through Limaye, who had brought him into the Hindutva outfit, entrusted him with significant organizational responsibility and acted as his first friend and sole guide in Sangli. And so Godse discussed with him the problem his family was facing because of his itinerant and poorly compensated career. Giving up his RSS work to revive his tailoring business in Sangli was out of the question, for his rising visibility and contacts built up in the course of his organizational work had begun, for the first time, to boost his esteem. It was one passion in Godse's life that never seemed to bore him. His ego and his ambitions were swelling. Yet, the misery of his family was real and he could no longer ignore it. The two, therefore, decided that Godse should operate from Poona, the metropolis that lay a relatively short distance from Sangli, close enough for a weekend commute by train, and which also offered him a chance to enhance his business prospects.

4

Sangh and Sabha

Poona in the 1930s was a bubble of conservative Chitpawan traditionalism in a fast-changing India. A sombre metropolis in the Bombay Presidency, it embodied the glory and heritage of centuries and acted as the unofficial capital of traditional Maharashtra. For almost a century before the British took it over from the Peshwas in 1818, Poona had governed a Maratha empire that extended up to Delhi at its peak. Partly because of this imperial hangover, the city remained a profoundly self-assured place, quite at ease in its own sense of superiority, of its history and cultured urbanity.

Yet, for all its self-belief, Poona was a world of yesterdays—full of remembrances of the past and deep-seated doubts about the future. It had emerged as a centre of old-style scholarship in the late nineteenth century, a few decades after the end of the Peshwa rule, but there was a palpable awareness that Poona had lost its vital force. What survived was a semblance of the past along with a sharp longing for the political revival of Peshwa glories. Nowhere else in India was the atmosphere of exhaustion and Hindu revivalism so tangible. The end of the Hindu era was nowhere experienced so despondently nor was the increasing craving for its revival as intense as it was in Poona.

If a section of Poona seemed extremely confident, it was because of a belief in its destiny to re-emerge as the pivot of a Hindu empire, one based on a Brahminical vision of politics since it would be like the kingdom the Chitpawans had built under the Peshwas. Naturally, this current of Hindutva politics of the period made itself felt with a particular force in this precariously balanced city. Right from the 1930s, when men sporting black caps representing Hindu supremacist bands strikingly affected its street scene side by side with Congressmen wearing white Gandhi caps, Poona was a battleground for forces against Gandhism.

During his previous sojourn in the city, Godse had spent a few years as a high-school student who failed his matriculation examination and then moved back home in 1929. The retiring strain in his nature had made him shy away from the outside world that was anyway yet to assume any sharpness during the 1920s. But when he arrived in Poona for a second time, both Godse and the city had changed. While he had become a dedicated swayamsevak, Poona was gripped with a Hindu revivalist feeling.

There is no record of exactly when Godse moved back. Years later, he said that shortly after he moved to Poona, he got the news of the end of Savarkar's confinement within Ratnagiri.[1] This watershed event took place on 10 May 1937. Perhaps Godse had come to Poona in late 1936 or early 1937, full of hope and intending to pursue his tailoring vocation in a more urban setting—an indication that he did not intend to explore new ways of earning money despite entering a new socio-economic milieu. 'I brought along all my tailoring equipments when I came to Poona,' he said in his statement recorded after the assassination of Gandhi.[2] Godse was around twenty-seven at that time.

It is probable that returning to the scene of a previous failure, he shied away from taking a risk by venturing into an unknown vocation. Even as he decided to stick to his tailoring business, he desisted from opening a little shop of his own. Instead, he became the partner of one Vishnupant Anagal, a local RSS hand, who already had his own tailoring shop in Poona.[3] Possibly, Godse's business experiences in Sangli had made him extremely cautious as he tried to make his way again in the city. There is no indication of how he met with Anagal. There is no evidence of a previous acquaintanceship. The sources are silent and Godse never recorded a word about it. It seems most likely that Limaye, while planning a safe course for Godse in Poona, put him in touch with Anagal and persuaded them to become partners in business.[4]

Limaye also seems to have opened the way for Godse to tap into the vast, distinctive clothing market of the RSS cadres in Poona. S.H. Deshpande recorded in his reminiscences that the tailoring shop was a favoured destination for swayamsevaks wanting to get their uniforms stitched.[5] Consequently, it didn't take much time for Godse's business to start looking up. He was now able to send around seventy to seventy-five rupees every month to his father in Sangli. Though the sum was paltry, it was a significant support to his family.[6]

By connecting his tailoring business to the cadre base of the RSS, Godse developed in Poona the kind of functional relationship with the Sangh that was quite unusual for any swayamsevak. For some time, Godse shared in equal measure in running the shop. As time passed, he started reverting to the habits of the aimless idler, while Anagal focused on the business. Godse's lack of involvement with the business increased in the months after restrictions were lifted on Savarkar. Anagal, however, seemed not to have held any grudges, for the business opportunities that had opened because of their popularity with the cadre base kept growing.

~

Savarkar was almost fifty-five when the British authorities removed the restrictions on his movement and political participation in May 1937. He had repeatedly petitioned the government since 1934, promising to remain on the right side of the law even while taking to politics. This might have influenced the decision but it did not clinch it.[7] Far more significant was a massive signature campaign led by Hindu Mahasabha leader Moonje and persuasions by Jamnadas Mehta, a staunch Savarkarite who was part of the interim government formed in the Bombay Presidency after the provincial elections across India in early 1937.[8] Savarkar was now free to join any political party and visit any place without obtaining permission from the district administration of Ratnagiri.

After years of restrictions—from January 1924 to May 1937—Savarkar chose his political track with care. It was to be a peculiar mix of collaboration and hostility. Perhaps it was the fear of the British government that weighed so oppressively upon him that he went beyond openly adopting a collaborationist's role and threw himself into the war against the enemies of the Raj—Gandhi and the nationalist forces.

With his freedom restored in full, Savarkar set out to shape the battlefield so strategically that it could host a war between Hindus and Muslims. He had already outlined the plan through his vision of Hindutva. Now he had to win the allegiance of Hindus—not just of Brahmins—to be recognized as the most prominent votary of the Hindu rashtra and therefore its natural leader. It was not without reason that his maiden foray was in Kolhapur, the seat of power of the descendants of Shivaji.[9] Savarkar then travelled to the Hindu pilgrimage town of Pandharpur to pay obeisance to the most venerated Hindu saints of Maharashtra.[10] Through these initial gestures, he principally sought to address the aspirations of Hindus, particularly the conservative section of the community, for it was among them that he hoped to find his most enthusiastic support.

He spent the next few months travelling extensively in the Marathi linguistic districts of western India, attending public receptions organized by his followers and addressing packed gatherings, before settling down in his ancestral house at Dadar in Bombay. These addresses were not meant to arouse any kind of anti-British feeling—they were simply aimed at underlining Savarkar's arrival in politics after his long exile—though it also perhaps helped to hold together his image of a former revolutionary. In fact, his incarceration in the Andamans was to be one of his proudest boasts, which his loyalists and he would later use to assert their superiority over Gandhian nationalists.

Perhaps because Mehta was responsible in important respects for Savarkar's freedom, the latter first joined Mehta's party, the Democratic Swaraj Party, an outfit of old Tilakites who had been against the Congress' decision to launch a radical civil disobedience movement and who favoured a cooperative approach towards the British government.[11] The party suited Savarkar also because, as he himself admitted, its principles were consistent with those of Hindutva.[12] But shortly afterwards, in October 1937, Savarkar left this party, which had its base only in certain pockets of the Bombay Presidency, and joined the All India Hindu Mahasabha, a loosely organized outfit with a presence in several parts of the country.

Established in 1915, the Hindu Mahasabha initially considered itself more of a sociocultural group than a proper political party and operated as an adjunct to the Congress. The idea of creating a national-level Hindu Mahasabha to defend and protect 'the interest of the entire Hindu community'[13] from western impact had emerged out of a regional initiative known as the Punjab Hindu Sabha. By the late 1920s, the Mahasabha had transformed its image to a hardline organization, marginalizing the moderate Hindu leadership from within and directing its activities against the Muslim League. It now moved steadily closer to the position of the Arya Samaj, a Hindu hardliner organization with its headquarters in Delhi and its roots in Punjab. Initiated in the late nineteenth century as a movement to reform Hinduism, the Arya Samaj had by now transformed itself into an anti-Muslim society, acting as a breeding ground for Hindu communal organizations.

Nevertheless, the Mahasabha remained, at least nominally, allied to the Congress. Throughout its early history, most of the leaders and members of the Mahasabha held the membership of the Congress as well. The Mahasabha, however, drifted away from the Congress and Gandhi on the issue of the communal award of 1932, which set up separate electorates for Muslims. The Mahasabha severely condemned the award, especially since it seemed to give Muslims the control of both Bengal and Punjab. Growing estranged, it started accusing the Congress and Gandhi of Muslim appeasement. Soon thereafter, the Congress forbade its members from being in communal organizations, including the Hindu Mahasabha.[14] This marked an important conjuncture in Indian politics as the development of Hindu communalism was firmly established, incorporating the idea of a militant Hindu party that was anti-Muslim.

As an organization, however, the Mahasabha resembled little more than a social group when Savarkar joined it. Most of its prominent leaders were already in touch with him and recognized him as the leading Hindutva ideologue. Two months later, at its nineteenth annual session in Ahmedabad in December 1937, the Mahasabha leaders were so awed by the presence of Savarkar that they unanimously elected him as the president of the organization.[15] During the session, he set to work with an energy and determination that even his severest critic could not ignore. 'There are two antagonistic nations living side by side in India,' he declared, addressing the session. 'Several infantile politicians commit the serious mistake in supposing that India is already welded into a harmonious nation, or that it could be welded thus for the mere wish to do so. [. . .] India cannot be assumed today to be a unitarian and homogenous nation. On the contrary, there are two nations in the main: the Hindus and the Muslims, in India.'[16]

The two-nation theory from Savarkar evoked as much ridicule as bitterness when it was first delivered in clear-cut terms. His enumeration of this idea in his monograph[17] fourteen years ago had mostly gone unnoticed except among his hardcore loyalists in the Mahasabha and the RSS. The disastrous political line that he expressed now eventually added to the deteriorating communal environment in the country, especially when the Muslim League picked up the thread and demanded the partition of India three years later. For the Mahasabha, however, this brought a sense of confidence it had never experienced before. Party colleagues and workers followed Savarkar's lead as the ground was set for refashioning the Mahasabha into a mass party. In doing so, Savarkar walked the tightrope, remaining on the right side of the government even while furthering the impression that he opposed Gandhian nationalists because they were not revolutionary enough.

~

No other organization in India was so exhilarated by the events and emotions of the removal of restrictions on Savarkar as the excitable RSS. Its cadres thronged the public receptions organized to celebrate his release.[18] In those intoxicated days of Savarkar's entry into active politics in 1937, Hindu nationalists of all stripes realized, for the first time, that they could hold their own beside the supposedly invincible Gandhi and his Congress party. If political leaders like Mehta and Moonje were instrumental in getting Savarkar out of confinement in Ratnagiri, the RSS led the way in infusing new spirit into small but action-hungry supporters of Hindutva by making the post-release celebrations a grand success.

It was also a time when the tumult of India had subsided into a mood of guarded watchfulness. The streets were quiet, the students had picked up their books again and the workers had gone back to the factories. The Congress, despite its reservations about the limited degree of self-rule under the Government of India Act of 1935, participated in the elections to provincial assemblies held in February 1937 and won most of the seats, convincingly routing the Muslim League. Gandhi, though party to the Congress' decision to contest the elections, had stayed away from canvassing; after the results, he advocated 'a gentlemanly understanding' between the governors of the provinces and their Congress ministers to give the Government of India Act a chance.[19] A sense of national unity seemed to prevail in the country.

But beneath the cloak of unity, the divergent forces attempted to turn the situation to their own advantage. The

Mahasabha and the RSS had not been able to grow beyond small pockets in the absence of a leader who could have an all-India stature despite all their efforts over the decade. Savarkar produced a sense of common purpose that had not been felt in the past. The Mahasabha and the RSS could hope that he would match Gandhi and help them counter Congress politics. All, therefore, joined hands to express the new self-confidence in a bold and provocative manner. The RSS, with a strong cadre base among Maharashtrian Brahmins, was naturally in the forefront.

In Nagpur and other Marathi linguistic districts of the Central Provinces, Hedgewar personally supervised the receptions planned for Savarkar. In a letter dated 23 September 1937 to Baburao More, one of his lieutenants, the RSS chief wrote:

> Swatantrya Veer Savarkar-ji will visit Central Provinces between September 24 and October 8. He will arrive in Akola in the morning of September 24. To welcome him personally, I am leaving for Akola tonight [23 September]. There I will stay with him for four days. I will return to Nagpur when he starts his journey for Vanhad. In the morning of 3 [October], he will come to Nagpur and stay here for two days. On 4th morning, he will be given guard of honour in military fashion at the central place of the Sangh by the Nagpur [unit of the] Sangh. He will then visit Bhandara, Chanda and Wardha during 5, 6, 7 and 8 [October] before returning to Bombay on 9th. The Sangh units of all these places will honour him in the best possible manner as per their capacities.[20]

In the Bombay Presidency, Savarkar attracted an even more enthusiastic response from the RSS. When he came out from his Ratnagiri confinement, Limaye, forming a pair with him, organized public receptions in various districts of the province and shuttled among these places along with him.[21] As head of the RSS in Maharashtra, Limaye planned the itinerary for Savarkar and was helped ardently by his followers and comrades in the organization. This he seems to have done instinctively, for Savarkar was not just the Hindutva ideologue but also his guide and mentor.

Godse, like most swayamsevaks of Poona, was an active participant in these events. He followed Limaye's example and attended Savarkar's public receptions not just in Poona but also in places like Kolhapur, Miraj and Sangli.[22] These events brought Godse close to Savarkar once again. In the last five years, after his first round of interactions with Savarkar between 1929 and 1932, Godse had seen him only once—sometime in 1935 when he travelled to Ratnagiri with a group of local youth from Sangli to meet the Hindutva ideologue.[23] Savarkar's influence on him, after his thorough assimilation into the RSS, had deepened further. Dazzled by stories of Savarkar's sacrifices and his sufferings in the Andamans, Godse adapted his work and his attitude to please his mentor. 'I was overwhelmed by the realization that this man in his fifty-sixth year, after spending twenty-seven years in jail, had once again resumed his work for the society,' Godse recounted, 'whereas I was busy just in earning money.'[24]

The realization marked the beginning of his break from the tailoring business, which had remained his main preoccupation since the time he had moved to Poona.[25] Though formally still a partner in the business, his main priority now was to cement his strong relations with Savarkar. Perhaps his instinctive rush was also guided in part by his lack of standing in the Hindutva circle in Poona. Godse, it seems, had got a sense of the full measure of the opportunity that Savarkar's entry into politics was offering. Godse's proximity to Savarkar was an asset, and he was determined to utilize it.

~

Before the assassination of Gandhi, the RSS and the Mahasabha showed a notable tendency towards close cooperation and often developed fluid and overlapping memberships.[26] There was nothing unique in what Godse was attempting—the two organizations were intertwined and reciprocally stimulated each other.

Throughout the years of their existence, they had followed this pattern. Most of those who had attended the foundation meeting of the RSS in 1925 had also been members of the Mahasabha. Hedgewar, the first sarsanghchalak of the RSS, was secretary to the Mahasabha from 1926 to 1931.[27] Although the official RSS literature, dating to the period after the assassination of Gandhi, gives all credit for the formation of the organization to Hedgewar, the truth—reflected as it was in the archival records—was different. These records reveal that Hedgewar, far from being the sole founder, played a minor role in the beginning and that the RSS might not have survived its failure to find a foothold in its initial years had Moonje and Babarao—both prominent leaders of the Mahasabha—not acted as catalysts and worked vigorously to transform it into a major force.

While Babarao merged his Tarun Hindu Sabha with the RSS in 1931, thus adding new accretion of strength to it, and facilitated its expansion in the Bombay Presidency,[28] Moonje's contribution to the organization was much more comprehensive. He was the political guru of Hedgewar, whom he had brought up in his own house in Nagpur and later sent to Calcutta to study at National Medical College.[29] An intelligence report prepared by the British government in 1933 ascribed to Moonje the responsibility of the reorganization of the RSS in the Marathi-speaking districts of the Central Provinces in 1927.[30] It was the same year that Moonje became the president of the Mahasabha. After his trip to Italy, where he met Mussolini, and visited the Balilla and the Avanguardie—two of the three keystones of the fascist system of indoctrination of youth—in March 1931, Moonje played a crucial role in moulding the RSS along fascist lines.[31]

In the following year, the Hindu Mahasabha connection opened new avenues for the RSS in northern and western India. In its Delhi session in 1932, the Mahasabha passed a resolution according official recognition to the RSS and commending its activities.[32] Later that year, Mahasabha leader Bhai Parmanand called an all-India Hindu youth conference—the Hindu Yuvak Parishad—in Karachi where another resolution was adopted, saying: 'Sangh work should be expanded all over the country'.[33] Hedgewar, who was taken to attend the Karachi conference by Babarao, stayed there for six days, discussing organizational issues with various Mahasabha leaders and youth who had gathered from the Sind and Punjab provinces.[34] The contacts Hedgewar gained at the Mahasabha meetings acted as the nucleus for the expansion of the RSS in later years.

Though Moonje did never hold any position in the RSS, he could, like any top office-bearer of the organization, interact directly with swayamsevaks. During an interaction with a senior British official on 8 May 1936, he confessed that he was very 'intimately' associated with the RSS leaders and volunteers. 'They [swayamsevaks] often consult me. I know them very well, more than anybody else, just like Dr. Hedgewar, the chief of the Sangh,' Moonje said.[35]

Savarkar, as a Hindutva ideologue, was indispensable to the RSS during the 1930s and 1940s, especially after he was freed from all restrictions in 1937. 'The intellectual food of the RSS volunteers has been the speeches and writings of Savarkar,' wrote S.H. Deshpande. 'How very dependent they were on Savarkar can be gauged from the fact that the day he was to address a meeting in Poona, it would be announced at the various shakhas of the town that the evening's proceedings stood cancelled and that the volunteers could "go home" (i.e. to Savarkar's meeting! This was never officially mentioned). This concession was not granted on any other occasion.'[36]

Savarkar's personality and habits of mind led him to hold himself above any organization. Simultaneously, as a leader in his own right, he attracted a following both in the Mahasabha and the RSS. He was very proud of the reputation he enjoyed among swayamsevaks, and left no opportunity to visit shakhas or address them when he went out on tour. The book compilation of Savarkar's diary entries, speeches, articles and notes—*Whirlwind Propaganda: Extracts from President's Diary of His Propagandist Tours, Interviews from December 1937 to October 1941*—shows that meeting RSS volunteers constituted an important part of his itineraries during this period.[37] On several occasions after becoming the president of the Hindu Mahasabha, Savarkar congratulated the RSS on its work and discipline while the latter regularly collected huge sums of money and presented it to him as a mark of respect. The British intelligence agencies recorded many instances of this nature from a period spanning the late 1930s to the early 1940s.[38]

Savarkar and the RSS continued to remain closely connected even after Madhav Sadashiv Golwalkar became the

RSS chief following Hedgewar's death on 21 June 1940. An Intelligence Bureau note giving a summary of field reports on the RSS stated that Golwalkar, while addressing a meeting of swayamsevaks in the Bombay Province in November 1940, propounded 'the pan-Hindu theory of one undivided India under the Hindu rule of the Mahasabha'.[39] Golwalkar had spent about five months as the chief of the RSS by then.

The fluid and overlapping relationship between the Mahasabha and the RSS would hold steady for most of the 1940s—until the events of 30 January 1948 precipitated its rupture.[40]

5

Ramachandra Becomes Nathuram

A dedicated RSS volunteer getting a glimpse of a new meaning to life under the guidance of a man who, despite enjoying the respect of the Sangh, was never its member and would soon become the leader of a distinct organization, the Hindu Mahasabha, was not in those days an ignoble idea. Godse did not immediately join the Hindu Mahasabha upon Savarkar's return to politics. He waited for a few months, weighing the situation before forging ahead. Though he held forth loquaciously about Savarkar's Andaman incarceration and claimed that the resumption of his life in politics even after 'spending twenty-seven years in jail' had inspired and transformed him, Godse appeared in no hurry to join the Mahasabha. His relationship with the RSS had deepened, and he considered the outfit a reservoir of militant energies even as he vaguely looked around for someone to lead him, and eventually became fixated on Savarkar.

Godse's cautious—and perhaps calculated—line of reasoning led him to write to Savarkar. In the letter he sought to bring the two organizations into active collaboration, apparently imagining himself as their spearhead. Though undated, the contents of the letter show that it was written sometime before August 1938. 'It is a fact generally accepted,' Godse wrote to Savarkar,

> that if there is to be a Hindu Sanghatan (Hindu Unity) not only in Maharashtra but in the whole of India, it would be systematically brought about by one, and the only one powerful institution, and that is the R.S.S. Its workers are really able leaders. At present they have the support of the youths. If in future, any work is to be undertaken, it would be advisable to carry it out in consultation with Dr. Hedgewar, who is a leader of your calibre and who is capable of doing a job which ten leaders cannot accomplish.[1]

This was Godse's sense of himself at that time: a hardcore Hindutva activist—someone so loyal to the RSS that he even tried to think ahead on its behalf. A mere four-year association with the RSS had hardened this touchy, sentimental, skittish and hesitant man and given him an exalted sense of responsibility for the Hindutva outfit. It seems that in joining the Hindu Mahasabha, he believed that he was working for the true interests of Hindu sangathan.

In the same letter, Godse also told Savarkar about his efforts to enlist new members for the Mahasabha. 'I have started the work of enlisting new members as far as I can. You will get the full information when you would come on 1st August [1938].'[2] In the strictest sense, the letter is not proof that Godse had formally joined the Mahasabha by the time he wrote it—he could well have been working informally for Savarkar's party. In fact, the first concrete evidence of Godse acting as its formal member belongs to 1 October 1938 when, alleging that religious rights of Hindus were being suppressed in Hyderabad, Godse suddenly emerged as an enthusiastic participant in the

Mahasabha's agitation against the Nizam, the Muslim ruler of the state.[3]

Still, the actual date of Godse's formal joining of the Mahasabha remains unresolved to this day. No evidence from any source—no document, no testimony—mentions it. None of the statements Godse made after the assassination of Gandhi—the Marathi statement recorded during the interrogation that concluded on 4 March 1948 and the English statement he read out on 8 November 1948 during the trial in the special court—give any specific date in this regard. The interrogation statement reveals that he started off as an active member of the RSS and then moved seamlessly to work for the Hindu Mahasabha without ending his previous allegiance.[4] His court statement, on the other hand, says he joined the Mahasabha after leaving the RSS but remains silent on when exactly he did so. 'Having worked for the uplift of the Hindus I felt it necessary to take part in the political activities of the country for the protection of the just rights of Hindus. I therefore left the Sangh and joined the Hindu Mahasabha,' he said during the trial.[5]

This was a claim that has remained one of the most debated aspects of Godse's life. In later years, pro-RSS writers saw in it an opportunity to exonerate the RSS from the charges of Gandhi's murder. They used the claim to quietly push the notion that Godse had already broken with the RSS and joined the Hindu Mahasabha almost a decade before he killed Gandhi. In time, most writers—both pro-RSS and their adversaries—started believing that Godse did leave the RSS before joining the Hindu Mahasabha, after Savarkar became its president. J.A. Curran Jr, the American researcher who is credited with the first scholarly attempt to study the RSS, is the only exception. A detailed report on the RSS, which he prepared for the Institute of Pacific Relations, New York, in 1951 stated: 'Godse had joined the R.S.S. in 1930, winning prominence as a speaker and organizer; he left the Sangh in 1934 because Hedgewar refused to make the R.S.S. a political organization.'[6]

Curran Jr is generally particular about referencing the facts he used in his paper, but in this case, his firsthand knowledge was limited. He cites no source—neither a document nor an interview—for this information, which completely contradicts the chronology in Godse's own statements and all other historical record. This is strange because Curran Jr must have been aware of the sensitivity of the issue as he did his field research in India during 1949–50—in the immediate aftermath of the assassination of Gandhi. That was also the time when serious efforts were being made by pro-RSS writers to tell the world that Godse's claim in the trial court was correct and that he had indeed given up his RSS membership and joined the Hindu Mahasabha long before he pulled the trigger. To lend credence to this argument, they emphasized that not only did the RSS and the Mahasabha exist separately, but also that there was discord between the two organizations, meaning thereby that Godse could not have remained a member of the Sangh once he joined Savarkar's party.

In the preface to the paper, Curran Jr wrote: 'The bulk of this study is based on a year and a half of frequent association with the R.S.S.'[7] Interestingly, Curran Jr was the first 'outsider', or a non-RSS member, who was given full access by the Sangh around the time when the organization was attempting to distance itself from Godse and his act of assassinating Gandhi. A possible explanation could be that Curran Jr's RSS informants, who were desperate to get rid of the Godse stigma, might just have planted this untruth which got reproduced in Curran Jr's paper as he lacked any means to verify it.

It is not just that Curran Jr got the timing of Godse's exit from the RSS wrong; there is a problem even with his estimation of Gandhi's assassin's entry into it. For, prior to 1934, there is no evidence that Godse was especially political. Back then, he lived the life of an eccentric, solitary young man who could not really aspire beyond finding a livelihood for himself until his father's pressure to share the financial burden of the family forced him into the tailoring business. Godse might certainly have listened to speeches and read books containing the Hindutva worldview after his nascent interest in anti-colonial politics was blunted—and he was virtually held back from joining Gandhi's Civil Disobedience Movement—by Savarkar in 1930. He might even have attended the RSS shakha during this period, but until he met Limaye at Sangli in 1934, he seems to have lacked any evident desire to plunge into Hindutva politics.

In any case, after he had spent a few years with the RSS, Godse's relationship with the Hindu Mahasabha seems to have had a muted beginning. It started off as his infatuation with Savarkar, intensified after the Hindutva ideologue became free of all his restrictions in 1937, and took a formal shape sometime during late 1938, almost a year after Savarkar became the Mahasabha president. Whatever the nature and extent of the new relationship, it—contrary to Godse's claim in the trial court—did not result in any rupture between him and the RSS.

~

It was at the time that Savarkar joined the Hyderabad agitation—often referred to as satyagraha—that Godse first emerged as a formal member of the Hindu Mahasabha. Immediately before, he appeared to be grappling with the excitement of his expanding political life. In the undated letter which he wrote to Savarkar just before August 1938, he made a strong case for the Mahasabha entering into the Hyderabad agitation, arguing that 'unless we take upon ourselves the task of undertaking such ordeals on behalf of Hindu Mahasabha, its strength would not increase'.[8] There is no way to ascertain in what capacity Godse made this suggestion to Savarkar and how important a role it played in the latter's decision to join the satyagraha. Though Savarkar did not personally enter the territory of the Nizam and led the agitation from outside, Godse participated in it as the Mahasabha's flagbearer.

The satyagraha had originally been launched by the Hyderabad State Congress, a provincial committee of the Indian National Congress, around the middle of 1938. Its objective was to obtain certain political concessions from the Nizam. It was a peaceful agitation in which Congress supporters, acting as satyagrahis, courted arrest in jathas or groups. Soon, however, the Arya Samaj, alleging suppression of the religious rights of Hindus by the Muslim ruler of the state, organized a parallel 'satyagraha'. The Hindu Mahasabha, which saw in the largely Hindu-populated princely state a potential reservoir of support, followed suit.[9] As the tone of the communal propaganda of the Arya Samaj and the Hindu Mahasabha became shrill, the Hyderabad State Congress, acting on the advice of Gandhi and Nehru, suspended its agitation in December 1938.[10]

Public sympathy for the satyagraha started to wane the moment the Hyderabad State Congress withdrew from it. Under the Arya Samaj and the Mahasabha, the satyagraha received a cool reception from the vast majority of the Nizam's subjects as the Hindu organizations were actually less popular in the Hyderabad state than it was made out to be by their leaders. The entire agitation was now financed and directed from outside, and the people courting arrest were mostly outsiders who were trucked in from neighbouring British Indian provinces in jathas.[11]

In Savarkarite parlance, the leader of each jatha was called 'dictator'—a term borrowed from the European dictatorships prevalent at the time. A fascination with Nazism and fascism was common to both the RSS and the Hindu Mahasabha, a fact that must have inspired Moonje's trip to Italy, where he met Mussolini. As pointed out by Italian scholar Marzia Casolari, beginning with the 1920s, Hindu militant organizations 'seemed to uneasily oscillate between a conciliatory attitude towards the British and a sympathy for the dictators'.[12] The two organizations saw the European dictatorships, especially fascism, as an example of conservative revolution—a concept that was discussed widely by the Marathi press right from the beginning of the Italian regime.[13] The aspects of fascism which seemed to appeal to the Hindu militants most were both its stress on militarization of society and the figure of a strong leader controlling a highly centralized organization.[14]

Maharashtrian Brahmins—the caste that manned the Hindu militant organizations—were the people who looked at European dictatorships as a source of inspiration. In fact, all Marathi newspapers and pamphlets that eulogized the fascist and Nazi regimes belonged to members of this caste. *Kesari*, which published a series of editorials on the subject, was the most prominent among them. Started by Tilak in the late nineteenth century, it now acted as the mouthpiece of the Hindu Mahasabha. The caste seemed filled with xenophobes who cherished ambitions of imitating the anti-Mughal exploits of Shivaji and the Peshwas, and saw in the fascist emphasis on discipline and respect of traditional values a reflection of their own deeply held desires. They marvelled at the martial traditions of the Chitpawans and considered the fascist advocacy for a militarized society a natural choice and a way to revive the Peshwa raj.

At the time the Hindu Mahasabha joined the Hyderabad satyagraha, the Hindutva forces had developed more than an abstract interest in the ideology and practice of European dictatorships—a fact summed up by their choice of calling the heads of their jathas dictators. Godse, as the first dictator of a Hindu Mahasabha jatha, entered the Nizam's state and courted arrest on 1 October 1938.[15] 'I was the dictator of the first batch of eight to ten people who took part in the agitation,' he later said.[16] He was sentenced to imprisonment for twelve months and sent to a Hyderabad jail.[17]

In many respects, the experience was momentous for Godse. It stretched his political fabric and offered him the first serious opportunity to grasp the real spirit of Hindutva in action. Years later, while recounting his experience, he would imply that his participation in the Hyderabad agitation was important not so much for his jail term as for the impressions of Gandhi and his approach to Muslims that it left in Godse's mind. 'This agitation was initially led by State Congress,' he said:

> But within two or three months, it withdrew from the agitation. [. . .] Gandhiji even tried to persuade Arya Samaj president Ghanshyam Guha to end the satyagraha, but he failed. Gandhiji also issued a statement in which he declared that [Hyderabad State Congress] had withdrawn from the agitation because he did not want to embarrass H.E.H. the Nizam. In a startling manner, it brought forth Gandhiji's principle of not opposing Nizam's oppressions just because it happened to be a Muslim institution. In one of his articles,

> written about the same time, he also gave the glorious title of Ram-Rajya [a term long used to signify an ideal of good governance sanctified by Hindu mythology] to Bhopal, another reactionary Muslim-ruled state. I felt irritated by Gandhiji's thinking in both these cases.'[18]

This was perhaps the beginning of Godse's ever-growing hatred for Gandhi, which lasted literally till the last hour of his life. Up till now, it was a mere echo of the speeches and writings of Savarkar or RSS leaders to which Godse owed the illuminations of his youth. The Hyderabad agitation gave him his own, never-to-be-forgotten experience that eventually shaped his mind.

It was also during the agitation that his name changed in the government records for the first time. From his childhood up till then, people used to call him Nathuram, though on paper he continued to remain Ramachandra, the name given at the time of his birth. In all his school records, this was the name that had been used. But he seems to have imagined himself unsafe in police custody on being arrested in Hyderabad. Fearing consequences in later days, he carefully concealed his original name and recorded 'Nathuram' in the register of the Hyderabad authorities.[19] Henceforth, he would use 'Nathuram' instead of 'Ramachandra' in all his paperwork.

Godse spent over ten months in jail, about a month and a half less than the prison term he had been sentenced to.[20] His release, along with other protestors, in August 1939 was part of the gesture of goodwill shown by the Nizam following the formal withdrawal of the agitation in July. Although the Hindu Mahasabha claimed that it withdrew the satyagraha because the Hyderabad government had promised some concessions to Hindus through a communiqué dated 7 July, the truth was different. With most Hyderabadis continuing to remain unmoved after the Hyderabad Congress's decision to suspend its satyagraha in December 1938, the agitation had started losing steam right since the beginning of 1939 and had virtually petered off when the Nizam announced the concessions. Even this gesture of the Nizam was more due to the colonial government's fears of communal repercussions in British provinces adjacent to Hyderabad than the satyagraha itself.[21]

~

It is clear that Godse joined the Hyderabad agitation as a Hindu Mahasabha member in good standing. Yet he did not abandon his parent body, nor is there any evidence of the RSS expelling him from the organization. His return to Poona from Hyderabad jail did not leave him isolated; he remained a star swayamsevak of the RSS. There was no change in his attire either. His usual clothes were a pair of khaki shorts, white half-sleeved shirt and the black RSS cap with a teardrop-shaped crown—as against the rounded crown and flat top of the Mahasabha cap of similar colour—and a pair of Maharashtrian sandals.[22] In later years, he also wore dhotis but never changed the RSS cap for that of the Mahasabha's.

In Hyderabad jail, he organized an RSS shakha and held regular exercises, thus inculcating the spirit and gospel of the Sangh even among those satyagrahis who belonged originally to the Hindu Mahasabha.[23] V.G. Deshpande, the Hindu Mahasabha leader who had led the second batch of satyagrahis and had been arrested and kept in the same Hyderabad jail, recounted in an interview, that he was administered the RSS oath in prison personally by Godse.[24] Clearly, Godse had cast himself not only as a leader of the Hindu Mahasabha jatha but also as a prominent worker of the RSS.

Two years after Godse assumed the new status, the overlapping and fluid relationship between the two Hindu militant organizations was publicly underlined by Paranjpe, the Hindu Mahasabha leader who had been one of the five founding members of the RSS in 1925 and had steered the Sangh as its sarsanghchalak for nine months when Hedgewar was in jail following his participation in the Gandhian Civil Disobedience Movement in 1930. Writing in the *Kesari* on 5 July 1940—a fortnight after Hedgewar's death—Paranjpe recounted his conversation with the first RSS chief months before his demise. 'He [Hedgewar] was himself for long the secretary of Hindu Mahasabha and was recently its vice president,' Paranjpe wrote. '[Hedgewar said that] swayamsevaks should give their maximum time to the Sangh, but there was no bar on those who desired to work for the Hindu Sabha. After all, we [the RSS] could not remain unresponsive to Hindutva ideology and the vision of a Hindusthan for Hindus.'[25]

The practice did not end after Golwalkar succeeded Hedgewar as the sarsanghchalak of the RSS. That it continued for most of the 1940s was confirmed by a report prepared by the Intelligence Department of Bombay Police in September 1947 on the membership pattern of the two organizations. The report said, 'Although not affiliated, most of its [the RSS's] prominent organizers and workers are either members of the Hindu Mahasabha or sponsors of the Hindu Mahasabha ideology.'[26]

With equal hatred towards Muslims and a similarity in the background of their members, the two organizations hardly differed in their ideology and orientation. Overtly, the RSS and the Hindu Mahasabha vowed to make India a Hindu rashtra after the termination of British rule and tried to articulate the Hindu search for self-esteem. Covertly, for the Maharashtrian

Brahmins, both promised to reinstate the dominance of the traditional Hindu leadership.[27] Although Savarkar was the supreme leader of the Hindu Mahasabha, his speeches and writings constituted the sole intellectual food for the RSS cadres as well.[28]

What distinguished the RSS from the Hindu Mahasabha was the secretive nature of its organization and the military discipline of its cadres. While the Hindu Mahasabha was a political party duly recognized by the government authorities, the RSS was a communal militarist organization without legal recognition. To the extent it formally existed, the RSS maintained utmost secrecy about its organizational proceedings and did not maintain any membership register. Its secretive nature would persist for years. In a report sent to Home Minister Vallabhbhai Patel in December 1948, months after the assassination of Gandhi, Congress leader Dr Rajendra Prasad, then the president of India's Constituent Assembly, noted:

> There are no records or proceedings of the R.S.S. organization; no membership registers are maintained. There are also no records of its income and expenditure. The R.S.S. is thus strictly secret as regards its organization. It has consequently developed along fascist lines and is definitely a potential menace to public peace.[29]

Based on inputs provided by the Congress government of the Central Provinces, the report of Dr Rajendra Prasad was hardly an exaggeration and largely summed up the true nature of the RSS. Barring a few stray records pertaining to the late 1930s and early 1940s, the investigative agencies could find nothing—and certainly no membership register—at the Nagpur headquarters of the RSS or any of its other centres after the assassination of Gandhi.

It is not inconceivable that the top leadership of the RSS might have considered legal advantages of not maintaining a membership register—the secrecy could easily allow them to disown their member in the event of his arrest for any violent and illegal activity. In later years, resuming a fresh journey after being unbanned in July 1949, the RSS would gain significantly from this fundamental aspect of its structure in its attempts to cover its tracks.

~

When he returned from Hyderabad jail, Godse seemed to lose some of his new-found sense of purpose. During his long stay in prison, his family had plunged into an abyss as the monetary support from his tailoring business had virtually stopped. 'On my return, I saw my family struggling for survival,' he said later.[30] The situation left him with a depressive propensity when he learnt that the tailoring shop was on the brink of closure despite his partner's best efforts.

The steep decline in their business was understandable. Over ten months, many of Poona's swayamsevaks—who constituted a significant part of the tailoring shop's clientele—had joined jathas going to Hyderabad to court arrest and many of them had been put in jail. Though the RSS had not formally joined the satyagraha, its members had enthusiastically taken part in it.[31] Thus, the euphoria among swayamsevaks over the Hyderabad agitation had also marked the concomitant dislocation of Godse's tailoring business.

For some time, therefore, Godse largely suspended his daily involvement with the RSS and the Hindu Mahasabha, focusing instead on his business so that he could help his family come out of financial distress. Together with Anagal, he laboured to revive the shop. From stitching clothes to dealing with customers and running around to deliver tailored items and fetch orders from new clients, this now became his daily routine. By the end of 1939, the business started looking up and Godse began to send some financial help to his parents.

Nevertheless, even during this period, he did not completely shutter himself inside his business. Though he remained oblivious to activities and meetings of the Hindu Mahasabha, he kept a window constantly open for the RSS, perhaps because the revival of his business required the local swayamsevaks' willingness to get their uniform stitched in his tailoring shop. He withdrew from the day-to-day activities of the RSS but attended important meetings which were held in Poona. That the RSS too counted him as one of its prominent members during this phase of his hibernation is reflected in documents seized by investigative agencies from the organization's Nagpur headquarters after the assassination of Gandhi about a decade later.

One of the documents talks of an important RSS meeting which was held in Poona on 9 December 1939, over three months after Godse's return from Hyderabad jail and more than a year after he joined the Hindu Mahasabha. The meeting was attended by all the important RSS organizers of Maharashtra as well as the organization's 'original members' in the region. Godse attended this meeting as 'the original member of the RSS of Sangli'.[32]

Another document pertains to a meeting of the Bombay provincial RSS unit held in Poona on 11 May 1940—almost two years after Godse joined the Hindu Mahasabha. The document recorded an upgradation in his position in the RSS since the meeting of 9 December 1939. Godse attended the 1940 meeting not merely as 'the original member of the RSS of Sangli' but as one of the organizers in Poona. 'In one file the details of Bombay Provincial RSSS[33] meeting held in 1940 were available,' the investigation report said, adding:

> In this file the name of N.V. Godse, tailor, has been noted on page 8 in the list of RSSS organizers of Poona, who had attended the meeting. The organisers' meeting was held on 11-5-40. In this meeting, Tatyarao Savarkar [another name of V.D. Savarkar], Kashinath Pant Limaya [Limaye], the Provincial Organizer of Bombay Province, Dr. Hedgewar Sar Sanghchalak Nagpur, Madhav Rao Golwalkar of Nagpur, Bapur Saheb Sohoni, Berar Provincial RSSS Organiser, Appaji Joshi, Wardha District Organiser of the RSSS and others from Nasik, Poona, Satara, Ratnagiri, Bombay, East Khandesh, etc., were present. The name of Godse was third from the top.[34]

In one respect, the meeting was of great significance for the RSS—it was the last major congregation of its leaders attended by Hedgewar before his death on 21 June 1940. According to Limaye's biographer D.S. Harshe, who witnessed its proceedings, the meeting was held in a large conference hall at N.M. Vidyalaya, a school run by RSS members in Poona, and was conducted by the 'three most prominent men of the Sangh' at that time—Hedgewar, Golwalkar and Limaye. 'Veer Savarkar attended part of the meeting. He also addressed it before leaving the venue,' Harshe wrote.[35]

By this time, Godse's circumstances improved, and he started sending Rs 125 to Rs 150 every month to his parents.[36] Soon his younger brother Dattatreya also shifted to Poona, where he set up his own business. 'With a small amount of Rs 75, Dattatreya began his business of iron work. His business grew fast, and within a year he also started supporting the family,' Godse later said. 'With Dattatreya pitching in to support the family, I started getting some spare time.'[37]

This appears to be roughly the time—around late 1941—when Godse again became eager to come out of his hibernation. 'After a gap of about two years, I began to take up the work of Hindu Mahasabha once again,' he recounted. 'Simultaneously, I became active in Rashtriya Swayamsevak Sangh.'[38]

In the years ahead, Godse's deep personal connections in the two organizations would prove critical in his aspiration to spearhead them.

~

Such an aspiration sprang up in Godse's breast owing to the idea of a 'Hindu National Militia', jointly cherished by the Hindu Mahasabha and the RSS since 1939. The idea must have been borrowed from the fascist concept of a 'National Militia' which would act as 'the bodyguard of the revolution'.[39] In India, the idea sprouted at the time of the outbreak of the Second World War and occupied the imagination of the Hindu militant organizations for some time before wartime restrictions on the RSS by the British government forced them to put it temporarily on hold. The initiative for the Hindutva joint venture came from the Hindu Mahasabha, which had been desperately looking for ways to remain relevant after the debacle of the Hyderabad satyagraha.

On 10 September 1939, a week after the beginning of the Anglo-German war, the working committee of the Hindu Mahasabha met in Bombay under the presidentship of Savarkar and adopted a resolution to create a Hindu militia. 'The Hindu Mahasabha calls upon the Hindus throughout India to organize Hindu National Militia in their respective provinces and Hindus between ages of 18 and 40 years should, in as large numbers as possible, immediately enroll as members thereof,' said the resolution.[40] From the start, the idea was conceived as an instrument of attack on Muslims, though, fearing a British government crackdown, it was presented as one of the steps required to be taken in order to prepare India to face the emergency provoked by the outbreak of the World War.

Soon after adopting the resolution, Moonje, who enjoyed the most personalized relationship with the RSS and Savarkar, and had already set up Bhonsala Military School at Nasik to impart physical as well as ideological training to Hindu youth, became the person in charge. He was made the chairman of a committee specially constituted 'to draft rules and regulations for the enlistment of members in the militia and for taking all steps necessary for arranging for their training and for enforcement of proper discipline'.[41] To enhance, apparently, the significance of the Hindu militia efforts, Savarkar, who was then the president of the Mahasabha, also became a member of this committee.

Moonje knew that the role of the RSS would be critical for building the Hindu militia. He, therefore, sent Paranjpe to persuade Hedgewar to support the proposed organization. 'On the advice of Dr. Moonje, I discussed the issue with Dr. Hedgewar,' Paranjpe wrote in *Kesari* on 5 July 1940. 'I requested him to provide some swayamsevaks for imparting training to the militia. He happily agreed to make some trained swayamsevaks available for the purpose.'[42]

Explaining the scope and objectives of the proposed militia, Moonje told the Hindu Mahasabha leaders at Poona on

8 October 1939 that the new body was being organized 'for the purpose of taking part in the defence of India both from external and internal aggression, whenever an occasion of emergency may arise during the course of the Anglo-German War.'[43] He also called upon the Maharashtrian youth to take the lead in the creation of the proposed militia. 'I believe that it will be quite in the fitness of things, in view of the historic All-India Military leadership of the Maharashtra, that a beginning should be made in the Maharashtra; so that the lead may be taken up by the whole of India afterwards,' he said.[44]

That attacking Muslims was the real motive of the proposed militia was not very hard to detect. Ten days after the Poona meeting of the Mahasabha, Moonje wrote a letter to an RSS leader explaining that Muslims were 'making themselves a nuisance', that the Congress government 'will not stand up' but would yield to them and that they [the proposed militia of Hindu Mahasabha and the RSS] would, therefore, have to 'fight both the government and the Moslims'.[45]

But on 31 July 1940, before the Hindu militia could be formed, the government, as part of its war efforts, banned the wearing of uniform and performance of drills by volunteer organizations, including the RSS, in British India.[46] 'The ban struck at the very core of the Sangh's existence by seeking to suppress those features of the organization which were its chief attractions in the eyes of its youthful recruits, viz., its uniform and its parade-ground activities,' noted a report prepared by the country's Intelligence Bureau Director, E.J. Beveridge, in 1942.[47] Regarding the observance of the ban by the RSS, he pointed out:

> While the official attitude of the Sangh to this ban is one of compliance with Government orders, there have been a

> number of instances of failure to comply either with the spirit or letter of the ban. Such cases have occurred repeatedly in the Central Provinces and occasionally in Delhi, Bombay, Madras, Sind, the Punjab and the United Provinces. Information on record shows that in only three cases have officers of the Sangh been persecuted (in Bombay, Madras and the Punjab). The Punjab case was under the Arms Act for unlawful possession of a store of swords and daggers.[48]

The ban in 1940 made the RSS operate under severe constraints. It halted the organization's expansion in British-controlled Indian provinces and dried up new recruits. S.H. Deshpande, an active member of the RSS in Poona from 1938 to 1946, noted that in the city, where the ban was taken seriously, drills stopped and swayamsevaks mostly occupied themselves with courses designed to make them 'tough and brave'.[49] The situation so threatened a section of the RSS that within a year after the ban they feared that they were destined not to control the country but to be recorded as one of the most spectacular failures in recent history.

The proposed Hindu militia, of course, could not have taken off at a time like this. Its main force, the RSS, had been hit hard, while the Hindu Mahasabha lacked the wherewithal to create a host of young people trained to take part in combat operations. The British government, fearing that a relaxation might hamper its war efforts, kept the restrictions on private paramilitary organizations enforced until the end of the Second World War and withdrew them only in 1946.

With deep personal connections in both the Hindu Mahasabha and the RSS, Godse must have been aware of the churning the two organizations had experienced during the early years of the Second World War. So, when he resumed political activities with a desire to become a crucial link between the RSS and the Mahasabha, the idea of a militia based on the joint efforts of the two organizations might have taken on new and seductive colours. 'The Sangh members in those days were debating the future course of action the organization should take,' Godse said years later. 'Should the Sangh stick to its original objective or it should modify itself and take part in politics were some of the issues which were discussed regularly. I was of the opinion that there should be a Hindu Rashtra Dal [HRD] with the objective to make our religion strong and protect the Hindu community.'[50]

It remains unclear whether Godse's proposal in the RSS circle of Poona was his own idea or it originated in the Hindu Mahasabha group which he attended simultaneously. It seems likely that the idea of the HRD first emerged in the Mahasabha circle and it won support from the section of the RSS which was extremely loyal to Savarkar.

6

An Army

Not far away, in the neighbouring town of Ahmednagar, a young schoolteacher, Narayan Dattatraya Apte, had tried his hand at a somewhat similar idea with the help of Savarkar but in vain. Since early 1941, he had been temporarily staying in Poona, deputed by his school, the American Mission High School for Girls, to complete a course in advanced teachers' training.[1] A native of Hangadi village in Sangli, Apte had studied science, graduated from Poona's Fergusson College in 1932 and then, around the mid-1930s, joined the American mission school.[2]

Like Godse, he belonged to the Chitpawan Brahmin caste and had become a devoted acolyte of Savarkar at least since February 1938—almost immediately after the latter took full control of the Hindu Mahasabha. 'Since the time you were released from your internment at Ratnagiri,' wrote Apte in a letter to Savarkar on 28 February 1938, 'a divine fire has kindled in the minds of those groups who profess that Hindustan is for Hindus; and by reason of the pronouncement which you made upon accepting the presidentship of the Hindu Mahasabha confidence is felt that that hope will materialize into a reality.'[3]

In the letter, Apte also expressed deep concern over the fact that the 'ideology' of the 'Hindu nation' was stagnating whereas the Congress, despite having a 'vacillating' ideology, was 'forging ahead'. As a countermeasure, Apte suggested the formation of a 'national volunteer army', which would consist largely of RSS members working under Savarkar's overall guidance. 'Mahasshaya, there are fifty thousand national volunteers of the Rashtriya Swayayamsewak [sic] Sangh who hold to their heart the uplift of the Hindu Nation, which is your aim [too], and this network is spread over from the Punjab upto Karnataka [. . .]. This fact is well-known to you. At this juncture the Hindu Society is standing [and] awaiting your guidance in all directions,' he wrote in his letter to Savarkar.[4]

It was clear that Apte was being very ambitious. He wanted nothing less than to be in a leadership role directly under Savarkar, bypassing the entire hierarchy of the Hindu Mahasabha. Like an astute marketing man, Apte sought to cultivate a personal relationship with the Hindu Mahasabha president in the name of laying down the foundation for a so-called 'national volunteer army'. The role in which he soon cast himself was that of a Hindu nationalist working on an ambitious plan to set up rifle training clubs in different parts of Maharashtra.[5] While doing so, he turned up frequently to obtain the help of Savarkar and his loyalists in securing licences as well as students for these rifle clubs.

From Apte's correspondence with Savarkar, it appears that the whole idea was to use the vast cadre base of the RSS and create innumerable hubs throughout Maharashtra of young men who would be trained in the handling of rifles. Together, these hubs, although it was never specified, could act as the core of what Apte described as the 'national volunteer army'—

akin to what the Hindu Mahasabha later called a 'Hindu National Militia'.

Apte's first success came on 27 October 1938, when he received the licence for a rifle club in Ahmednagar. 'It is a pleasure to inform you that due to your blessing a licence was granted to us by the Collector of this place on the 27th [October] to use four rifles (miniature .22 bore) on certain conditions,' he wrote to Savarkar on 29 October. 'This work took so much shape only because it was started on your inspiration and because you sustained (our) enthusiasm by writing letters again and again,' he added.[6]

In another letter dated 13 January 1939, Apte informed Savarkar that the rifle training had already started in Ahmednagar. 'At present three rifles are purchased,' he wrote:

> The licence is for four rifles. We will purchase the fourth soon. At present ten persons are taking instructions [in rifle]. We had already written to you that air gun class is going on. In that class as up to this date a total of hundred students have finished training. [. . .] The ten students for rifle are chosen out of those (hundred). [. . .] It is felt that mostly there will be no [dearth] of students.[7]

By May 1939, Apte had started rifle clubs in Ahmednagar, Poona, Satara and Sholapur, and completed the preparatory works in places like Chalisgaon, Jalgaon and Dombivali.[8] He now decided to speed up the opening of the club in 'every district' of Maharashtra, rapidly connect them together and bring them under one umbrella organization led directly by Savarkar. 'In the last letter I had mentioned (about my intention) of going to every district in the Maharashtra and to furnish the requisite information in the matter of opening rifle clubs, and I had said that after (the clubs are) actually opened I would write to you,' he said in a letter to Savarkar written on 10 May 1939.[9] In the same letter, he also proposed the creation of a central body under the leadership of the Hindu Mahasabha president to govern all these clubs. 'Some institutions like the Maharashtra Rifle Club may be created,' he continued:

> This institution should take into hand such important matters as what policy should be followed in all these clubs, to aid the establishment of Rifle Clubs at other places, to solve the difficulties of all the clubs, etc. My idea is that the experts in Maharashtra in this kind of matter, and eminent men like Dr Moonje [. . .] should be included in this (proposed central) institution and you should become the President.[10]

Savarkar seemed to have full knowledge of the real motive of these rifle clubs. He recognized this in a letter written to Apte on 28 June 1939. 'Of course you have already assured me in your letter that the practical work will be conducted in such a manner as to compass our end,' his letter said, adding: 'Great care should be taken in enlisting members, gentlemen who take lead at the very beginning of starting a club should be of a homogenous element.'[11] To Savarkar, the rifle club plan was clearly 'one of the most useful national activity' which should be protected and promoted through 'a special department' created in the Hindu Mahasabha and 'entrusted' to Apte.[12]

When, on 10 September 1939, the working committee of the Hindu Mahasabha adopted a resolution for setting up a National Hindu Militia, Savarkar seemed to know how to begin. But the events following England's increasing involvement in the Second World War shattered their hopes. Restrictions on the RSS in 1940 represented one aspect of the new approach of the British government in India, the refusal to renew licences for Apte's rifle clubs the other. Together, these developments turned the idea of a 'national volunteer army' a non-starter.

~

As a cigarette-smoking, whisky-loving, English-educated man in his late twenties, Apte was hardly the prototype of a Hindutva activist when he collaborated with Savarkar, but he did not lack ambition. During the approximately two years Apte spent in setting up rifle clubs, he became a member of the Hindu Mahasabha and read the Hindutva ideologue enormously.[13] But the real influence on Apte seem to have stemmed not so much from the intellectual realm as from his unbridled ambition. The degree of prestige and power that he hoped to attain through his association with Savarkar was something he could not even imagine aspiring to as a schoolteacher. Apte's loyalty to Savarkar had a basis that was totally different from Godse. Apte, unlike Godse, was not overwhelmed by Savarkar; it was Apte's ambition that most firmly bound him to Savarkar and made him one of his loyalists.

Similarly, even though the RSS had figured in his plans during the late 1930s, Apte, unlike Godse, had never been its member. He, therefore, did not know Godse previously. The first time Apte met Godse was in 1942, when the two got together to establish the HRD in Poona. No one knows as to how they met or who arranged their meeting. Though Savarkar may be suspected of the service since both were, by then, hardcore loyalists, neither Apte nor Godse disclosed the details in this regard. Nor is there any third-party account of the time to throw any light on the genesis of their relationship.

Apte had entered the world of Hindutva because he dreamt of creating his own army of young men trained in the use of firearms. The circumstances of 1940 blocked his project but he remained wedded to his dreams, so much so that he seemed ready to prefer a life of disaster to a life of disillusionment. Godse's aspiration to spearhead the RSS and the Hindu Mahasabha, and his advocacy of an organization of stormtroopers in the form of the HRD, almost aligned with Apte's dreams. The meeting of the two men in 1942 was, therefore, also a meeting of the two dreams. It marked the beginning of a long, though unlikely, friendship, one that lasted till the two were sent to the gallows.

At twenty-nine in 1942, Apte was three years younger than his friend. He was a teacher of mathematics and had come from a highly educated family. His father, Dattatraya Apte, was a reputed Sanskrit scholar and his uncle, Hari Narayan Apte, a well-known Marathi novelist.[14] Apte revered Shivaji as the symbol of Maratha pride and dreamt of re-establishing the Peshwa raj, but unlike Godse, whose chauvinistic feelings rested solely on Savarkar's writings and speeches, Apte derived his consciousness largely from reading the biography of Shivaji his father had written when he was still young.

Apte was about 5'8", and his persona exuded confidence and an irrepressible charm. He had thick black hair, large, expressive eyes and a ready smile. He was enterprising, extremely extroverted, wise in the ways of the world and capable of calculating his way to his advantage. Godse was just his opposite. He was slightly over 5-feet tall, considerably shorter than Apte, thin but taut like a coiled spring, quiet and watchful. Godse had round, protuberant eyes and the high-pitched voice of a man who lives on his nerves.

He, to be sure, entirely lacked confidence and was far from imposing in appearance.

Even their choice of clothes differed drastically. Compared to Godse's spartan wardrobe, Apte always wore western clothes, grey or black trousers and soft sports shirts being his favourite. In winter, he loved to wear a tweed jacket with the open collar of his shirt pressed neatly over the lapels. Godse was unbending and had a fussy personality, but Apte was supple and accommodating, and always eager to discreetly acquire a few rupees. Godse was mostly indifferent to food, except for his irrepressible fondness for coffee. Apte took the time to leisurely smoke cigarettes, and took pleasure in a glass of whisky, or rich food.

Above all, it was their attitude towards women that set them poles apart. Godse seemed to believe that as a righteous Hindu and true swayamsevak of the RSS, he should not cast his eyes even in passing on women other than his wife, sister and mother. In fact, he was awkward around women and remained unmarried. Perhaps he could not bear their physical presence because of his childhood experiences. Apte, on the other hand, always seemed bent on finding a woman he could seduce. Though he was married since 1932 and had even fathered a son, nothing deterred him from looking for new sexual escapades.

Godse and Apte, therefore, had little in common, but they did not realize it for they shared several surface traits. They were both united in taking instructions from Savarkar and reflecting the desire prevalent among a section of Chitpawan Brahmins for a return to Peshwa raj. They also understood instinctively that despite all their differences, they would sail only if they stayed together, else they would drift aimlessly. In fact, the unity in their dreams more than made up for the differences in their character.

~

Contrary to what is widely believed, the birth of the HRD in the summer of 1942 owed not so much to the efforts of Godse and Apte or the Hindu Mahasabha as to the RSS itself. Of course, the two friends took the lead and the Mahasabha leaders concretized the plan, but much of the new outfit's energy was channelled through the Sangh. Though the RSS never admitted to this, instead maintaining that the HRD was an informal wing of the Hindu Mahasabha, the overlap between the Sangh and Godse's new outfit was more than evident.

Once a tight band of Hindutva volunteers, the RSS had been in some disarray since 1940. Many of its testosterone-driven young swayamsevaks who, at one blow, found themselves deprived of the thrill and glamour of a potential soldier's life, found the early 1940s grim. The British government's ban, apart from dampening their morale, had lowered their self-esteem. Their very virility and masculinity, the notions generated every day in the shakha, seemed to recede. In the absence of parade-ground activities, they had ended up as mere spectators and listeners of speeches. Such a life seemed, to them, wretched and utterly unworthy.

The same impulse that had led Godse to the RSS, now brought swayamsevaks to Godse. Amidst growing despondency in the aftermath of the ban, his views and outlook were shared by an increasing number of swayamsevaks in and around Poona. They came in large numbers to take part in the eighteen-day-long foundation camp of the HRD. 'The first camp of the Dal was organized in Poona from May 1 to 18. A total of 160 swayamsevaks and sympathizers took part in it,' said Godse.[15] According to Laxman Ganesh Thatte, a Hindu Mahasabha member who, as a close friend of Godse, had actively participated in the formation of the new outfit, 'The Hindu Rashtra Dal was formed out of trusted R.S.S. men.'[16]

Curiously, the HRD worked in harmony with the RSS. No swayamsevak was expelled for joining the HRD, nor was there an official announcement by the top RSS leadership asking its members to stay away from the new outfit. And this was perhaps one of the strongest indications that, instead of representing a split in the RSS, the swayamsevaks attending the meeting of the new outfit enjoyed some kind of an official sanction.

In fact, since the inception of the HRD, Limaye, who at that time was the sanghchalak of the Maharashtra unit of the RSS, acted simultaneously as the prant pramukh or state chief of the new outfit as well. 'Shri Kashinath Limaye started working as prant pramukh [of HRD],' Godse revealed years later.[17] The revelation is at odds with the commonly accepted opinion that the HRD had nothing to do with the RSS and was essentially, though not formally, a Hindu Mahasabha offshoot consisting of hardcore Savarkar loyalists. As the sanghchalak of the most important state unit of the RSS, Limaye was one of the main decision-makers in the organization.

In the Poona camp, according to Godse, 'discussions and classes focused primarily on the means to improve the overall condition of Hindus, strengthen the Hindu religion and other related subjects'.[18] But behind this avowed goal, the HRD had sinister motives. The ostensibly non-political organization was meant to carry out secret and violent operations—those which an open organization like the RSS and the Hindu Mahasabha could not have undertaken.[19]

The combination of promised violence and conspiratorial ideology must have exerted a strong allure for a section of swayamsevaks. In thinking out ways to satisfy the desires of these young men, the organizers of the Poona camp included in the martial training programmes for HRD members a segment dealing specifically with horse riding. 'Apte was the in-charge of training the swayamsevaks in horse riding. In the camp he taught them how to mount and dismount a horse,' wrote Vasudev Balwant Gogate, a Savarkar loyalist and one of the organizers of the Poona camp, in his memoir.[20] Gogate had earned a name for himself in 1931, when as a young student he made a failed attempt to assassinate Sir Ernest Hotson, the acting Governor of Bombay, during the latter's visit to Fergusson College. None of the two shots he fired hit Hotson, who immediately secured the assailant with the help of his bodyguard. Gogate was tried and sentenced to imprisonment for ten years. Later, his prison term was reduced to six years and he was released in 1937.

In 1942, he was one of the prominent organizers of the HRD camp apart from Godse and Apte. 'Apart from a large number of swayamsevaks of Poona, those from Miraj, Sangli and Satara also attended the camp. I was in charge of ideological classes,' Gogate wrote. 'Godse acted as the host, looking after the arrangements and conduct of classes and training programmes in the camp.'[21] According to Gogate, the camp was organized in the campus of a private residence opposite Fergusson College and was attended by several important Hindutva leaders, including Savarkar and Jamnadas Mehta. 'The camp was concluded by Savarkar. He watched various programmes and activities in the camp and gave a very passionate speech to wrap it up,' said Gogate.[22]

The formation of the HRD was a major milestone in Godse's life. He seemed to have largely achieved his goal of becoming a link between the Hindu Mahasabha and the RSS. None of the two organizations officially owned up to the new outfit in view of the wartime restrictions imposed by the government, but both covertly treated it as their joint venture. In particular, the RSS seemed to have found a way to keep even despondent swayamsevaks, for whom its charm was wearing off in the absence of parade-ground activities, involved in a cause it cherished. The politically lean—and frustrating—time for the RSS was, therefore, the best time for Godse.

~

The launch of the HRD instantly elevated Godse's profile among the followers of Hindutva in Poona. It glorified his 'commitment' to the idea of a Hindu rashtra, his organizational abilities, and his oratory and clear intellect. He was now certified as worthy of the Hindu organization's attention. The launch swelled his ego and ambitions, but he instinctively understood where he must stop. Even though he had begun to think of himself as a fighter for an independent Hindu rashtra, he seemed to be cautious not to do anything that might annoy the British government.

Three months later, on 9 August, when India exploded following the arrest of Gandhi and other top Congress leaders, Godse, following the approach of the RSS and the Hindu Mahasabha, sat on the fence, watching the development indifferently. The framework he had put himself in did not allow any resistance to the colonial masters. A day before the arrest the All India Congress Committee (AICC) had passed the 'Quit India' resolution, asking for the immediate end of British rule. The resolution declared that the Congress would 'no longer [be] justified in holding the nation back from endeavouring to assert its will' and, therefore, sanctioned 'a mass struggle on non-violent lines under the inevitable leadership of Gandhiji'.[23]

The Bombay Presidency, Godse's entire world, was the nerve centre of the Quit India Movement. In Bombay, where the AICC adopted the Quit India resolution, trouble erupted on a wide scale as soon as news of Gandhi's arrest spread. Crowds vandalized local trains, cut telephone wires, damaged post offices, street lamps, etc. Schools and colleges were closed, so were markets and bazaars in most parts of Bombay. Similar protests were recorded in other towns of the Presidency, including Poona, the heart of Chitpawan activities.

From Bombay, trouble spread to the rest of India. There were Quit India hartals across the country and many of them turned into anti-government riots. Security forces sought to brutally suppress the movement, causing a massive death toll. Though the official estimate of civilian loss of life was 1,028, Nehru put the death toll at 10,000.[24] Bengal, like Bombay, emerged as a major flashpoint for intense protests, witnessing hundreds of incidents of cutting of telegraph wires and burning of mailbags and letter boxes as well as attempts to force village headmen and petty officials to resign.[25]

The upsurge complicated Godse's position, but he seemed to remain careful, perhaps aware that a nationalistic position was not in his interest. In fact, in both the statements he made after the assassination of Gandhi—the pretrial statement and the statement he gave in the special court set up at Red Fort for the murder trial—he skilfully skipped any reference to the Quit India Movement. His motivations become easier to understand if one looks at the approach of the RSS and the Hindu Mahasabha towards the Quit India Movement.

S.H. Deshpande, who was about to complete his high school in Poona and was a very active member of the RSS at that time, was shocked to see the Sangh's approach to the movement since he had been given to believe that his organization had transformed itself into a 'truly revolutionary' one. 'However, when the Quit India movement gathered momentum the RSS remained a passive onlooker,' he wrote in his reminiscences. 'In one of the theory classes, this isolation was justified on the grounds that neither the RSS nor the country was yet strong enough to overthrow the foreign yoke. The speaker [of the RSS] told us that all the blood that was being spilled in the firings was in vain!'[26]

According to S.H. Deshpande, the argument seemed convincing to him because he did not believe in a violent revolution to free India, and as such, the Quit India Movement left him unmoved. In fact, his school, N.M.V. High School, had a very strong RSS base, all its teachers being staunch supporters of the Sangh. 'I was now in the matriculation class and held a position of some importance and authority as a leader of my school-mates who were in the RSS,' he wrote, adding,

> I could therefore see to it that not once during the days of the '42 movement did our school remain closed, although we had often to face Congress-sponsored picketing by students from the other city schools, who would stand outside our school gate and shout slogans. Once when a batch of demonstrators threatened to stop classes, we got together a small band of RSS volunteers outside the gate, broke their cordon and forced them to beat a retreat.[27]

Not everyone was as convinced by the RSS stance as S.H. Deshpande. Shrinivas D. Acharya, who was a sixteen-year-old boy and a member of the RSS at that time and one year junior to S.H. Deshpande in the same school, found himself burdened by pangs of conscience over not being able to take the risk of violating the diktat of the Sangh and taking part in the Quit India Movement. 'On the whole, it was a mentality rather than a class of people which marked the members of the Sangh in those days,' Acharya recounted. 'It was an ostensibly revolutionary but actually a servile state of mind, and one that existed both inside and outside the Sangh. We as the RSS workers were given to believe that the Quit India movement was the movement of Congress and that we would have our own separate movement which would be much more decisive for setting up a Hindu rashtra. A small number of swayamsevaks could make out that such a movement would never happen, and they left the Sangh. I could not because I feared being left isolated in my group.'[28]

Acharya, in fact, never left the RSS. Even in his nineties, he would attend a nearby RSS shakha in Poona whenever his health permitted.

~

After the camp of the HRD in May, the world around Godse began to change, slowly at first, and then faster and faster. His sense of self bloated, but he never entertained truly revolutionary ideas perhaps because he owed his sense of personal value to identification with his political group, which was rooted deeply in the conservatism of the Chitpawan Brahmins. He flirted with rebellion but never embraced it. He postured as an angry young man but avoided most serious risks. His views were nuanced but riddled with contradictions.

He rose by denouncing the status quo in the RSS and the Hindu Mahasabha. But when the Quit India Movement began to shake the earth beneath and forced a section of the Hindu Mahasabha, especially its Bengal unit, to try and change the party's line of cooperation with the government, he was found defending what he had repudiated—the status quo. It seems that Godse's anxiety complex, which was at the root of the contradictions in his character, reasserted itself even as his stature grew sharply and he became an important voice in the Hindu Mahasabha.

Nevertheless, the predicament was real in the Hindu Mahasabha's unit in Bengal, where leaflets and posters had declared the Quit India Movement as 'Azadi ki Ladai'—battle for Independence—and the mobilization of almost all sections of society was virtually complete in every part of the province. The Bengal unit's predicament is reflected in a letter that Mahasabha leader N.C. Chatterjee wrote to Moonje on 14 August, five days after the arrest of Gandhi kick-started a nationwide movement. The 'present position in Bengal', Chatterjee wrote,

> is that the entire Hindu population is with Gandhiji and his movement and if anybody wants to oppose it, he will be absolutely finished and hounded out of public life. The unfortunate statement issued by Veer Savarkar [opposing Quit India movement] made our position rather difficult in Bengal. It is rather amusing to find that Mr. Jinnah wants the Mussalmans not to join the Congress movement and Mr. Savarkar wants the Hindus not to join the same.[29]

It was primarily because of this realization of the Bengal leaders, who received support from party units in some other parts of the country as well, that the working committee of the Akhil Bharat Hindu Mahasabha was forced to adopt a resolution in a meeting in Delhi on 31 August, demanding an immediate declaration of India's independence and the formation of a provisional national government. 'If the British Government still persists in its policy of callous indifference to India's national aspirations and does not respond to this demand for the recognition of India's freedom and the formation of a National Government, the Hindu Mahasabha will have no other alternative but to revise its present programme and to devise ways and means whereby Britain and her Allies will realize that India as a self-respecting nation can no longer be suppressed,' said the resolution.[30]

According to a report prepared by the Intelligence Bureau, Hindu Mahasabha leader Shyama Prasad Mukherjee, during his tour of Punjab on 9 September, asserted that if forced to act, his party would launch a 'civil disobedience—though not on Congress lines which had impeded the [Second World] War effort. He gave the impression that if Government failed to meet the Mahasabha demands there would be no alternative to "direct action".'[31]

To Godse, this was rank heresy. He watched with increasing uneasiness the success of the Bengal unit of the Mahasabha in building up a vigorous campaign inside the party to discard the old line of cooperation with the British government. If left to itself, the Bengal unit might have captured the party and overturned the Maharashtra line, and for objectives which Godse violently opposed.

What the Bengal unit of the Mahasabha was experiencing for the first time—the temptation to take a nationalist position under popular pressure created by the Quit India Movement—Godse had long ago gone through. Ever since Savarkar had stopped him from taking part in Gandhi's Civil Disobedience Movement in 1930, he had known the anguish of a reality that had run counter to his own temptations. But he had also learnt long ago that no matter how tempting the desire to deviate from the path shown by the Hindutva ideologue had been, he must resist it to remain connected to the goal of a Hindu rashtra.

All along, the Maharashtra unit of the Hindu Mahasabha had given the political line to the party. No alteration in the arrangement was acceptable to Godse and most members of the Maharashtra unit of the party. The inevitable showdown came in less than a month. In another working committee meeting of the Akhil Bharat Hindu Mahasabha held at Delhi from 3 to 5 October, a fresh resolution was passed, putting the 31 August resolution on the backburner, thus taking the organization back to its original politics.[32]

Just before the October meeting, Godse, along with Hindu Mahasabha leaders M.B. Udgaonkar and D.G. Abhayankar, had written a joint letter to Moonje, demanding: 'No resolution passed by the Mahasabha should in any way compel Hindus to start civil disobedience or "direct action" involving an endless strife at this most inappropriate time and on such a fundamentally radical issue as "independence".' The letter stressed on the need to 'save the Mahasabha from being engulfed in a bottomless pit'.[33]

Clearly, Godse had now become a strong voice in the Hindu Mahasabha and a dedicated political leader. His speeches were forceful and attacks outlandish. 'His facts were often wrong, his opinions usually contradictory and aggressively didactic, and his attitudes theatrical,' Acharya recounted. As a young swayamsevak in the 1940s, Acharya had attended several of Godse's meetings. 'His voice was shrill and he used vigorous gestures while speaking. He tried to arouse emotion by building up a series of apparently disconnected sentences delivered in repetitive bursts but in varying tones,' Acharya added.[34]

7

And a Newspaper

The strengthening of the HRD continued the following year. More units of the outfit were formed and their activities became more structured. A saffron cap was adopted for the HRD swayamsevaks in contrast to the black cap of the RSS members.[1] It was probably a deliberate move to make two sets of swayamsevaks look slightly different from each other. The rest of the uniform remained the same. Better coordination also began between the RSS and the Hindu Mahasabha in the running of the HRD and the training of its cadre.

In May 1943, the HRD organized its second annual camp, this time in Ahmednagar. By then, Apte had returned to Ahmednagar after completing his teachers' training course in Poona. He and Godse worked hard to make the camp as successful as the one in Poona. Held for fifteen days, the Ahmednagar camp was attended by around 100 swayamsevaks.[2] This camp was much more organized than the previous one. Each swayamsevak attending the Ahmednagar camp had been told in advance to bring a set of khaki shorts and white shirt—the uniform of an RSS member—along with a saffron cap and charged Rs 14 as fee for lodging, food and other facilities.[3] They were also asked specifically to wear the saffron cap, along with khaki shorts and a white shirt on special occasions in the camp.[4]

Every morning, the swayamsevaks would assemble in rows for a military-style call to order, followed by exhaustive physical exercises. The camp's curriculum included training in the handling of airguns and theoretical instructions—*baudhik varg* (ideological classes)—delivered by teachers from the Hindu Mahasabha and the RSS. Apte, who had the experience of running rifle clubs, personally supervised the airgun training. G.V. Ketkar and 'Professor Mate' were among the prominent teachers sent by the Hindu Mahasabha for theoretical instruction to the HRD camp.[5] Ketkar, a senior leader of the Mahasabha, presented an assessment of the works of his party, while Mate, who taught at Poona's S.P. College, spoke on the need for promoting unity among Hindus, though, of course, without challenging the Brahminical hegemony.

The involvement of the RSS in the running of the camp and training of the HRD cadres now became more elaborate and complex than in the past. For theoretical classes in the Ahmednagar camp it sent two of its best teachers—P.G. Sahasrabuddhe and D.V. Gokhale.[6] Sahasrabuddhe taught Marathi literature at Poona's N.M.V. High School in 1943 and was one of the most prominent members of the ideological branch of the RSS.[7] During the ideological classes of the RSS, Sahasrabuddhe used to sermonize on subjects like capitalism, socialism, fascism, and social and political philosophy.[8] At the Ahmednagar camp of the HRD, he delivered lectures on the subject of 'socialism and the Hindu Rashtra'.[9]

D.V. Gokhale, the other RSS man who addressed the HRD members attending the Ahmednagar camp, was considered the Sangh's rising star in Poona. He was just over twenty in 1943 and had become a pracharak or full-time member after passing his intermediate exams from Poona's S.P. College in 1942—the year when the RSS created its first batch of pracharaks who vowed to remain celibate and dedicate their lives to the expansion of the organization. D.V. Gokhale was a strict disciplinarian and was considered in the RSS circle an expert on war-related issues.[10] In the HRD camp, he spoke on the subject of 'current war [Second World War] and Hindusthan'.[11]

Overall, the training seemed to draw on the tested practices of the RSS and was meant to prepare the HRD cadres for specific political purposes. It could be that the Hindu Mahasabha also provided teachers for the Ahmednagar camp but it was the imprint of the RSS which was most visible. In fact, even the training framework—the baudhik varg—belonged to the RSS, which had used it for the last many years. The atmosphere in the HRD camp, therefore, was no different from any RSS baudhik varg, in which the combination of a call to arms, exclusive association of Hindu men and conspiratorial ideology always exerted strong allure. Teachers evoked the 'glorious' past of Hindus while ridiculing the democratic polity or finding fault with the Indian National Congress because it was 'founded by the British'.[12] Their lectures were profusely illustrated with stories from history and the Puranas but carefully avoided serious analysis of any problem—contemporary or past—of history, philosophy, economy, politics or social life.[13]

Given the primacy of the RSS in the HRD camp, no other teacher could excel as much as Sahasrabuddhe. A vocal admirer of the European dictators of the time, he was known for using his lectures for promoting a pro-authoritarian state of mind among swayamsevaks. Referring to a series of lectures by Sahasrabuddhe to RSS volunteers in 1942, an Intelligence report said:

> On 4.5.42 he [Sahasrabuddhe] announced that the Sangh followed the principle of dictatorship. Denouncing democratic government as an unsatisfactory form of government, he quoted France as a typical bad example and, praising dictatorship, he pointed to Japan, Russia and Germany. He particularly praised the Fuehrer principle of Germany. On 21.5.42 he drew attention to the value of propaganda, quoting Russia and Germany as examples, and again extolled the virtues of the Leader principle, citing Mussolini's success as a further example.[14]

Sahasrabuddhe's effectiveness was due as much to the choice of his topic as to his oratorical powers. 'P.G. [Sahasrabuddhe] was a teacher in school,' remembered S.H. Deshpande. 'He was a brilliant orator and was held in awe by his pupils. There is no doubt that it was his untiring efforts that had won for the RSS hundreds of my schoolmates.'[15] There is every reason to believe that Sahasrabuddhe might have reflected the same spirit at the Ahmednagar camp, especially at a time when the underlying principle of training seemed to be to develop the HRD into not only an instrument for the protection of the Hindu nationalist movement but also primarily the training school for the future struggle that might be required to make India a Hindu rashtra.

Heading it all as the leader, star speaker and organizer was Limaye himself, the RSS's Maharashtra chief, who had doubled as the state president of the HRD since its foundation in 1942. This fact had been widely advertised by Godse and Apte in their bid to attract the maximum number of RSS workers to the annual camp of the HRD. A printed advisory sent jointly by the duo to potential participants ahead of the HRD's Ahmednagar camp stated: 'Rashtriya Swayamsevak Sangh's prant sanghchalak KB Limaye will stay in the camp for two to three days. You will, therefore, get an opportunity to listen to his precious thoughts.'[16]

Limaye's stay at the Ahmednagar camp signified the close association of the RSS with the HRD. In fact, the lines between the two outfits were not always easy to discern. Many years after the assassination of Gandhi, a section of the RSS, which was constantly aware of the presence of this uncomfortable link of the organization with Godse and the HRD, quietly circulated stories suggesting that Limaye had stayed out of the RSS from 1943 to 1945 and that the Sangh had nothing to do with his activities during that period. If anything, the myth of Limaye breaking away from the RSS exemplified the paranoid attitude of the organization, which scrambled for an escape route when confronted squarely. That is the only way to explain the fake narrative. A distortion of history of this magnitude could not have been successfully accomplished during Limaye's lifetime. For Limaye might just have spoken in his defence. After his death in 1980, Walter K. Andersen, the American researcher whose access to the Nagpur headquarters of the RSS was rather conspicuous, and co-author Shridhar D. Damle allowed a lie into their 1987 book, *The Brotherhood in Saffron: The Rashtriya Swayamsevak Sangh and Hindu Revivalism*. Without giving a reference to a document or an interview, the book—partly in its main text and partly in its endnotes—quietly claimed that Limaye, due to his differences with Golwalkar, resigned from the RSS in 1943 and stayed out for three years, joining back and resuming the charge only in 1945.[17]

This was a clear case of myth-making, for archival documents and reminiscences of the period simply reject the theory of any rupture in Limaye's relationship with the RSS during the years preceding the assassination of Gandhi. Of the various sets of records seized from the RSS headquarters at Nagpur during the investigation of the assassination, one pertained to letters from the organization's satraps in different parts of the country informing about the funds collected during the day of 'Guru Dakshina'—the offering made by swayamsevaks on a particular day every year—in their respective areas. Limaye's name as the RSS leader operating from Sangli figures prominently in the list prepared based on the correspondence received during 1944 and 1945, the years Andersen and Damle claimed Limaye had stayed out of the Sangh.[18]

The myth is also punctured by reminiscences of the period. In his account, Narhari N. Kirkire, a swayamsevak who lived in Sangli from 1937 to 1945, mentions an episode of Limaye representing the RSS in a meeting with the ruler of the princely state in 1944.[19]

A similar reminiscence was provided by Pujari. A Sangli-based swayamsevak, Pujari was eighteen in 1944 when Limaye organized a three-day winter camp of the RSS men of the region at Kurundwad, a neighbouring princely state. 'About 400 swayamsevaks from Sangli, Miraj, Kurundwad, Kolhapur and nearby areas attended the winter camp of 1944,' Pujari remembered. 'Around 11 o'clock on the very first night, while Kaka [Limaye was affectionately called Kaka by RSS men] was addressing us, a swayamsevak left for toilet without taking permission from him. Kaka continued to address us, but when that swayamsevak returned, he stopped his speech and ordered all of us to pack up, lift our beddings and march for three miles to Narsobawadi [a township close to Kurundwad] and return to the camp site. He was a strict disciplinarian and used to give severe punishments for any breach of discipline. It was only around three in the morning that we returned and then went to sleep.'[20]

The fake narrative, not possible without encouragement or even direct support from the RSS, fits with the organization's penchant for making myths aimed at facilitating its expansion or hiding the sordid events of its past. Distorting history to create Islamophobia among Hindus or to push the notion that their sense of being a nation arose in the Hindus' fight against Muslim rulers offers a hint about how important a strategic tool myth-making has been for the RSS. In the decades after the assassination of Gandhi, the RSS would use this tool in a much more comprehensive way in its bid to set itself apart from the assassin.

In the case of Limaye, however, the myth-makers missed what he was worth to the RSS, particularly between 1940 and 1946, when the paramilitary outfit had to operate under severe constraints due to the ban on parade-ground activities. As the ban was enforced in the British–Indian provinces, the RSS, for the entire period, tried desperately to keep itself alive by expanding its activities in states ruled by Hindu princes—a requirement that constrained the organization in the Bombay Presidency and made it even more dependent on Limaye than it had ever been. An Intelligence Bureau report of June 1943 said that 'the Rashtriya Swayam Sevak Sangh, in its anxiety to avoid any action which would draw the attention of the authorities in British India to its activities, is endeavouring more and more to entrench itself in the Hindu States where, according to one report, it hopes to perfect its organization and training unhindered'.[21] The pressure on the RSS might just have increased after September 1944, when the British government issued a fresh order—Camps and Parades (Control) Order, 1944—providing more power to provincial governments for the control of parades and camps.[22]

When the ban came into effect in 1940, of all the Marathi princely states, the RSS was the strongest in Sangli thanks to Limaye. From this bastion, Limaye oversaw the expansion of the Sangh's activities in the neighbouring princely states of Kolhapur, Ichalkaranji, Jamkhandi, Miraj, Kurundwad, Budhgaon, Aundh, Kirloskarwadi, Kundal, Phaltan, Bhor and Akkalkot till the government ban of 1940 as well as the control order of 1944 were withdrawn in September 1946.[23] Relying on Limaye's contacts, Golwalkar was able to obtain permission to hold their annual military style conclave, called the Officers' Training Camp, in 1943 in Sangli and Kolhapur.[24]

Given the pivotal position Limaye occupied in the network of the RSS in Maharashtra, his absence from the organization during the critical years of 1943–45 couldn't have remained a secret affair—a fact that various myth-makers did not respect as they set out to sanitize the history of the Sangh in later years.

~

The credo of the HRD was inseparable from the political ideology promoted by the RSS and the Hindu Mahasabha. The name of the new outfit was not idly picked; it signified the sense of purpose that fuelled the two parent organizations at the time the run up to India's independence began. The secret nature of the new outfit also indicated the dubious means through which the goal of making India a Hindu rashtra after independence was being contemplated. The Congress party's unyielding command over most of the Hindus made the RSS and the Hindu Mahasabha uncomfortable because it challenged their claim to represent the community. Democratically, therefore, the RSS was in no position to secure their idea of India. Yet, it was determined to forge ahead. Branding Gandhi and the Congress as enemies of

Hindus was a conspicuous example of their strategy to achieve the objective through undemocratic means.

As an increasingly active member of the RSS and the Hindu Mahasabha, Godse identified with their campaign against Gandhi and the Congress—after all, he was spearheading the goal of a Hindu rashtra by virtue of being the leader of the HRD. His radicalization as a leader of the HRD did not merely carry him into a state of opposition towards a democratic India, in some respects, it deepened his alignment with the antipathy of the RSS and the Mahasabha to Gandhi and the Congress.

Strictly speaking, the HRD did not develop any distinctive ideology except for a generalized Hindutva belligerence and some training in the handling of airguns. It had no strategy, merely an enormous restiveness. Most of those who joined its ranks were not even political soldiers. Rather, their temper was that of fake mercenaries and their passions were roused by high-sounding political slogans—'Hindustan belongs to Hindus', 'saffron flag is our national flag', 'one nation, one leader' and the like. But they knew nothing about how to translate these slogans on the ground. As most of them originally belonged to the RSS, they gave their allegiance not to a programme but to the parent organization and then to an individual leader—Savarkar, whose personality and habits of mind had led him to hold himself above all the Hindu militant organizations. He, however, was always in a double mind as he remained acutely conscious of the risk involved in being seen publicly leading an organization which had secret motives and was developing into a body of stormtroopers. It did not bother him in the least if his follower Godse ran the same risk; indeed, Savarkar seemed to prefer it. 'All of us wanted Savarkarji to act as the dictator of the Dal. But he refused to accept this position. He only assured to provide guidance to the Dal,' Godse said later.[25]

The double standard Savarkar practised in this regard sometimes puzzled Godse. The outfit was Savarkar's personal initiative, yet he dithered when it came to leading it from the front. Godse felt annoyed when, despite his repeated requests, Savarkar declined to attend the second annual camp of the HRD. At one point, Godse was so anguished that he shot a very harsh letter to Savarkar. 'People at Nagar [Ahmednagar is also called Nagar] are greatly disappointed on account of your decision not to visit Nagar,' he wrote to Savarkar a week before the HRD camp was to begin. 'I have not got enough words to describe it. Similarly, Hindu Rashtra Dal considers you as its Supreme Head. I cannot describe adequately the mental anguish caused by the disappointment resulting from the fact that our supreme head cannot attend even the annual session of the youths in connection with the "Shibir" [camp].'[26]

Savarkar's approach reflected an uncomplicated opportunism but that did not diminish Godse's reverential attitude towards him. Despite the occasional rebellious gestures, Godse remained meekly subservient to Savarkar, perhaps because of his intrinsic craving for approval and a sense of belonging. On 29 May 1943, two weeks after the Ahmednagar camp, following instructions from Savarkar, Godse hosted him for a private discussion with members of the HRD at Poona. According to an Intelligence report, Savarkar told the HRD members 'to vow implicit allegiance to him' and 'to remain a distinct body from other Hindu institutions'.[27] Private discussions, in fact, formed a key element in Savarkar's strategy to sustain his relationship with the HRD.

Nevertheless, the HRD carried its success deeper and deeper into new pockets of Maharashtra. Sometime in the second half of 1943, Apte got selected for the Royal Air Force, and the entire burden of the HRD fell on Godse. The latter, however, remained relentless in his efforts. He drank coffee and saved himself from all vices, throwing all his energy and the drive of his growing ambition into the new outfit. It was mainly because of his hard work—helped ably by Limaye—that several new units were set up under his leadership in places like Bombay, Miraj, Sholapur, Barshi, Pandharpur and Indore by the end of 1943.[28]

Godse connected well with the HRD swayamsevaks, who shared many traits with him. They jotted down lectures he delivered in 'the study classes of Hindu Rashtra Dal'.[29] But beyond these classes and periodical camps, there was virtually no specific action on the ground. The high-sounding political slogans they used in their meetings were only a cloak for their inaction. The approach of the RSS not to indulge in any activity that might attract government reprisal and to remain on the right side of the British seemed to also restrain the HRD. The new outfit's collaborationist approach was exhibited most remarkably early in 1944 when Godse—apparently with the help of Apte—got the British Indian Army to set up a 'war exhibition' in the outer compound of Poona's S.P. College while an ideological training camp for HRD members was conducted in the college's conference hall.[30]

In a broad sense, Godse had come to enjoy the undeclared leadership role in the HRD in quite the same way as his masters did in their respective organizations—Savarkar in the Hindu Mahasabha and Limaye in the Maharashtra unit of the RSS. The mental distance between a follower and the followed had shrunk. The initiatives he would take up in the ensuing months would alter his destiny.

~

Around the end of 1943, only months after joining the Royal Air Force, Apte had to abruptly quit the job and return to Poona. At the time, Godse was working at a hectic pace, trying to create as many units of the HRD as he could. Apte's decision to leave the job was due to the death of one of his brothers who headed the family.[31] As the situation burdened Apte with family responsibilities, he had to restrain his political ambitions and look for gainful employment. He had resigned from the American Mission High School before joining the special duty branch of the Royal Air Force, so returning to the Ahmednagar school was not an option. His teaching experience finally helped him obtain a job as a teacher of mathematics at a local school in Poona, Bhavi School, around the beginning of 1944.[32]

Godse's ambition leapt the moment Apte's feet touched Poona's soil. Though the family responsibilities forced Apte to live the quiet life of a teacher for a few months, he remained restless and envisioned diversifying his activities to meet his political ambition. Not long after coming to Poona, Godse and he began to discuss ways to widen the compass of their pursuits. Without much delay, there were stirrings of a business venture in their discussions. The venture—the launch of a Marathi newspaper—would be based on an alliance and division of labour between Godse and Apte. It carried two components: the promise of a sustained income and an opportunity of actively taking part in the political project of a Hindu rashtra.

During the Second World War, newsprint was a scarce commodity, so there was a restriction on starting a new newspaper. *Agrani* was an old Marathi title which had stopped its publication from Poona for some time.[33] 'We decided to take over *Agrani* and revive it. We obtained permission from its editor, Shri Shikhare, and then submitted necessary declarations in the office of the Magistrate of Poona,' Godse said later.[34] Thereafter, the duo started a vigorous campaign to collect money for the launch of the newspaper. 'We needed at least Rs 20,000 to start the newspaper,' said Godse. 'We first approached Advocate Savarkar. He had received Rs 200,000 as contribution [from his followers] on the occasion of his sixtieth birth anniversary the previous year. We requested him to give us some money for the newspaper. He gave us Rs 15,000 as loan. We also collected small amounts of two-three thousand each from several other people.'[35]

The first issue of *Agrani* with Godse as its editor and Apte as its general manager was published on 25 March 1944. With the launch of the newspaper, their acquaintanceship deepened into a partnership. There was, however, no question about who was in charge. More often than not, Apte took decisions and Godse responded with obedience. But there is no evidence of this hierarchy ever coming in the way of their mutual trust.

Years later, after he had assassinated Gandhi, Godse said that as Hindutva activists Apte and he had been fired by anger over the general attitude in the contemporary press not to give proper coverage to activities of Hindu organizations. 'On 16 January 1944, we discussed this issue in detail and concluded that there was no point in crying over our failure to get our activities covered in the press,' he recounted. 'We were of the opinion that things would work out only if we brought out our own newspaper and published our activities in it. We, therefore, decided to start a newspaper, and from the next day we began our preparation.'[36]

To some extent, Godse was not completely off the point. But he seemed to have concealed the more compelling factors from his interrogators. For there is no evidence to show that the decision to start a newspaper was taken spontaneously.

The two friends might certainly have felt resentment over the Hindu organizations' inability to make headlines in the general newspapers of the time. But Apte—if not Godse—also seemed to be looking for ways to draw a sustained and regular income while getting involved in Hindutva politics and might just have sought to exploit the situation, which had become a matter of concern for Hindu organizations, to his advantage.

Also, Godse and Apte were not the only ones in the Marathi linguistic region who felt the need for a local newspaper to promote Hindutva ideology. In 1944 itself, two more Marathi newspapers besides *Agrani* came into existence with the overt backing of the RSS. One of them, *Vikram*, was started from Sangli by the RSS chief in Maharashtra and one of Godse's mentors, Limaye.[37] The other, *Tarun Bharat*, was launched in Nagpur by Narkesari Smarak Mandal Trust, a body close to the RSS.[38] All three papers shared the same tone: they were bitterly critical of the Congress and detested Gandhi for his philosophy of non-violence and his idea of Hindu–Muslim unity, and their approach to communal problems was aggressively communal.

'I was in high school when the three newspapers began their publication,' said Pujari. 'Apart from *Vikram*, which was published from Sangli, we also used to get *Agrani* regularly. Young swayamsevaks like me used to go door to door to distribute them and convince people to become their subscribers. That was the usual practice those days in Maharashtra. As far as I remember, *Tarun Bharat* hardly ever reached Sangli till I completed my matriculation in 1946, and so we believed that *Vikram* and *Agrani* were the only two newspapers that carried our viewpoint at a time when all prominent newspapers were pro-Congress.'[39]

A similar enthusiastic reception to the new newspaper was given by the RSS members of Poona. 'For young swayamsevaks of Poona, the publication of *Agrani* was a very special occasion. Restrictions on our drills had taken away the thrills of regular shakhas. For some time, therefore, the distribution of *Agrani* became one of the new attractions for us,' recalled Acharya.[40] *Agrani* carried Savarkar's photograph on its masthead and positioned itself as an informal mouthpiece of the HRD.

'Apte and I became so busy after the launch of the newspaper that it became difficult to find time for the activities of Hindu Rashtra Dal. So around the end of the year [1944], we told the swayamsevaks of Hindu Rashtra Dal that because of our engagement in the newspaper we won't be able to spare time for them and that they should themselves run their branches,' Godse said later. 'We also informed the [HRD] swayamsevaks that the newspaper was facing a financial crisis and that we would be able to spare time for Hindu Rashtra Dal only after the crisis was over. The expansion of Hindu Rashtra Dal stopped after we diverted our attention.'[41]

After launching himself on a journalistic career, Godse began to follow politics more keenly.[42] From now on, his life as a political activist was driven by a ruthless determination to achieve the goal set by his masters—of a Hindu rashtra. It seems that he had also developed an exalted notion of his own abilities, recognizing himself as a leader in a chrysalis. Whether he was taking part in public events or writing articles for his newspaper, his overriding concern was himself. He was incandescent in the articles that appeared in *Agrani*, in each piece roundly denouncing Gandhi, non-violence and the idea of Hindu–Muslim amity. In course of time, the paper frequently carried articles which were outright communal and had a good deal of abuse for Gandhi.

~

It was a heady time to be starting a newspaper and hurling oneself into a journalistic career. After the Quit India Movement subsided and while Gandhi and other Congress leaders were still in jail, the prelude to the post-Second World War negotiations for the transfer of power by the British rulers was being staged. As the government had declared that any move towards Indian statehood would be possible only if the Congress and the Muslim League resolved their differences, the issue of Pakistan now became the main point of debate in political circles. The League was adamant on a separate state of Pakistan, while the Congress was not ready for India's partition. The Hindu militant organizations, with no history of ever organizing any agitation for India's independence of their own conception, got an opportunity to enter—for the first time—into the larger political debate. They stoked communal hatred against Muslims and demanded exclusive right for Hindus over India, thus deepening the fears of Muslims, while at the same time declaring that in no case would they allow 'vivisection' of the country.

As the deadlock threatened to perpetuate the colonial domination instead of hastening its fall, Congress leader C. Rajagopalachari, or Rajaji, came up with a proposal, suggesting a post-war commission to demarcate contiguous districts in the north-west and east of India where Muslims had absolute majority; plebiscite of all inhabitants in such areas to decide whether they would prefer a separate Pakistan; mutual agreement for cooperation on defence, commerce and communications in case of separation; and the implementation of the whole scheme only after the League endorsed the Congress demand for independence and the British transferred power to Indian hands.[43]

The Hindu Mahasabha and the RSS immediately launched a propaganda campaign against what they dubbed as the tacit acceptance of the concept of Pakistan by the Congress. They dubbed Rajagopalachari's proposal—known as the 'Rajaji Formula'—as evidence of the Congress' capitulation to the League. Almost out of nothing, the Hindu Mahasabha and the RSS sought to create a potentially huge stake for themselves. The occasion was a real baptism of fire for a newly born journalist in Godse who, for the first time, came out of his constant indulgences with trifling local matters to comprehend and reflect on a national political issue, though he looked at it in a piecemeal and communal manner. 'It became clear to me that Congress and Muslim League were cooperating and that this cooperation might lead to the formation of Pakistan,' said Godse.[44]

His newly acquired understanding, though faulty in every respect, was in accord with the propaganda campaign of Hindu organizations. 'We started opposing Congress' cooperation with the League. We wrote a series of articles denouncing it. After that the politics of Hindustan started changing fast,' he continued.[45] Godse's attunement to the mood of the Hindu Mahasabha and the RSS, and his sense of what they wanted from him, seemed to lay at the root of his faulty comprehension of the Congress' position vis-à-vis the League's Pakistan demand. To a great extent, these initial political observations of Godse also signalled his sense of increasing personal value, perhaps because of his rising visibility through *Agrani*.

Weeks after the launch of his newspaper, the entire debate on Rajaji Formula reached Poona. In April 1944, Rajagopalachari visited the city's Aga Khan Palace—which had been turned into a jail where Gandhi was kept after his arrest in August 1942—to discuss his proposal. 'On coming out of the Aga Khan Palace, he [Rajagopalachari] declared that Gandhiji had approved his plan,' said Godse.[46] From this point on, Godse seems to have begun holding Gandhi singularly responsible for appeasing Jinnah. Until then Godse had acted either by instinct or by imitation and had always been plagued by self-doubt. Now, as he put some of his thoughts down on paper in the form of articles, his ideas started getting firmer.

Soon, they started translating into concrete action. Gandhi was released from jail on 5 May 1944 because of ill health. After spending a week in Poona, he moved to Bombay and stayed for almost a month in a seaside cottage in Juhu. From there he went back to Poona and then on to Panchgani, a beautiful hill station in the Western Ghats where he could escape the fierceness of the Indian summer.[47] As his health improved, he gradually started engaging in the political process once again. On 17 July, Gandhi wrote to Jinnah and sought a meeting with him. 'Please do not regard me as an enemy of Islam and the Muslims here,' he remarked. 'I have always been a friend and servant of yours and of the whole world. Do not dismiss me.'[48]

A week later, Godse's men showed up. Just when Gandhi was concluding his prayer meeting at Panchgani on 22 July, a group of young men led by Apte stood in protest against his approval of the Rajaji Formula. According to a news report published in the *Times of India* on 23 July 1944:

> The hostility of a militant section of Hindu Community to Mr. Gandhi's blessing of Mr. Rajagopalachari's communal formula was reflected immediately after the termination of prayers on Saturday [22 July] when the spokesman of a group of a dozen Hindu youths rose suddenly and asked Mr. Gandhi questions and expressed "resentment".
>
> Mr. Gandhi in a low tone replied, but the Hindu youths were not satisfied. They waved black flags for five minutes

> outside the hall and then left. Mr. Gandhi remained calm and drove away to his residence. [. . .]
>
> The youth who asked the questions is understood to be a Poona journalist, named Mr. ND Apte, while his companions are also from Poona. They are said to belong to a fairly militant Hindu organization. He asked Mr. Gandhi who was seated on the "dais" whether it was true as reported in the press, that he had approved of the communal-Pakistan formula. Mr. Gandhi replied that that was so. The youth said that they were there to express their resentment against his blessing of the Pakistan scheme. Mr. Gandhi asked him whether he had any written statement to give him. The reply was that the opposition had already been voiced and that he and his friends had come personally to voice their protest. Mr. Gandhi remarked that it could hardly be the time or place for such a course.[49]

It is not clear whether Godse was part of the group or he was involved in dispatching the protestors to Gandhi's prayer meeting. His name was not mentioned in the news report. Nor did Godse or Apte say anything in this regard in their respective statements, both stating that it was the latter who led this protest.[50] Yet, the protest signalled Godse's new direction at a time when he seemed set not to live placidly.

8

Psychosexual Pangs

On a personal level, talk of marriage surrounded Godse. It had come up in the past too, particularly after his shift to Poona from Sangli, but had subsided after he was jailed in the course of the Hyderabad satyagraha. The launch of *Agrani*, which promised a regular monthly income for Godse, revived this talk again. Generally, in those days, Chitpawans married young, but Godse remained unmarried even though he was past the age of thirty. In 1944, he was thirty-four years old, and the family agreed that the time had come for him to marry.

Godse, however, seems to have been afflicted by a revulsion for women. Perhaps it was memories from his unusual childhood, of a boyhood spent garbed as a girl, which informed his later life. Except for his mother and his elder sister Mathura, he could not bear the physical presence of women in his private life. Sometimes it created embarrassing situations for him. In one instance, Godse, who suffered from excruciating migraines, was so grievously affected by its attack that Apte had to deliver him half-conscious to a Poona hospital. When he woke up and found himself in a ward serviced by nurses, he panicked and, pulling a sheet around him, ran away from the hospital rather than allowing female hands to touch him.[1]

He took more pleasure in the company of men than women and, therefore, overrode family expectations. This did not go down well with his family, certainly not at a time when he had started living independently and almost stopped providing financial assistance to his parents. His parents, who had moved by now to Poona from Sangli and lived on his father's pension, did not approve of Godse's 'indifference to household matters' and grudgingly expressed this to one of their relatives, Narain Vithal Paranjpe, who lived in Jubbulpore.[2]

Godse's choice fitted with the Hindutva world view in which the assertion of masculinity, power and virility—both discursively and institutionally—occupied the central position. In that world, non-association with women is even today extolled as something akin to the vow of brahmacharya, the voluntary renunciation of sex in all its form, said to have been practised in ancient times by Hindu seers. The pledge of celibacy was, and still is, a condition for an RSS man desirous of becoming a pracharak of the organization. Though there is no evidence to suggest that at any point he formally became a pracharak, a position created within the Sangh only in 1942, Godse was a member of the RSS and stayed away from women.

His close association with Savarkar seems only to have sharpened his uncompromising views on women. Savarkar was a man who believed females to be only slightly above beasts of burden and that a woman was nothing but a vessel to bear sons. In a speech delivered at Nagpur in 1937, he advised women 'to be mothers of fine, healthy progeny' and declared that the 'kitchen and children' were their main duties.[3] In an essay titled 'Women's beauty and duty', Savarkar argued that 'the primary duty of a woman is to the home, children and the nation'.[4] He believed that since there was a fundamental and natural difference between man and woman and since 'their duties are different', their education must also 'necessarily differ'.[5] Although he was not against formal education for women, he felt that they should be trained in areas suited to their 'temperament' and that they were primarily needed to be educated as mothers so that they could 'enrich the nation with a generation stronger, more beautiful, and more patriotic than the past'.[6] According to Savarkar, any woman who digressed from her duty in the domestic sphere became 'morally guilty of a breach of trust'.[7]

Savarkar's ideas were not unusual. In traditional Brahmin families most men scorned and mistreated women, and nearly all Brahmin women of that generation lived in subjugation verging on slavery. The preservation of Hindu spiritual values by subjugating women was, and still is, considered necessary by Brahminic Hinduism in the making of a Hindu rashtra. Perhaps it was the masculine content of Hindutva that led Savarkar to call India a 'fatherland' rather than 'motherland'.

In the summer of 1945 when Savarkar came to Poona for the marriage of his daughter Prabhat, Shantabai Gokhale, an important woman leader of the Hindu Mahasabha in the city, saw Godse hovering on the periphery of the Savarkar family. Shantabai was trying, at that time, to resolve a conflict between Savarkar and his wife. The mediation had been necessitated because Savarkar had decided not to spend on the wedding ceremony, which he wanted to keep extremely puritanical, while Yamuna desired a celebration of the marriage of their only daughter. Of the four children born to Savarkar and Yamuna, two had died young and only Prabhat and Vishwas, a son, had survived. But since Savarkar had given his mandate, Yamuna felt too intimidated to revive a discussion on the subject with her husband. Shantabai, who sympathized with Yamuna, decided to take up the issue with Savarkar and persuade him to allow his wife a say in the decision for as important an occasion as the marriage of an only daughter. Shantabai's biographer recorded her conversation with Savarkar:

> 'What is your estimate? How much it should cost?' Savarkar asked as Shantabai tried to reason out with him.
>
> 'Not more than five hundred rupees,' Shantabai replied.
>
> Tatya [Savarkar] then called for Nathuram and asked him to give five hundred rupees to Shantabai. While giving the money, Nathuram asked her: 'When will you give me the details of the expenditure?'
>
> 'Within eight days,' she replied before taking the money and coming out of the room.
>
> When Shantabai informed all that to Yamunatai, the latter said: 'It could become possible only because of you.'[8]

The vignette, though small, is adequate. Savarkar treated his wife Yamuna peremptorily, as if some dignity to her might have endangered his political project. As a loyal follower, Godse willingly sided with him, never being able to see the ill-treatment for what it was. Godse—the ideologically driven man buffeted by forces that he neither controlled nor fully understood—must have imbibed his ideas considerably from his ideological master.

~

Apte was different. He did not suffer from quite the degree of contempt for women that surrounded his friend. But he was compulsively sexual. Though he had been married for over a decade, nothing, not even extremely urgent matters, could deter him from a possible seduction. During the time Godse was trying to save his private sphere and protect himself from the touch of a woman, Apte had already begun a deeply emotional affair with a young Christian woman.

The young woman's name was Manorama Salvi and she was the daughter of a doctor posted in a hospital at Shegaon, a small Maharashtra town about 500 km east of Bombay. Manorama had met Apte at American Mission High School, where she was a student and he a teacher of mathematics. Even after he left the school and joined the Royal Air Force in 1943, she was among the girls with whom Apte corresponded regularly. In 1944, she completed her matriculation and moved to Bombay, where she took admission at Wilson College and started living in Pandita Ramabai Girls Hostel at Alexandra Road, Gamdevi.

In July that year, Apte made his first overtures—he came to Bombay and took Manorama and two of her friends to an afternoon film show at Roxy Cinema, followed by a walk to the Chowpatty seashore.[9] He returned a week later to invite Manorama to a late-evening film show, to be followed by dinner. Manorama, as she later recalled in her testimony, was not surprised.[10] She had, in fact, expected it. Yet, she was in two minds. Although she had known Apte had changed from the time she had first met him, she decided to discourage his advances. Possibly, she wanted to focus on her studies. So, she turned down Apte's invitation. But when he insisted, she could not but agree to accompany him to lunch the next day.[11]

Apte came a bit early, at 11.30 a.m., and took her to a restaurant at Sandhurst Road. The two then spent the whole afternoon talking and parted ways only in the evening at Victoria Terminus (V.T.) railway station. While Apte went to

Poona by Deccan Queen, Manorama returned to her hostel by tram.[12] This was the first time she had gone out alone with Apte but he made no attempt to exploit the occasion. This seems to have both delighted and frustrated her. Yet, that afternoon transported her in a world of dreams.[13]

During the next few months, this became a routine; Apte would come all the way from Poona to take Manorama out to lunch and to the cinema. They developed a close friendship, spending hours together, exchanging their intimate thoughts and sometimes just sitting across from each other in absolute silence. When they were away from each other, they exchanged letters. 'I became very friendly with Apte,' she confessed years later.[14]

They even devised a code to keep their friendship a secret. It was imperative. The hostel warden, who kept an eye on all resident girls going out with men who were not family, had become suspicious of Manorama's friendship with Apte and had even reported this to her father, Dr Daulatrao Salvi. 'I had asked Apte to adopt a pet-name "Nirmala" as our warden Dr. Miss Hewat had reported to my father that Apte was corresponding with me. My father had requested me not to meet Apte,' she said.[15]

When she went to her father's place at Shegaon during her vacation in October 1944, they corresponded regularly—Apte wrote under the pseudonym 'Nirmala' and Manorama poured her heart out in her replies. The month-long separation brought them even closer to each other, and when she returned in November there was nothing to stop them. Apte went to see her in the hostel and she went to meet him at Arya Pathik Ashram, a guest house at Sandhurst Road where Apte usually stayed during his visits to Bombay. 'After [writing] my Previous [pre-graduation] examination, I visited Apte at Arya Pathik Ashram and I spent the night with him at Gujarat Niwas. The next morning, I returned to the hostel and Apte left for Poona,' she said.[16]

Apte had got what he wanted but Manorama was engulfed by the sheer joy of love. She was a pretty girl, slim, fair and had long hair. In 1944, she was sixteen, obsessively sentimental and extremely naive. Her devotion to Apte was touching; in fact, it was so complete that she didn't even bother to find out if he was married or not. She was totally clueless about his Hindutva ideology and the politics of the time, and could hardly fathom the way Apte was headed. Every time Apte came, he gave her a copy of *Agrani*.[17] She read it but never concurred with its contents. Nor did she agree on many things she discussed with him. But she trusted him and found him gentle, and once they made love, she thought, they had become inseparable.[18]

However, Apte always seemed to reserve information about himself—he'd never discuss his family and would always remain secretive about his activities. Despite Manorama's devotion, he had never for a moment considered himself unjust. Neither did she pursue the information that he withheld. For in those days, nothing mattered to her as much as the sheer bliss of being with the man she loved.[19]

~

Godse admired Apte's trait of effortlessly keeping his thoughts a secret. He considered this ability of his friend as an essential ingredient of a man striving for as big a mission as setting up a Hindu rashtra. He even tried to reshape himself in Apte's mould. But he never managed to accomplish it, and every time he visited Poona's Tilak Smarak Mandir he blurted out whatever he thought he was trying to conceal. 'Godse was unconsciously imitative. On one occasion he seemed to copy

Savarkar's attitudes and mannerisms, and on the other, Apte's. But Godse was not a good actor. He could not carry his pretentious behavior too far and always reverted to his original self rather quickly,' recounted Acharya.[20]

Tilak Smarak Mandir, situated on the site where Tilak had lived and died, was in those days one of the centres of ferment and swarmed with Hindutva activists living in Poona. M.S. Dixit, who was an active member of the Hindu Mahasabha in Poona at the time, recalled that Godse was a regular visitor. 'Every evening [Hindutva] activists used to gather near Tilak Smarak Mandir for [an] informal chat and discussions. Students, youths, middle-aged persons and old people all used to come there. Sitting on stones around the temple and forming groups, they used to discuss political issues and events,' Dixit wrote in his memoir. 'Sometimes even senior Hindutva leaders like L.B. Bhopatkar, Sundartai Bhopatkar, G.V. Ketkar and Shantabai Gokhale visited the area. Godse and Apte also used to take part in these political discussions,' he added.[21]

Godse was not a regular visitor to Tilak Smarak Mandir till the time the HRD was formed. Until then, even when he visited, he was hardly recognized by the people there. But from the day the HRD was founded, he had the floor in Poona and Hindutva activists started paying attention to him. In the political circles of Tilak Smarak Mandir, his stature grew more after the launch of *Agrani*, and so did his frequency at these discussions. The accolades cast upon him by Hindutva activists for starting an ideologically driven newspaper were so frequent and so unequivocal that he had no trouble in believing that he was indeed one of the greatest leaders born to protect Hinduism.[22]

In a milieu that favoured Hindu supremacists and assumed that eccentric opinions and manners were signs of a sharp mind,

Godse's views did not seem peculiar. 'If a question excited him, he frequently shouted,' according to Acharya, 'But what he said, no matter how excessively he behaved, struck his listeners as consistent.' Sometimes Apte also accompanied Godse to Tilak Smarak Mandir. But instead of taking part in discussions there, he mostly remained a mute spectator. He stood one degree away from Godse and two degrees from the other visitors and yet, in his own way, he seemed quite comfortable in the company of the Hindutva activists. 'Apte spoke only occasionally. Most of the time he smoked and simply watched people discussing among themselves,' said Acharya.[23]

Godse rarely laughed, and when he did, it sounded more like the shoulder-heaving laugh of a man who feels he ought to be amused but is not. But a smile sometimes flashed across his usually grim face. By Acharya's account, Godse was not a patient listener either, and sometimes when things were not moving in the manner he wanted, he would get up abruptly and start walking out in short, quick strides.

At Tilak Smarak Mandir, Godse often liked to predict political developments in prophetic tones, though no one took them seriously. 'Till the end of the Second World War, he was seen predicting victory for Axis powers [Germany, Italy, and Japan]. He used to give long arguments to defend his prediction. But when Axis powers surrendered, he quickly changed his position and started arguing why their defeat was inevitable right since the beginning of the War in view of the invincibility of the United States and England,' remembered Acharya. 'In later years, the death of Gandhi and extermination of Muslims in India became the subject matter of his prophesies.'

Godse, in any event, was hardly the only Hindutva activist of his generation to treat Gandhi as the source of all political problems in the country. Most men like him believed that there was once a golden age when Peshwas ruled the country and that Gandhi, instead of working for the revival of the Peshwa rule, was trying to undermine the glories of the past. 'Gandhi bashing was the most common subject of discussion among the [Hindutva] activists,' recounted Acharya.

'In spite of his fickleness and his inconsistency, which sometimes left visitors to Tilak Smarak Mandir with a genuinely perplexity, Godse was generally mild-mannered,' said Acharya. He was not as quick-witted and attractive as Apte, but he seemed to be committed to the ideology, and there was hardly anyone in Poona's Hindutva circle who disliked him. 'Generally, people did not dislike him, but at no point he was considered a leader,' said Acharya, 'and that is because his leadership qualities were not visible to people. In his approach, he was considered superficial and vain. He was always so anxious to prove his point that his behavior was often absurd.'

In discussions, Godse was known for his extreme and violent views which were sometimes heard with a sense of alarm. Despite the communal temper at Tilak Smarak Mandir, many were not favourably impressed by him as they didn't support taking such positions in public. 'I couldn't make much of that strange fellow Godse,' said Acharya, 'but I knew one thing—he was going to get somewhere.'

~

Agrani's aggressive campaign for a Hindu rashtra and its attempt to become a voice of all Hindutva organizations signalled Godse's new direction—more systematic, better organized and more distinguished. In the absence of another such platform in Poona, it was perhaps a welcome change for him from the volatility and peculiarity of his life so far. But

Godse was not destined to live placidly. Very soon, as *Agrani*'s stock rose and people started taking note of it, he began to confront problems and choices of extraordinary importance and complexity. Though Godse never recognized it, the reason for this to a great extent was himself.

As the editor of *Agrani*, he wrote whatever he pleased and did not feel the need to follow any journalistic ethics. As the idea was to champion the cause of a Hindu rashtra, he aimed his venom at the Congress and its idea of Hindu–Muslim unity. By 1946, the authorities in the Bombay Presidency became aware of the newspaper's provocative anti-Muslim stance and its advocacy of violence. Before long, the government descended upon it, and a heavy security was demanded against the good behaviour of the newspaper, which meant the money would be forfeited the next time it prejudiced law and order.[24]

The newspaper managed to meet the penalty demand largely because of the active support of Savarkar—a fact revealed by a set of letters seized from the latter's residence after the assassination of Gandhi. In one letter, dated 10 October 1946, Apte thanked Savarkar for his appeal to his supporters to help the newspaper overcome the crisis and informed him that 'a sum of Rs 3000 to pay for the security of Agrani' had already been received apart from 'promises regarding further financial help'.[25]

One of the donors at this stage was Jugal Kishore Birla, the businessman who contributed Rs 1000 to *Agrani* in October 1946. 'I received yesterday morning the cheque for Rs. 1000 (one thousand only) which Shriman Sheth Jugal Kishore Birla of Delhi had sent from his office at Bombay [. . .]. A receipt for this Rs. 1000 on the receipt-book of Agrani has been sent separately to Shri Birla,' Apte wrote to Savarkar on 30 October.[26] Birla had emerged as an important benefactor of the

Hindu Mahasabha and the RSS; for the latter's swayamsevaks he bought a large number of steel helmets early in 1947.[27] For some undeclared reasons, the RSS had added for a brief while in 1947 a steel helmet to the uniform of its swayamsevaks—a fact that lent encouragement to theories that the Hindu paramilitary outfit was gearing up for some impending showdown.

The security demand imposed on *Agrani* also led Godse to hold several rounds of meetings with Congress leader Morarji Desai, who was the home minister of the Bombay Presidency.[28] In his memoir, Desai mentioned his meetings with Godse, whom he described as 'a worker of the Rashtriya Swayamsevak Sangh in Poona' and 'also the editor' of the paper.[29] 'Godse's writings [. . .] were full of incitement to the Hindus. [. . .] Whenever he came to see me I expressed my disapproval of his activities. He visited me sometimes to discuss the security order which I had passed against his paper for carrying writings inciting violence,' he wrote.[30]

Although there is enough evidence to suggest that *Agrani* was being subsidized by Savarkar right since its inception, the Hindutva ideologue himself had been cautious not to be seen as part of a newspaper involved in inciting hatred and violence. Nor did he have any wish to sully his reputation by open contact with the adventurers Godse and Apte. Savarkar had, therefore, written to Godse and Apte on 4 April 1945 advising them 'to keep proper accounts about the paper' and asking them that 'the policy of the "Agrani" paper should be definitely maintained within the sole rights of both of them'.[31] This in no way meant that his help to the paper was selfless. For, merely a day before the above instructions, Savarkar's secretary G.V. Damle had written to Apte, asking him 'to attack the attitude of the Associated Press [a news agency] through his paper Agrani' because the agency had not carried Savarkar's exact quote on the Congress.[32]

In any event, the security demand imposed on *Agrani* had the opposite impact on Godse. Instead of making him see his folly, the penalty only highlighted for him the enduring righteousness of his cause. 'I was commenting on atrocities on Hindus. But [. . .] the Congress government started seeking explanations from me. This happened with some other papers also. The government stopped me from ventilating Hindu feelings [through *Agrani*],' he said years later.[33] As it gradually became clear, nothing—not even a hefty fine—was going to change Godse. He remained as rigid and unbending as ever and continued to write like an outraged editorialist. He even seemed to regard that his newspaper was being persecuted at the behest of Gandhi, on whom Godse increasingly focused his wrath.

Thus, after Gandhi toured the riot-hit areas of Calcutta and Noakhali in Bengal and from there to Bihar during November 1946 and March 1947, the lead headline of *Agrani* published on 12 April 1947 was: 'The Thirst for Blood of the Advocate of Non-violence has not been Quenched'. The article declared that 'Gandhiji is anxious to see Mr. Jinnah the first president of India'.[34] It also said that Gandhi was 'not satisfied with the bloodshed of Hindus' and that he wanted 'more bloodshed and massacre of Hindus'. Another article in the same issue said Gandhi was 'asking Hindus to be non-violent so that they should not take objection to remain under the rule of Jinnah or Muslim League'.[35] Yet another article in the same issue of *Agrani* had the heading: 'Gandhi, Commit Suicide'. The article asked Gandhi to 'commit suicide' or 'withdraw himself from the Indian politics' and said that 'it is utter shamelessness that a coward person who always moves under the police and military escort should ask the Hindus to sacrifice themselves without defending'. The article added that 'those who do not wish to have bloodshed in India should disregard Gandhiji's suicidal advice and should chalk out a new policy suitable to the present society'.[36]

Articles that Godse wrote in *Agrani* left no doubt about what he was against, although there was still considerable doubt about what he was for. He was gravitating towards his destiny, and quite fast at that.

~

Godse expressed his new self-confidence in a bold and provocative gesture: he whipped out a knife and tried to stab Hindu Mahasabha president L.B. Bhopatkar in December 1946 when he felt the party was not honouring his wishes.[37] Godse's outburst coincided with his rising irritation at a time when the partition of India became inevitable and the Mahasabha decided to join the provisional government headed by Nehru. The provisional government had been set up in September 1946 from among the members of the Constituent Assembly elected early that year. This government was to ensure smooth transition from British rule to Independence.

Godse believed that the Hindu Mahasabha should stay away from the government led by Nehru. Perhaps he felt that by joining the government the Mahasabha would deviate from its special mission of converting India into a Hindu rashtra. He, therefore, resented the party's decision to let its leader, Mukherjee, accept a seat in the Nehru cabinet. When a resolution to this effect was moved by Bhopatkar at the Barshi session of the Maharashtra provincial Hindu Mahasabha, Godse pulled out a knife in anger. The conference was held between 13 and 16 December 1946.[38]

Though Apte backed him, Godse could not make common cause with most of the party leaders, who seemed to fear being left out at a time when the limelight was set to shift to the provisional government leading the transition to Independence. Perhaps it was the insecurity of his situation that forced Godse to take a violently antagonistic position, for the idea of reconciliation implicit in the Hindu Mahasabha resolution threatened to rob him of the sense of purpose critical for his own existence.

Godse's obstructionist tactics did not work. His act and his extremist position annoyed many leaders attending the conference. The resolution was adopted and Mukherjee was allowed to join the provisional government.

However, Godse, who had worked himself into an almost hopeless position, refused to back down. Now he shifted his focus to what he seemed to have thought an imminent showdown, under the leadership of Savarkar, with the Congress and Gandhi for the setting up of a Hindu rashtra. Already, months before the Barshi session, Savarkar, addressing a group of around fifty swayamsevaks of the HRD at his residence in Bombay, had called for preparations to boycott Muslims in all forms and to retaliate against 'aggression' by them.[39] Once isolated in the Mahasabha at its Barshi session, Godse might just have lost faith in the party's ability to convert India into a Hindu rashtra, and this might have heralded his shift from collective action to individual acts to achieve the goal. It is possible that with this transition, he came to regard himself as the saviour the Hindus awaited.

Though the communal tension had not yet reached the grotesque extremes of August 1947, it had already led to the virtual collapse of religious harmony in several parts of India. In a gradual but very concrete way the communalists of both sides were spreading venom, thus reinforcing each other's prejudices and hatred. Maharashtra was not the focal point of these tensions but, in view of the determined efforts by various organizations and individuals to target Muslims, it was unlikely that the calm would remain for long.

9

'Gandhi, Commit Suicide'[1]

By early 1947, Godse had already come out of painful obscurity. The personal progress he had made in the past five years was astounding. He was quite a different person from the inconsequential drifter he had been in the beginning of 1942, before he launched the HRD. With extraordinary dedication to his sense of purpose, he had emerged from his status as underling. Soon, in keeping with his new role, he would become more aggressive in his writings.

The cynic in him was transformed into a man of action, and his self-doubt gave way to a bubbling self-confidence. The desire to prove himself, which was present almost from the start, even during his brief career as a child mystic, drove him; his act of whipping out a knife at Bhopatkar in December 1946 was, in part, a reflection of that aspect of his personality. His emotions, fears and obsessions seemed fixed. In fact, Godse's world view had not changed since the time he came under Savarkar's spell in 1930; it only sharpened over the course of time, much more during the last five years.

Perhaps, this was essential for Godse to become the assassin of Gandhi. From late 1946 onwards, the nation reeled under the immense anxieties of an impending partition. Seldom had India seemed more divided than it was in those months. The Islamists' determined bid for Pakistan had brought India on the verge of Partition. Hindu supremacists hoped that the crisis would end up marginalizing Gandhi—the advocate of Hindu–Muslim unity—and the Congress and create the grounds for the transformation of India into a Hindu rashtra.

Godse was intensely attuned to the feelings of those championing a Hindu rashtra. He shared their aims and longings, but more sharply, more radically, more mulishly. Whereas his contemporaries in Poona felt discontent, he felt desperation. His articles, like his speeches, incited communal violence and cheered attacks on Muslims. They viewed the communal crisis as a purification process that held great hope of liberation for Hindus and marked the end of one age and the making of a new one. When Gandhi fought against the crisis, he was declared anti-Hindu and Godse aimed his venom at him. In none of his articles did he ever refer to the widely known fact that his own outfit, the HRD and the organizations he was associated with, the RSS and the Hindu Mahasabha, were as responsible for the communal crisis as the Muslim League.

More than any single article Godse is known to have written before Independence, the one published in *Agrani*'s issue of 3 July 1947—six weeks before Partition—seemed to carry an open subtext of resentment and disapproval directed at Gandhi: 'Everywhere Hindus are being killed but Gandhiji is always eager to start on tour in order to add a new province to Pakistan.' Another article in the same issue exhorted 'Hindus' to take the law in their own hands by pointing out that 'the creation of "Pakistan" is a reality but we [Hindus] are still at the stage of holding meetings, taking out processions and passing resolutions only.'[2]

Around this time, in the first week of July, Apte was arrested by the Poona Police in connection with a bomb case. For a brief while there existed a palpable danger of fresh government crackdown on the paper. Godse betrayed his fear in an article published in the issue dated 6 July. Titled 'Let Hundreds of Such Oblations be Offered in Quick Succession Now', the article said:

> If the paper is successful to some extent in creating extreme contempt for the partitioners of India, the editor of 'Agrani' is prepared to sacrifice both himself and the paper. The only innermost desire is that the Goddess of Freedom should be pleased at least by the offering of many such oblations in quick succession for the sake of this unfortunate country.[3]

In another article published three days later, on 9 July, Godse solicited the support of Hindu supremacists of Poona for Apte's release. Titled 'Sharp Steel Edge in the Battle Field of Akhand Bharat: Mr. Narayanrao Apte's Inspiring Introduction', the article described him as 'the manager of "Agrani", a close friend of Mr. N.V. Godse, a founder of Hindu Rashtra Dal, an outstanding orator, a sincere worker of Hindu Mahasabha and a devotee of Savarkar's doctrine'. The article also eulogized 'the action taken by Mr. N.D. Apte at Panchgani in Mahatmaji's prayer meeting'.[4]

In the absence of any serious investigation into the bomb case, Apte was let off and the danger passed. In fact, since the time a penalty was imposed on *Agrani* in 1946, Godse found himself imperiled only once—when the government demanded another security from his paper in the beginning of August 1947, days before Independence.[5] Godse ducked the penalty by dissolving *Agrani,* only to restart it under another name: *Hindu*

Rashtra. Apte and he occupied their respective positions in the new paper, which was a replica of *Agrani* both in its tone and content.

Partition gave Godse endless material for denouncing Gandhi and inciting violence. Godse used the plight of Hindu refugees to whip up communal frenzy and spread hatred against Gandhi, the Congress and Muslims. On the day of Independence, Godse wrote: 'India on this day is divided into two parts and the Congress is responsible for reaching this stage.'[6] Months later, after he had assassinated Gandhi, he maintained this sentiment. 'Congress asked us to celebrate that day [the day of Independence],' Godse told the interrogators, 'But crores of our [Hindu] brothers were becoming victims of atrocities. The government had made no plans for their security. In such a situation, the celebration of that day would have meant overlooking the sin of letting Pakistan born.'[7] This was in consonance with the official attitude of the RSS—nowhere in the country did swayamsevaks participate in Independence Day celebrations.[8]

On 6 September 1947, Godse denounced Gandhi's fast in Calcutta and questioned its purpose. His article said the Hindus 'in Sind, the Punjab and Noakhali' were regularly massacred while Gandhi and the Congress were 'asking people not to be restive'.[9] In another article, which appeared the next day, Godse branded Congress leaders as 'the assailants of all our [Hindu] valour, courage and manliness' and suggested 'the removal of such leaders who are obstacles in the path of bravery'.[10]

For the rest of 1947, Godse seemed content to drift along through regular articles of this nature. He imagined himself as a writer-activist representing the extreme radicality of Hindutva politics. He cast himself as the star of the Hindutva narrative, as a warrior fighting for the political ascendency of Hindus.

As a political project, the idea of a Hindu rashtra had failed to take off despite the Partition-induced communal frenzy; as propaganda, it could be salvaged.

~

Apte's arrest in the bomb case was an indication that the two friends were doing more than authoring and publishing inflammatory articles, and occasionally providing support to those who wanted to convert India into a Hindu rashtra. To the extent it formally existed, the office of their newspaper in Poona was as much a newsroom as a space to conceive and execute subversive plans. A temporary shed made of bricks, the newspaper office had a tent pitched in the compound that served as the workplace for the pair. Evidence of specific details of the conspiratorial use of the office space in those months is fragmentary, but it suggests, unsurprisingly, that Apte—and not Godse—was in the lead role.

Godse seemed to believe that without the knowledge and shrewdness of Apte, underground politics was not possible. One of the principal reasons for his sense of inferiority was that there was no convincing personality in the Hindutva circles of Poona whose bearing was as modern and point of operation as communal as Apte. Isolated from modern ideas and incapable of recognizing their growing importance, Godse remained frozen in stubborn conservatism. Arrogant and unimaginative, he clung to traditional positions. As he seemed to think only in terms of the effect, he admired the perceptions of Apte being a doer and a mover, an organizer and a planner.

Perhaps this was the reason why Godse did not mind carrying the entire burden of running the newspaper while Apte roamed around in Poona and Bombay, sometimes to prepare his secret plans and more often to spend time with Manorama. Godse saw in this arrangement a division of labour of sorts that was imperative for the success of his vision. The arrangement suited Apte, too. He appreciated the crusading zeal with which Godse worked for the newspaper—the mainstay of their income and activity—and made it seem that with the help of two other Savarkar loyalists, Vishnu Ramakrishna Karkare and Digambar Ramchandra Badge, Godse was promoting their collective vision through secret operations. Godse had scarcely anything to oppose to this method of executing subversive plans.

In 1947, Karkare, who was of the same age as Godse, lived in Ahmednagar, where he headed the local unit of the Hindu Mahasabha and ran a restaurant-cum-guest house, Deccan Guest House. He had known about Apte for almost a decade since the latter became a teacher at American Mission High School but came in direct contact with him and Godse during the second annual camp of the HRD at Ahmednagar in 1943. It was Karkare who had managed the food requirements for those attending the camp.[11] Later, when *Agrani* was launched, he acted as its agent in Ahmednagar and became even closer to Apte and Godse. When communal riots broke out in Calcutta and Noakhali during late 1946 and early 1947, the trio began to hold regular discussions, mostly in the newspaper office, making wild plans of terror attacks in Muslim localities of Poona and other parts of Bombay province.[12]

When the question of procuring ammunition for their subversive plans arose, Apte suggested the name of Badge, a local arms peddler who was already known to all of them. Badge's business depended largely on his association with Hindu communal groups. His arms shop, Shastra Bhandar, at Sadashiv Peth in Poona displayed only permissible weapons like knives and tiger claws, but he also dealt in contraband firearms and ammunition, which he acquired and disposed of surreptitiously through his 'contacts' spread across the Bombay province.[13]

Badge was thirty-eight and, like any arms trafficker, cunning to the core. His flowing beard and long black hair allowed him walk about in Poona, Bombay and other parts of the province disguised as a sadhu, peddling arms kept hidden in his multifold robe and in two huge gourds attached to a veena that he carried on his shoulder. Several years ago, he had met some members of the Hindu Mahasabha and quickly realized that Hindutva activists, who cherished visions of guerrilla attacks in Muslim localities, constituted a huge market for arms. He became a member of the Hindu Mahasabha and started attending its sessions where, mixing the politics with his business, he primarily looked for potential customers.

By the time Badge joined the trio, India's political fabric was stretched thin. Muslim League leader Jinnah had stuck to his position. Partition had become imminent, and Gandhi and the Congress leaders seemed helpless. One day in May 1947, Godse, Karkare and Apte met at Badge's residence to plan something big. 'It was suggested by Apte that a direct action should be taken against Muslim League [leader] Jinnah who was fighting tooth and nail for creating a separate state of Pakistan,' Karkare subsequently said. 'He further suggested that Jinnah should be assassinated as a solution to the question of Pakistan.'[14]

Godse clapped his hands in excitement. Karkare was asked to wait in Poona till the plan was executed, while Apte took the responsibility for making necessary arrangements and procuring arms for the planned murder of Jinnah.[15] Though Godse was an accomplice, he was asked to focus on the newspaper. Karkare felt that Apte was not divulging full details as he had withheld for some time the precise source of the arms he was seeking to acquire.[16] Karkare, however, kept quiet thinking that Apte was perhaps consulting someone who didn't want to be named.

'Once, I was told by Apte to go to Badge and bring a box containing bombs,' recounted Karkare, 'Accordingly, I went to Badge and got a box of bombs, about six in number, and kept the same in the corner of the "Agrani" office. [. . .] I think that this must be in the month of June or July.'[17] To guard the explosives, Karkare mostly stayed in the newspaper office, awaiting additional instructions from Apte.

A few days later, Apte gave him some cash and asked him to hand it over to Badge in exchange for a Sten gun. According to Karkare, Badge took him to a desolate place close to Yerwada jail, where they procured two guns from someone who had already been informed about the deal. After they returned to the *Agrani* office around midnight, Badge took one of the guns and left. 'I took the other Sten gun and kept it in my bedding, which was in the "Agrani" office,' said Karkare. 'I then went to Apte's house. I informed Apte that I had kept the article in the bedding and left it hidden near a tree in the compound of "Agrani" office. I then went to the "Agrani" office and slept there.'[18]

Almost immediately after that, things began to go wrong. A bomb, which had nothing to do with the conspiracy to kill Jinnah, exploded in some other part of Poona. This led to a series of arrests of Hindutva activists, and one of them, a man known simply in history as Athavale, disclosed Apte's name as an accomplice. Apte was picked up and put behind bars. Karkare panicked and ran away to Ahmednagar with all the explosives. 'As soon as Apte was arrested I thought that the police would conduct a search of the "Agrani" office. I therefore took charge of the box and went to Ahmednagar and kept this box with me for about four months,' recounted Karkare, who took along the Sten gun too.[19]

Karkare's worries were misplaced. In a political atmosphere already full of uncertainties ahead of Independence and Partition, the local authorities were too occupied with larger issues to investigate deeper into what seemed to be a minor incident of a blast. About a month after the arrest, Apte was released from jail and the case was closed as his involvement in it could not be ascertained due to a lacklustre probe. 'The case against us was later withdrawn by the government. In fact, in that case I had no connection whatsoever with Athavale,' Apte subsequently said.[20]

Apte's arrest did not interrupt their lives, but it forced them to immediately abandon the plan to assassinate Jinnah. Godse, who had been thrilled to be involved in a plot to kill the Muslim League leader, was dejected. According to Karkare, 'Godse was perturbed in his mind because of the arrest of Apte and the failure of the plan.'[21]

~

Apte's true attitude towards Godse's violent plan is more difficult to discern. Apte was thirty-three. His faith in the concept of a Hindu rashtra, in which he had so deeply immersed himself, was stirring. Beyond Poona, Hindu supremacists in north and west India were gaining strength. Gandhi and the Congress might have held the ground despite Partition, but their political critique was stimulating. Still, there is hardly any evidence to suggest that Apte was willing to take significant personal risks in the name of a Hindu rashtra. He seemed to live in a mental world totally different from that of Godse. While Godse, a trained RSS worker, was unwaveringly loyal to the idea of a

Hindu rashtra and wanted to do everything to achieve it, Apte seemed to be exploring how he might have it all—money, multiple sexual partners and staying in good standing among the supporters of Hindutva.

He was quick to figure out the best course to obtain the desired result—a quality that eluded Godse, who always relied on someone to guide him. Like most canny swindlers, Apte waited patiently for the opportunity and grabbed it the moment it came to him. He did not think twice before discarding an idea if it went awry or did not match his expectation. In any case, he always looked strangely peaceful, as if he had nothing at stake, again unlike Godse, who could neither conceal his excitement nor his disappointment.

After the plan to kill Jinnah was jettisoned, Godse was disconsolate but Apte remained as unperturbed as ever. He, however, started pondering over another wild plan in September when he met Goswami Shri Krishnaji Maharaj, a wealthy religious preacher of Vaishnav persuasion who was popularly known as Dada Maharaj. A hardcore Hindu chauvinist, Dada Maharaj claimed to be the descendent of medieval saint Vallabhacharya and had ashrams at several places, including Bombay and Pandharpur. The property owned by his family fetched an annual income of over Rs 2 lakh. Besides, he had huge earnings from private offerings made by his disciples and followers.

Dada Maharaj was not a man to flinch from speaking his mind. After the communal carnage in Noakhali he had addressed several meetings, calling upon Hindus to take the law in their own hands in order to defend themselves against the attacks of 'goondas'.[22] Days before Independence and Partition, he presided over the All India Hindu Convention held in Delhi and attacked the Congress government for its 'appeasement policy'.[23] Partition of India outraged him and made him eager to financially support violent attacks on Pakistani establishments and its leaders. The idea that Apte used to make this wealthy Hindu communalist loosen his purse strings was particularly outlandish—a plan to attack the Constituent Assembly of Pakistan. 'Mukund Malaviya, son of Madan Mohan Malaviya, told me that one Apte was going to blow up the Pakistan Assembly,' Dada Maharaj said after the assassination of Gandhi.[24]

Dada Maharaj met Apte in Poona sometime in September while he was on his way to Pandharpur. 'From his conversation with me I understood that he wanted to blow up the Pakistan Constituent Assembly. He told me that he had the required men for the job but what he lacked were arms and ammunition,' Dada Maharaj recounted. 'He [Apte] also said that he could at least kill Jinnah and Liaqat Ali Khan [the President and Prime Minister of Pakistan, respectively, at that time] only if he had dependable arms. The two pistols he possessed, he said, were not dependable. He requested me to get two revolvers for him, because, as he revealed, if he got two good revolvers he would succeed in accomplishing the job. I promised to discuss the subject further on my return.'[25]

The meeting gave Apte an opportunity to merge his ideological and avaricious sides. He seemed to have realized that everything he did for ideological reasons also simultaneously offered him an opportunity to raise funds. Partly this reflected Apte's communal beliefs, but partly it was a marketing strategy crafted by a man who was as passionate about his hatred for Muslims as he was about making money. Godse seemed to instinctively understand where his own passion for a Hindu rashtra overlapped with Apte's desire for easy money.[26] At the time, these lines of activity did not seem to be burdened by contradictions.

In any event, Apte had, by now, learnt to adjust with both Godse's constant yearning to prove himself and his own self-indulgence. He knew he wanted something big from Dada Maharaj and, therefore, worked out several proposals to which he could react. Apte then sent out a message to him that on his way back from Pandharpur, he would like to see him again in Poona.[27] 'In October, Apte came to my place in Poona,' Dada Maharaj said:

> He made over two pistols to me and requested me to get two revolvers in exchange. [. . .] I did not, however, give him any revolver the same day because I could not lay my hands on any. It was then that Apte revealed to me that a train containing arms and ammunition was soon to proceed to Pakistan and he wanted to blow up that train by means of a flame-thrower. That expedition, he said, would cost ten thousand rupees but he had only half the amount.[28]

When Dada Maharaj refused to contribute the required amount, Apte suggested another plan—he would go in the former's motorcar and loot the octroi post on the border of the Nizam's state of Hyderabad. The idea impressed Dada Maharaj, who happily offered his car for the operation. On hearing nothing for several days about the fate of the octroi loot plan, he became suspicious and went looking for Apte at his residence. He was shocked when Apte told him that he was not successful in the plan. According to Dada Maharaj, Godse often accompanied Apte to the meetings, generally in RSS uniform. 'At Poona and [later] at Bombay, I had always seen Apte with a man of 35 years with grey hair, thin and tall, wearing khaki short and shirt. Later I came to know him as Godse,' he said.[29]

Despite Apte's failure to loot the octroi post, his relationship with Dada Maharaj survived, with the latter still hoping that one day he would inflict a serious blow on Pakistan. When Godse and Apte set up a printing press for their paper in November 1947, Dada Maharaj performed the puja. 'At Diwali [1947] Apte invited me for opening ceremony of Hindu Rashtra Press which took place on 17-11-47,' Dada Maharaj said later. 'I had a talk with Apte regarding the flamethrower. I promised to pay for them if the articles were produced. Badge brought 40 packets containing a yellow substance partially green bearing no. 808. I bought them at Rs 32 per packet and handed them over to Apte. The same evening I performed the opening ceremony of Hindu Rashtra Press,' he said in his statement.[30]

Dada Maharaj bought the explosives because Apte had promised that he would use them as the substitute for the flamethrower to blow up the train carrying arms and ammunition to Pakistan. But even this plan was not carried out. No one knows what happened to those packets of explosives—whether they rotted or were returned to Badge on the condition that the latter, after keeping a commission, would hand over the rest of the money to Apte.

~

Manorama began to suspect that Apte was up to something dangerous towards the end of August, about a month after he was released from jail. 'He appeared to be making some plans. His thought was to destroy the Muslim localities in Bombay by fire,' she recounted. 'I tried to dissuade him from such plans but he had made up his mind. He was arrested and afterwards discharged.'[31] This was no doubt a horrible situation but she thought it was a temporary phase that would eventually pass.

She was not interested in his public life but just wanted to see him happy, and she knew that was all he expected or wanted from her. Every time he visited Bombay, he would take her to a hotel room where they would make love before parting. She understood little about Apte's politics and less about his work and always irritated him when she attempted to advise or warn him. She never resented this, nor did Apte care to change his behavior.

Manorama knew that Apte was a staunch disciple of Savarkar. There were several times when he asked her to meet him, but she never showed any interest. Over a year ago, while on her way to her father's place in Shegaon, she had broken her journey in Poona where she lived for two days in a hotel with Apte. Savarkar also happened to stay in the same hotel.[32] So Apte took her to Savarkar's room and introduced her as his wife.[33] Though she didn't like the man, she felt elated because the way she was introduced reassured her that Apte meant to marry her. She, of course, had no idea that he was already married.

It was also during that stay in Poona that Manorama first met Godse.[34] It was not a formal meeting like the one she had had with Savarkar. Godse just dropped in looking for Apte, who then introduced him to her. She did not form any opinion about Godse, except that she did not dislike him. What, however, struck her was that Apte, who had introduced her to Savarkar as his wife and had even written the same in the register at the reception, as he used to do every time they visited a hotel, said nothing of this sort when he introduced her to Godse. Thereafter, she saw Godse a few more times but they never talked.

She, however, never met Savarkar again as she seemed to hold him responsible for what she thought was the communal turn Apte was taking. She felt agitated a few months later when Apte, in a casual conversation, expressed his hatred towards Gandhi. Though she had no real interest in politics and was not a follower of Gandhi, she, like any ordinary Christian of the time, had a very high regard for him. She, therefore, did not say anything when Apte described a past incident in which 'he had put some questions to Gandhiji and was pleased to find that Gandhiji could not answer him'.[35]

It was hardly surprising that the naïve Manorama would think Apte an 'innocent' man who was under the spell of 'fanatics' like Savarkar. Her own insecurity almost always stopped her from sharing her feelings about Savarkar freely with Apte. Once, when she wrote 'something against Savarkar' in a letter, Apte 'got intensely annoyed' and wrote back 'a scolding letter'.[36] Thereafter, she refrained from voicing these thoughts, reasoning perhaps that she should learn to endure the state of affairs, at least long enough for the communal frenzy to die down, and for Apte to return to his old self.[37]

~

If the moment was turbulent for Manorama, it was doubly so for Godse, although for a different reason. The repeated failure of the ambitious plans through most of the later part of 1947—first to assassinate Jinnah, then to attack the Constituent Assembly of Pakistan and finally to blow up the train carrying arms to Pakistan—had shattered all his hopes of shaking the country. Though these plans had been conceived by Apte, who was also to supervise their execution, Godse had earnestly believed in them and had enthusiastically supported them. In a way, therefore, Godse was still adrift, but the direction in which he was now floating was getting increasingly defined.

Added to the frustration was his failure, as the editor of *Hindu Rashtra*, to rouse the communal feelings of Poona's Hindus against Muslims. The psychological impact of all this seems to have started mounting on him, reflected as it was in the rather frequent bouts of depression he now seemed to be experiencing.

One such occasion was recorded by Dixit, who was a regular contributor to Godse's newspaper.[38] In his memoir, Dixit recalls Godse asking him why the thirteenth-century Marathi saint Dnyaneshwar died prematurely. Dixit replied that he did not know.

> 'I will tell you,' Godse said. 'With all the suffering, this saint kept preaching karmayoga'—a concept that calls for good works—'but people remained inactive. This annoyed him and he took "Samadhi"—embracing death by entering into deep meditation. 'This was in a way suicide. Do you agree?'
>
> 'Is it an issue worth contemplation?' Dixit asked him.
>
> 'Then leave it.'[39]

Godse's depressive thoughts may have surprised Dixit in some respects because he had mostly seen him full of energy and making bombastic claims. This conversation, which took place in the office of *Hindu Rashtra*, reveals a couple of important things about Godse's mental state at the time: a depressive streak and an exaggerated sense of self-importance as he compared his inability to rouse Hindu passions with Dnyaneshwar's failure to make people respond to his preaching. It was a presumptuous self-reference but one that spoke of Godse's rising sense of himself as both righteous and little understood.

Godse lived as a subtenant in a small room of a three-storey building in Sadashiv Peth, Poona. Dixit, who lived only two rooms away in that apartment since the beginning of 1947, noted the frequent change in his mood. 'Soon after the conversation, Godse gave a speech at Shiv Mandir,' wrote Dixit. 'At the end of his speech, he said in crude language: "And this old man believes that he will live for hundred and twenty-five years. Let's see how he remains alive.".'[40] Godse was referring to Gandhi in his speech. The shift in his mood seemed to have exacerbated his temper, though his outbursts usually passed quickly.

It remains unclear how frequent these bouts of depression were. What seems likely is that such an instance was followed instantaneously by a reawakened sense of self-importance, producing a return to his ambition and boastfulness.

Section II: Plot

10

The Plan

By the end of 1947, Godse had no coherent plan for his life. He was getting fatigued with his journalistic career. His newspaper would still have another month to go and some of his most provocative articles had yet to appear. Nevertheless, his interest in it had diminished. Despite the mental turmoil, there was a vague sense of direction, one that seemed to be pointing towards an act big enough to shake the country. But what that act would be was still unclear in his head.

Towards the end of December, Godse was already having a series of lengthy and reflective conversations with Apte regarding the future course of action.[1] It was in these meetings that the idea to kill Gandhi germinated. The idea was not new to Godse; he had discussed it five months ago, weeks before India became independent. In a meeting of Hindu activists held at Shivaji Mandir in Poona, Godse had mentioned that some RSS men who were present in the congregation considered Gandhi and Nehru as roadblocks to a Hindu rashtra and therefore favoured their elimination. According to an account provided by Gajanan Narayan Kanitkar, a Poona-based Gandhian, the mandir meeting was held in July and was presided over by Apte and addressed by Godse. 'He [Godse] also mentioned that the R.S.S. volunteers who were in the meeting were remarking that Gandhiji and Nehru were thorns in the way of establishment of Hindu Raj and hence they should be removed,' reported Kanitkar.[2] Himself a witness, he instantly informed B.G. Kher, the then chief minister of the Bombay Province, about the matter through a letter dated 23 July 1947—six months before Gandhi was killed.[3]

But the idea was not pursued then. Perhaps it got lost in the din created by Partition. Godse and Apte, on their part, had been overtaken in those days by a craze to assassinate Jinnah and hit at some vital establishments of Pakistan. It was a heady time and they had boasted about their plans, and amassed arms and ammunition for the purpose. However, they could not succeed in executing these plans. Godse took no noticeable part in them. Yet, he felt so attached to them that he was at a loose end following their failure. Afterwards, as he craved to emerge from the anonymity that had so long concealed and depressed him, the idea which had been put on the backburner before Independence resurfaced.

The only question was who would assassinate Gandhi. Apte was clever enough to steer clear of that part of the debate. Godse, at this stage, could not muster the resolve to perform the act either. It seems that he, like Apte, was less interested in becoming a 'martyr' than in creating a movement based on the emotional power of someone else's 'martyrdom'. Godse's instincts were hardly surprising; he had spent much of his adult life only talking of acts of courage. Even when Apte made plans against Jinnah and Pakistan, Godse only concurred with him and never offered his service. Godse had put himself forward as the saviour of Hindus, but he was not prepared to assume the task of personally committing the assassination. His views on the use of violence were egregious, a great deal more egregious, in fact, than those held by even the worst of the Hindu fanatics of Poona, and the speeches and writings in which he expressed them were simply appalling. But assassinating Gandhi was different. It required much more courage than authoring threatening articles and giving provocative speeches, the kind of courage that Godse did not exhibit at this point.

The issue, however, was resolved at the beginning of 1948. On 2 January, the two friends travelled to Ahmednagar to discuss the issue with Karkare. The closed-door meeting, in which they succeeded in identifying the man who could kill Gandhi, took place in a small room on the top floor of Karkare's guest house.[4] 'During the discussion about the Congress Policy, we came to the conclusion that the policy of the Congress was manipulated as per wishes of the Mahatma Gandhi,' recounted Karkare. 'Godse also stated that whatever we may do, Mahatma Gandhi will never change his attitude towards the Muslims and as such he decided that Gandhiji should be killed. Apte and myself concurred with this view and promised assistance towards this direction.'[5]

When the issue of who would kill Gandhi was raised, Karkare resolved it quickly. He introduced Godse and Apte to a young refugee who had been cut off from his family, had been staying with him for the last couple of weeks and who would be 'ready to perform any daring act' suggested by Karkare. 'I came out of the room and called out to Madanlal [Pahwa], who was somewhere in the hotel,' said Karkare, 'I took him to the room where Apte and Godse were seated. I told them that this is the refugee who is known as Madanlal.'[6]

And so Godse set foot on his final course.

~

Pahwa, a twenty-year-old refugee from Pakistan, was seething with anger at the fate that had befallen him. Like many refugees, he held Gandhi personally responsible for his sufferings. Born in 1927, he grew up at Pakpattan in Montgomery district of west Punjab. In 1944, at the age of seventeen, he left school before his matriculation examination and ran away to Lahore to join the Royal Indian Navy (RIN). He was sent to Bombay for training but failed in the examination that took place a month later. Once discharged from the RIN, he went to Poona, where he joined the civil unit of the British Indian Army and was shifted to Lahore after a short training. It was a temporary job concerning the British government's war efforts. Around the end of 1946, on being released from the army, Pahwa went back to his home in Pakpattan. At the time of Partition, he had been staying with his maternal aunt and was evacuated to India around the third week of August.[7]

In the months following Partition, Pahwa meandered through Punjab and Gwalior and reached Bombay in October. He was in search of employment for a while and then, with the help of Prof. Jagdish Chandra Jain, a professor at Ramnarain Ruia Autonomous College, Pahwa took to selling books door to door. His hard work and charming ways opened up new contacts for him. One of them, a middle-aged businesswoman who he knew as Mrs Modak, was particularly helpful. Pahwa's search for a stable livelihood, however, continued. Soon, he moved to selling fruit, which took him to Ahmednagar, where he met Karkare, who offered to help him set up a coconut shop. Prof. Jain and Mrs Modak asked him to stay in Bombay, but Karkare's offer had left Pahwa in two minds. For a while, he tried to establish himself in Bombay but then, on failing, he accepted Karkare's offer and moved to Ahmednagar around mid-December.[8]

Karkare, however, had something else planned for Pahwa. He asked Pahwa to have his meals at Deccan Guest House and arranged for his stay in the local office of the Hindu Mahasabha. Karkare first set him to organize refugees settled in Visapur, a semi-urban settlement close to Ahmednagar. Then, he started using Pahwa as his henchman to torment local Muslim hawkers and shopkeepers, hurl bombs on their settlements and break up meetings of political leaders opposed to the Hindu Mahasabha. Pahwa was now totally dependent on Karkare, who started looking after his daily expenses too. The new job did hold an appeal for Pahwa—he could regale his friends with surreal stories and boast of his prowess. Something of the school bully seemed to have persisted in him[9] and had taken on a grotesque form in Ahmednagar.

There was one other reason he felt so attached to the place: merely days after moving to Ahmednagar, he had become enamoured with a singing girl who was known for her beauty. 'On 25th December at about 6.30 P.M. after attending a cinema show in the Chitra Talkies, I met a friend named Chabbu from Ahmednagar. He was with me in the Military for training at Poona,' Pahwa told his interrogators after Gandhi's assassination. 'While talking about our past friendship, we started talking about girls and he took me to the residence of a singing girl. Chabbu knew one girl by the name of Shewanti but she was not at home at this time.'[10] Pahwa visited Shewanti's house a second time two days later. Chabbu's description of her beauty seemed to have stuck in his mind. 'On the night of 27th December I went to the house of Shewanti and there I met her and became friendly with her,' he said.[11] Pahwa fell for Shewanti and started visiting her almost every evening.

Shewanti was nineteen when Pahwa met her. She had inherited her good looks from her mother, a commercial sex worker living in the red-light district of Bhagat Gali next to Chitra Talkies. Shewanti was little over 5 feet, with thick and long hair framing her round face, large black eyes and delicate nose. She was also an emotional creature, always dreaming of getting out of the wretched world of prostitution. For over two years, Shewanti had resisted her mother's repeated persuasions to join the sex trade, telling her confidently that one day a man of her choice would come into her life and take her away to a world where she could live with dignity. Her mother would say nothing but laugh.[12]

With Pahwa, Shewanti began to feel that she had found true love at last. He seemed to adore her, according to her acquaintance Sumanbai, and showered her with gifts of things she had never possessed.[13] Yet Pahwa never lost his balance; he learned to serve both his love and his 'Seth'. Though he was too young to bat in the same league as Karkare and his friends, Pahwa seemed content to drift along with them. Shewanti, from whatever she had heard of Karkare, didn't like him and believed that he was instigating violent attacks on Muslims and might one day get Pahwa in serious trouble.[14]

'Don't you realize that people respect you because they are afraid of you?' Shewanti once asked Pahwa, according to Sumanbai. 'He only smiled,' Shewanti told Sumanbai years later, 'as if he were happy he was so important.'[15]

~

On Thursday, 1 January 1948, a day before Karkare introduced Pahwa to Godse and Apte, the police raided Deccan Guest House. It was late in the evening and Pahwa had just started dinner. That very day he had succeeded in snatching a coconut shop from a Muslim resident of Ahmednagar and handing it over to a Hindu refugee. 'At that time the police came to the Hotel and surrounded the place in order to carry on the search. The police gave instructions to the persons in the Hotel not to leave the place,' said Pahwa.[16]

Pahwa left his meal midway and started arguing with the police inspector. 'I also told the Inspector that if Karkare was to be arrested, I should be first taken into custody,' he said. While the arguments continued, about forty to fifty refugees gathered there and started shouting slogans against the move to arrest Karkare, who was present in Deccan Guest House at the time. Fearing a showdown with the refugees, the police backed off.[17]

The next day, Pahwa was talking to a group of refugees who had come from Visapur when Baban, a helper of Karkare, came scampering from Deccan Guest House. Karkare had sent him to summon Pahwa. 'I went to the room where Karkare and two others were seated,' said Pahwa. 'Karkare called me inside the room and introduced me to the two others as a hard-working refugee named Madanlal. [. . .] I did not talk to them but just said Namaste and went back to the Hindu Mahasabha office.'[18]

Unaware of the plot, Pahwa continued his normal routine for the next two days. During the day he organized refugees and planned with them the ways to displace Muslim shopkeepers, and in the evenings, he spent time with Shewanti. On 4 January, as he needed some money to shop for Shewanti, he revealed to Karkare about his new-found love. Karkare didn't question him and just gave him the money. 'Thereafter, I purchased a silk odhni worth Rs 19 and went to Shewanti's place,' said Pahwa, 'I took Shewanti for a cinema show at Chitra Talkies where a picture *Chabukswar* was running. At about 10.0 p.m. I returned to Karkare's hotel and after my dinner there I slept in the mahasabha office.'[19]

The next day was to mark the beginning of a new chapter in Pahwa's life, one secretly designed for him. Though he would still meet Shewanti a few more times, his life as a free bird was about to end. At around 11 a.m. on 5 January, while having his meal at Karkare's hotel, Pahwa heard the announcement that Rao Saheb Patwardhan, a local Congress leader, would address a public meeting in Ahmednagar at 9 p.m. Karkare, who sat nearby, told him that Patwardhan had returned from Jammu and Kashmir, and would speak about his visit and that Pahwa would attend the meeting to listen to what the Congress leader had to say.[20] Most of the afternoon that day, Pahwa spent with Shewanti and they saw a feature film in Chitra Talkies.

Around nine in the evening, Pahwa reached the venue of the public meeting along with some of his refugee friends. About 200 refugees were already there. When Patwardhan began his speech, a few of his supporters raised a slogan which the refugees found objectionable. The refugees started shouting a counter slogan. This led to chaos, followed by police lathicharge. As Pahwa was among those leading the refugees, he was arrested along with his friends. They were taken to the police station and kept there for the whole night. The next morning, the police summoned Karkare and told them to leave town in the next twenty-four hours. To avoid police action, Pahwa and Karkare immediately returned to Deccan Guest House and started preparing to take the afternoon train to Poona.[21]

It was then that Karkare made the first oblique reference to the secret plan he had hatched along with Godse and Apte—that Gandhi would be killed because he was an impediment to the establishment of a Hindu rashtra. 'Karkare had told me in the presence of Chopra and Bhatia [Pahwa's refugee friends] about the secret scheme of taking the life of Mahatma Gandhi. He had said that Gandhiji was the only obstacle in the establishing of the Hindu Raj,' Pahwa said later.[22] Karkare did not mention the other part of the plan—that Pahwa would have to do the killing.

As Pahwa had no idea about his own role in the plan, he didn't pay much attention to the revelation.[23] He was seemingly on a different plane, which was not the same as the period immediately after Partition. He still felt resentment against Gandhi but seemed comfortable with the situation in Ahmednagar. Charmed by Shewanti, he now stood one degree separated from Karkare and two degrees from Gandhi.

~

In the aftermath of Gandhi's assassination, Godse would try to connect his extreme step with his outrage over Gandhi's support for Pakistan. 'In the first week of January 1948, I came to the conclusion that Gandhi, who had been constantly helping Pakistan, had to be killed. There was no other way we could have dealt with Pakistan,' Godse said in his pretrial statement, recorded at the stage of interrogation.[24] Later, during the trial, as he anxiously tried to remove any traces of guilt from Savarkar, Apte and the other co-accused by denying the existence of a conspiracy, Godse pushed up the timeline and gave a totally different account, one that contradicted his previous argument. In the revised account, he said the assassination decision was taken after Gandhi had on 13 January started his indefinite fast, which Godse viewed as a move to 'compel' India to pay Rs 55 crore to Pakistan. The amount, which was due to Pakistan as part of its share of the cash balance of undivided India, had been withheld by the Indian government because of Pakistani incursions in Jammu and Kashmir. 'But this decision of the people's Government was reversed to suit the tune of Gandhiji's fast,' Godse claimed during the trial. 'In these circumstances the only effective remedy to relieve the Hindus from the Muslim atrocities was, to my mind, to remove Gandhiji from this world.'[25]

Although it would be a mistake to attribute statements Godse made after the assassination to his state of mind before the act was committed, there is continuity in his opinions. His repeated references to Gandhi's pro-Pakistan attitude as a turning point in his own thinking and as a touchstone of his anti-Muslim viewpoint suggest the resonance of that feeling in his life. Everyone who was familiar with Godse knew that by the time he decided to kill Gandhi, that feeling had developed deep roots amidst the communal passion generated by the RSS and the Hindu Mahasabha over the last two decades. This passion of the RSS and the Hindu Mahasabha was at the core of the idea of a Hindu rashtra and was, by no means, an aberration caused by Partition. Gandhi had comprehensively countered this communal feeling through his open politics and marginalized the idea of a Hindu rashtra, reducing the RSS and the Hindu Mahasabha to the stature of lunatic fringe outfits in Indian public life. Thus, if Godse, imagining himself as the deliverer of this idea, killed Gandhi, he seemed to have done so with considerable faithfulness to the project of a Hindu rashtra.

The virulent idea fuelling this project—which demanded that Hindus must be granted an exclusive right to define India's national identity—was in a nebulous form when Savarkar propounded it. But Golwalkar added considerable details to the idea in his book, *We or Our Nationhood Defined*,[26] which was first published in 1939, almost a year before he became the RSS chief. Golwalkar unambiguously compared the project to promote a Hindu rashtra with German anti-Semitism. He presented Hitler's treatment of Jews as a model to be applied on Indian Muslims and Christians.

'To keep up the purity of the Race and its culture, Germany shocked the world by her purging the country of the semitic races—the Jews,' Golwalkar wrote. 'Race pride at its highest has been manifested here. Germany has also shown how well nigh impossible it is for Races and cultures, having differences going to the root, to be assimilated into one united whole, a good lesson for us in Hindusthan to learn and profit by.'[27] He then argued:

> From this standpoint, [...] non-Hindu peoples in Hindusthan must either adopt the Hindu culture and language, must learn to respect and hold in reverence Hindu religion, must entertain no idea but those of the glorification of the Hindu race and culture [. . .] and must lose their separate existence to merge in the Hindu race, or may stay in the country, wholly subordinated to the Hindu nation, claiming nothing, deserving no privileges, far less any preferential treatment not even citizen's rights.[28]

Even if an RSS activist had not read the book, through the ideological classes during shakha training, he might still have repeatedly heard much of what it contained. In fact, virtually all RSS members knew that their objective was to capture the Indian state in the name of the Hindu faith. They carried in their veins a deep hostility towards anyone who seemed to be a threat to their objective. Though Golwalkar's book fuelled Hindu supremacist feelings and stoked general hatred for non-Hindus, particularly Muslims, it suggested no practical way to convert India into a Hindu rashtra, thus leaving it up to swayamsevaks to look for ways to remove hurdles.

Thus, by 1947, it was common within the Hindutva circles to refer to Gandhi as the real problem whose active presence was detrimental to their idea of a Hindu rashtra. Though the nation did not look at it in this way, those belonging to or sympathizing with the RSS and the Hindu Mahasabha seemed obsessed with the idea. By the time Partition became imminent, they had freed themselves from much of the strain and awkwardness that had accompanied their political idea. They were still secretive, and they still did not always seem comfortable with the way India was taking the initial steps towards a secular democracy, but by now, in the aftermath of Partition, there could be no doubt about their determination to push their idea through.

The RSS and the Hindu Mahasabha had lakhs of members between them. They had expanded their geographical reach: their area of influence now included the whole of central, western, northern and eastern India. They expected to become a substantial player in deciding the ideological direction the nascent nation was to take, using the unique opportunity Partition and the increased intolerance among the Hindu and Sikh refugees offered. During the first few months after Partition, they even seemed to succeed in pushing through their vision for India's post-colonial society.

But with Gandhi, the most famous and the most popular Indian leader, firmly opposing them, the tide started to turn. The seventy-seven-year-old man, who was known for producing miraculous results through fasts, had grown in a short span after Partition into his role as the supreme deity of communal harmony. It was largely due to his immense moral power that within four months of Independence and Partition, the victory of the idea of a secular democracy seemed beyond question. It rose above the turmoil of the times as the unifying principle in post-Independence India. The spirit of the age seemed to be pointing towards a political system devoid of any differentiation based on religion.

Full of resentment and refusing to learn from history, Hindu organizations withdrew into their reactionary doctrines and set themselves against the mood of the times. Gandhi was now the target, both for these organizations and their individual members. The resentment was noted by the Intelligence Department of Delhi Police on 8 December 1947, when Golwalkar, addressing a group of RSS members at Rohtak Road in the national capital, said: 'The Sangh will not rest content until it had finished Pakistan. If anyone stood in our way we will have to finish him too, whether it was Nehru Government or any other Government.'[29] In the closed-door meeting, the RSS chief especially targeted Gandhi and revealed that he had means to 'silence' him. 'Mahatma Gandhi wanted to keep the Muslims in India,' Golwalkar said,

> so that the Congress may profit by their votes at the time of election. But, by that time, not a single Muslim will be left in India. If they were made to stay here, the responsibility would be Government's, and the Hindu community would not be responsible. Mahatma Gandhi could not mislead them any longer. We have the means whereby such men can be immediately silenced, but it is our tradition not to be inimical to Hindus. If we are compelled, we will have to resort to that course too.[30]

It was only about three weeks after Golwalkar threatened to 'silence' Gandhi that Godse, along with Apte and Karkare, got preoccupied by the plan to complete the task. Whether he was asked to 'silence' Gandhi remained a mystery. There were theories, but in the absence of a thorough investigation into the conspiracy angle of Gandhi's murder, there could be no certainty or pat explanations.

~

'For the [Gandhi murder] plan to be successful, it was necessary to put the reins of command in the hands of one man,' Godse later remarked, 'So, I asked Apte to take all the decisions in this regard.'[31] But the group which had been gathered for the purpose was characterized more by diversity than discipline. This was partly because Godse himself remained uncertain about his own participation in the plan. Apte too was prompted by his own acute and highly developed sense of self-preservation. Nevertheless, under his direction, the plan seemed to proceed on several fronts: from the preparation of the blueprint and the identification of the man who would assassinate Gandhi to the identification of the source of arms for the purpose. But some means had to be devised to get the would-be assassin to take on the task before this plan could be implemented.

At the time, Pahwa was in a state of flux. He was occupied not so much by his hatred for Gandhi as his infatuation for Shewanti. On 6 January 1948, he, under instructions from the police, was to leave Ahmednagar along with Karkare for Poona, where they were to meet Godse and Apte. But a brawl at Ahmednagar railway station gave him a pretext to stay back for two more days. He had sustained a minor head injury and had to be hospitalized for a couple of hours. The next day, Karkare proceeded to Poona and asked Pahwa to complete his preparation and meet him in the office of Godse's newspaper in a day or two.[32] For Pahwa, however, preparation meant only one thing—meeting Shewanti as many times as possible. Before leaving for Poona late on 8 January, he told her that he would be back 'in a few days'. The two then exchanged addresses, Pahwa giving her Prof. Jain's postal address for any correspondence.[33]

The pace of events quickened when on 9 January, Pahwa met Godse and Apte in the presence of Karkare for a second time—this time in the *Hindu Rashtra* office in Poona. Even here, Pahwa was not told about the plan. While Pahwa was busy talking to his friend, who had accompanied him from Ahmednagar, Apte quietly told Karkare that it had been decided to kill Gandhi 'within five or six days'.[34] According to Karkare, Apte then 'asked me if Madanlal was prepared to come with us. I told him that Madanlal was ever ready to do any act and would be taken with me'.[35]

Though Godse made the requisite preparations with Apte, he stayed aloof while the latter interacted with Pahwa and Karkare. Perhaps he was simply obeying the command structure he himself had put in place. He remained silent even when Apte asked Karkare to check the arms which were with Badge and were to be taken to Delhi. In less than half an hour, Badge arrived and gave the details of the arms with him. Later that day, Karkare, along with Pahwa and his refugee friend, went to Badge's house to inspect the arms. 'At about 12.30 p.m. Madanlal, myself and Om Prakash [Pahwa's friend] went to the house of Badge,' recounted Karkare. 'Badge asked his servant to bring the "stuff". The servant whom I subsequently came to know as Shankar went in the inner room and brought a bag before us. Badge opened the bag and showed me 1 hand grenade, 2 revolvers and 1 gun-cotton slab and explained the method of using the arms.'[36]

On their return, Apte asked Karkare to proceed straight to Bombay along with Pahwa and wait for them in the

Hindu Mahasabha office. Karkare followed the instructions, and that very night caught a train to Bombay. Pahwa accompanied his master but without any hint of what they were up to.

11

Alibi

Godse seemed confident that Pahwa could be relied on. At this stage, Godse wanted to stay safe from the murder plot he and Apte had devised. And so, he had also been secretly planning a parallel narrative that would act as a 'cover story' and preclude his friend and him from being dragged into the murder controversy once Pahwa had carried out the job. Accordingly, shortly before embarking on a journey from Poona to launch the operation, Godse created the impression that Apte and he were going not to Bombay and then on to Delhi, but to Nagpur to attend a marriage ceremony. 'We left the management [of *Hindu Rashtra*] in the hands of Apte's younger brother Madhavrao Apte and told everyone that we were going to Nagpur for eight to fifteen days, although we boarded Poona Express on January 14 for Bombay,' he said later.[1]

To make the 'cover story' appear convincing, a letter was dispatched the same day from Poona to Godse's sister Mathura, who lived in Nagpur along with her husband Prabhakar Trimbak Marathe. The brief letter, which stated that Godse was on his way to Nagpur, was sent by Mathura's daughter Watsala, who studied at a high school in Poona and stayed with Godse's parents. Nagpur, the heart of Hindutva and the headquarters of the RSS's countrywide network, is located to the east of Poona, while Bombay is to its west. 'My daughter Watsala [. . .] sent a chit [. . .] to the effect that Nathuram Godse was to go to Nagpur in the near future,' said Marathe subsequently. 'This chit was received [on] 16th or 17th January 1948.'[2]

The parallel narrative, it was felt, would erase Godse and Apte's footprints and cover their tracks. The pretext had been provided by N.B. Khare's invitation to Godse for the marriage ceremony of his daughter in Nagpur.[3] Khare, the prime minister of the princely state of Alwar, was a native of Nagpur. He was a bitter critic of Gandhi and had been closely associated with the Hindu Mahasabha and the RSS. In Alwar, he was known for 'heavily financing' the RSS 'through the state agencies'.[4] The marriage ceremony of his daughter was to be held on 20 January.[5]

It seems likely that Godse saw himself presented with an unexpected opportunity when he received the invitation from Nagpur. Perhaps soon thereafter he began to synchronize the timings of his operation with the marriage event. He did assent to attend the marriage of Khare's daughter but went on to plan Gandhi's murder on the very day, apparently to obfuscate his presence in Delhi. Watsala's 'chit' could have served some purpose had the murder plot been executed in the manner Godse had expected. As it happened, Gandhi was indeed murdered, not on 20 January by Pahwa but through a revised plan ten days later when there was nothing to hide.

Nevertheless, the move revealed Godse's overwrought but megalomaniac temperament. It was in accordance with his history of caution and care in the planning of violent operations, and it showed his scant sense of reality. It seems that he never doubted the viability of the plot to assassinate Gandhi, and so while heading out to launch the operation, he naïvely thought that if he spread a rumour all would end favourably. Perhaps this attitude of Godse's came from his long association with the RSS, in which mere physical exercises and conspiratorial talks regarding revolutionary plans were used to foster mistaken notions of manliness among youth.

In fact, Godse and Apte themselves blew their 'cover' the moment they left Poona on 14 January. As they boarded the train for Bombay, they encountered an attractive young woman seated opposite them. Shanta Modak was an actor in Marathi films and popularly known by her screen name 'Bimba'. She was also on her way to Bombay. Apte immediately recognized her and, seized by a sudden excitement, started a conversation with her. He introduced himself as the proprietor of *Hindu Rashtra* and Godse as its editor.[6] The conversation continued for the entire journey, and they even went together to the train's buffet car where they had coffee.[7]

Apte also told her that they were headed to Savarkar Sadan, which was in the same locality in Bombay's Shivaji Park where her brother lived. 'At Dadar station we got down. I met my brother at the station,' Shanta Modak said subsequently. 'I told the gentlemen I could give them a lift to Shivaji Park. They accepted the lift. My brother's house and Savarkar Sadan are on the same side of the road. [We] dropped the two gentlemen opposite Savarkar Sadan, and I saw them heading towards Savarkar Sadan.'[8]

The odd thing about their conversation was that the two friends, who had taken so much care to deflect attention before they left Poona, revealed all about themselves and their destination so easily. Perhaps they gave little thought to the danger of such chit-chat with a person they hardly had any possibility of meeting again. After the murder of Gandhi,

Shanta Modak not only recorded her testimony in front of the investigators but even appeared as a prosecution witness during the trial to identify the two 'gentlemen' as Apte and Godse.[9]

The parallel narrative, devised so elaborately and with such secrecy by Godse, never really stood a real chance of success.

~

How much interest Savarkar took in the secret plan is particularly difficult to assess. In the absence of a proper investigation into just the plot to murder Gandhi, he could not be convicted and eventually got released. But on 14 January, his house, Savarkar Sadan, was the locus of a meeting he had with Godse and Apte. This meeting marked the beginning of a series of events that preceded the murder of Gandhi. The details of this meeting are not entirely understood. In his testimony, Savarkar did not talk of any such meeting. Godse, too, remained silent about it even while admitting that he and Apte headed to Savarkar Sadan from Dadar railway station in the jeep driven by Shanta Modak's brother.

The only narrative confirming this meeting is one that was provided by Apte. According to him, the meeting took place around 7.30 p.m., immediately after he and Godse were dropped at Savarkar Sadan. 'At the gate of Savarkar Sadan was a Gorkha watchman who informed Veer Savarkar about our arrival,' Apte recounted. 'Nathuram Godse and myself thereupon went to the first floor of Savarkar Sadan where we met Veer Savarkar. We had a talk with him for about 30 minutes.'[10] According to Apte, they discussed only Savarkar's newly published book, *Samajik Kranti*, and the functioning of the 'Daily Hindu Rashtra'.[11]

Irrespective of what they discussed, the very fact that their mission to kill Gandhi started off with a meeting with

Savarkar was significant, at least in the evaluation of those who investigated the assassination plot. After the meeting, their numbers swelled as other accomplices started joining them. Badge met them first, at 8.15 p.m., as Apte and Godse walked out of Savarkar Sadan. After dropping his helper Shankar Kistaiyya at the Hindu Mahasabha office, Badge had left to try and trace them. Badge and Shankar had come to Bombay on the same train as Godse and Apte but could not see them as they were in a different compartment. Shankar carried a khaki handbag containing two slabs of guncotton and five hand grenades, along with fuses, wires and detonators.

'Badge told me that [they] had arrived from Poona with necessary ammunition which will have to be kept at a safe place somewhere,' Apte said later. 'I stopped Badge there and alone went back to Savarkar Sadan, had a look at the ground floor of that building, did not find a suitable place for keeping that stuff there.'[12] Nor was the Hindu Mahasabha office safe for keeping the explosives. Apte, therefore, decided to take the help of Dixit Maharaj, who lived in the famous Bhuleshwar temple of Bombay. Dixit Maharaj, like his brother Dada Maharaj, was a religious preacher and known for his sympathies for the idea of a Hindu rashtra. Apte knew both brothers and was confident that the temple was unlikely to be raided by the police.

So, all four of them—Godse, Apte, Badge and Shankar—sat in a taxi and proceeded to Bhuleshwar temple. By the time they reached their destination, it was late and Dixit Maharaj had gone to sleep. As meeting with the religious preacher was not possible, Badge left the bag with Dixit Maharaj's helper, who was known to him and Apte. 'Whereupon I asked him [the helper] to keep the bag which I was carrying until the morning and that I would see the Maharaj the next day,' Badge said subsequently.[13] They returned to the Hindu Mahasabha office by the same taxi. 'Apte handed over Rs 50 [. . .] to Godse who in turn handed over the amount to me. This was for expenses of our travel from Poona,' said Badge, 'They asked Shankar and myself to sleep in the Mahasabha office for the night and told that they would meet us the next morning. They then drove away in a taxi.'[14]

But before leaving, Godse quickly entered the amount he had given to Badge in a small notebook that he always carried in his pocket. It was his habit to keep a record of even the most trivial expenses he made. After Gandhi's assassination, the notebook was to provide a mine of information to the investigators. Back then, however, it was perhaps seen as too insignificant an issue to be taken note of. Maintaining an account of expenses was, in fact, the only job he seemed to do after he left Poona. Beyond that, he acted virtually as Apte's subordinate, following him unquestioningly. This was partly because of his belief that a mission could be successfully accomplished only if its command structure was clearly defined—something that he revealed at the time of his interrogation. But perhaps his own sense of inferiority also played a part, for Godse seemed to believe that his gifts of foresight and objective planning had always been limited. This sense of inferiority had made him look for—and in course of time become accustomed to—strict subordination and devotion to someone he trusted.

Apte, on the other hand, seemed to enjoy the leadership role. In the span of barely a couple of days, he had succeeded in providing the group with a firm inner structure and all its members were increasingly getting dependent on him. He was not only coordinating among them but also taking decisions on their behalf. He moved swiftly, as if he knew Bombay like the back of his hand. Even the room in the city's Sea Green Hotel, where he and Godse spent that night on 14 January, was booked by him under an assumed name.[15]

'The following morning we proceeded in a taxi from Sea Green Hotel to Hindu [Maha] Sabha Office, Dadar, where Nathuram and myself met Karkare, Madanlal, Badge and his servant,' said Apte, 'I told all these people that we had to go to Dixit Maharaj's place at Bhuleshwar.'[16] Soon thereafter, they set off together for Bhuleshwar temple in a taxi. When they reached their destination, Pahwa carried Karkare's canvas holdall to the outer room of Dixit Maharaj's residence. 'Nathuram and myself requested [Dixit] Maharaj to give us a new revolver. Maharaj told us at the moment he had not one but he will be in the position to secure one in the afternoon,' recounted Apte.[17] When Dixit Maharaj wanted to know why they needed a gun, Apte gave an explanation aimed at making Dixit Maharaj interested in the project—to carry out some operations in the Nizam's state of Hyderabad.[18] As they talked, Dixit Maharaj's helper brought the bag of explosives that was left with him at night. Badge opened the bag and checked the goods inside.

Apte took the bag and called Karkare aside. Once again, he asked him whether he was confident of Pahwa carrying out the assassination. On confirmation, Apte handed over the bag of explosives to Karkare, who quickly put it in his canvass holdall. Apte also gave him Rs 500 as travel expenses and asked him to proceed to Delhi the same evening along with Pahwa.

~

Pahwa got wind of something serious the moment Karkare put the bag of explosives in his holdall and asked him to get ready for a journey to Delhi. 'I became inquisitive and asked him as to why we wanted to go to Delhi. He tried to give me vague explanations,' Pahwa said later. 'I was wondering why ammunition, etc., was being taken to Delhi. I therefore came to know that these persons had an idea of attacking Gandhiji or some other prominent leader.'[19]

Pahwa was learning of the plot, but not fast enough. The latest revelations made him suspicious of Godse and his friends. But Pahwa still hadn't realized that he and not Godse or Apte or anyone else had been chosen to carry out the attack. Still, he didn't want to leave Karkare, who had been looking after all his needs. At least, Pahwa decided not to leave Karkare until he'd made more sense of his own role in what currently seemed to be an irrational plan. Pahwa was obliged to assist his master, and he perhaps thought that he would restrict himself to that. Yet, he seemed to become desperate to meet those who genuinely wished him well.

The train bound for Delhi was to leave V.T. railway station at 9.30 p.m., and Pahwa had a few hours to kill. He told Karkare that he was going back to the Hindu Mahasabha office to pick up his trunk and that he would meet him at the station. However, once out of the station, he went straight to the house of Mrs Modak at Gaiwadi, Girgaon. He had known her since his arrival in Bombay after Partition. She was beautiful in spirit and in appearance, and Pahwa seemed to be attached to her. 'I told Mrs Modak that I was going to Delhi and that she should not worry about me,' he recounted. 'I told her that I would bring a *galichya* [carpet] for her from Delhi. She asked me to take some money from her but I told her there was no need of money. I was with her for about half an hour. She was seated at that time in her button factory which is at her residence.'[20]

From there, he went to see Prof. Jain. 'I reached his house by about 6 p.m. and Dr Jain was in the house,' Pahwa said.

> I opened the topic to him and told him that Karkare and myself were going to Delhi and I feel that he is going either to kill Gandhiji or Jawaharlal Nehru. Dr Jain told me not to listen to anybody and that I should not go to Delhi but remain at his house. He further said that I should not do such thing. I however told him that I would go to Delhi and meet my relatives. I did not tell him that we were taking any ammunition with us.[21]

But Prof. Jain was shocked. 'Before me stood a young man, who was being exploited and misguided,' he later wrote in his reminiscences. 'Possibly because he was poor and a helpless refugee, money had enticed him or perhaps he was given false hopes and promises of some kind. But it was clear to me that he was basically a decent young man, otherwise he would not talk to me with such a childlike faith. I watched his face closely and could not decide as to what he said was true or false.'[22]

Before Pahwa could leave, Prof. Jain took him for a walk to discuss the issue in detail, to find out more about the conspiracy and dissuade him from taking part in it. 'At first, I had a general talk with him. Then I asked him to return to Bombay and take up some job,' Prof. Jain wrote. He warned Pahwa about the dire consequences he would have to face if he participated in the conspiracy. 'If you mix with such treacherous and anti-national people, you will repent greatly,' Prof. Jain told him, 'If what you have told me is true, remember you will have to undergo untold sufferings all your life and you will be completely ruined.'[23]

Like a teacher trying to persuade a pupil to shift to the right track, Prof. Jain also explained to Pahwa the aims and objectives of various political groups, underlining the communal agenda of the Hindu Mahasabha in contrast with the progressive programmes of the communists and the socialists. Pahwa listened to him like an obedient student and then left. 'I was with him till about 7.45 p.m.,' Pahwa said subsequently. 'I assured him that I would not take any part in such activity and then left his house.'[24]

By the time Pahwa came out of Prof. Jain's house, he was no longer as tense as he was when Karkare had told him about the plan to visit Delhi. He went to the Hindu Mahasabha office, picked up his trunk, which contained his clothes and other things of daily use, and quietly proceeded to V.T. At 9.15 p.m. Karkare joined him carrying his canvass holdall. Together they entered a third-class compartment of the Frontier Mail bound for Delhi.

~

How did Godse and Apte regard the progress of their plan at this stage? The evidence is thin, but it nonetheless makes it plain that at least Apte was thinking of a contingency plan even as Karkare and Pahwa set out for Delhi. Apte, therefore, asked Badge whether he would be interested in becoming a part of the plan to kill Gandhi, claiming that the task had been 'entrusted' to them by none other than Savarkar himself.[25] Apte also promised to bear all expenses for Badge's journey to and back from Delhi. Badge heard Apte out but did not make any specific commitment to the plan. Perhaps it was because, as Badge said later, he saw the plan as a bit too ambitious. As a cunning arms trafficker instinctively alert to danger, Badge replied in a characteristically ambiguous way that did little to boost the prospect of the plan in actual terms. 'I agreed to accompany them to Delhi but said that I would first go to Poona and make all arrangements and return,' Badge recounted.[26]

Yet, Badge's reply infused Godse and Apte with a sense of relief and confidence. Godse, especially, seemed to think the plan was progressing swiftly. He was also impressed by Apte's handling of the operation. So, Godse did not mind when late on 15 January, after finalizing the plan with Badge, Apte expressed his inability to accompany Godse to Poona, where they had to make some arrangements to ensure the paper ran smoothly in their absence. Though Apte told him that he was not feeling well and required some rest, Godse did not seem to believe him. He possibly concluded that it was not Apte's health but his desire to spend some intimate moments with Manorama that was holding him back. Nevertheless, he was happy to let Apte stay back and proceeded alone to Poona.

'I stayed that night in the [*Hindu Rashtra*] office in Poona and made necessary arrangements there,' Godse said later.[27] The next morning, he visited Kirkee, a small town close to Poona, where his younger brother Gopal lived. Godse and Apte had already taken him into confidence. Gopal agreed to accompany them and promised to arrange a revolver for the operation. 'Gopal told me that he would join us [in Delhi] and that he had already arranged a revolver,' recounted Godse.[28]

For the most part, their pursuit of a revolver had remained unsuccessful. Dixit Maharaj had promised a firearm the previous day and even arranged an American revolver for them when they met in the afternoon. However, he had demanded a price of Rs 500, which they didn't want to pay. They had expected him to hand it over to them free of cost. Dixit Maharaj, however, seemed to have learned from the experiences of his brother Dada Maharaj, who had in the past been fooled by the pair to pay up for arms and ammunitions for absolutely no operation as such. Thus, they could not strike a deal with Dixit Maharaj. It was for this reason that Gopal's announcement was considered a significant development by Godse.

On his way back to the newspaper office, Godse dropped in at Badge's residence just to make sure that he was still a part of the team. At that time, Badge was not at home. Godse, therefore, left for his office. After some time, Godse checked at Badge's residence again but he was still out. 'When I returned to my residence, Shankar informed me that somebody from the *Hindu Rashtra* office had come twice to see me but I was out. I at once understood that the individual must have been Godse,' Badge recounted. 'I therefore went to Godse's office. He was alone there in the office. On seeing me he came out and asked me whether I was ready to proceed to Bombay. I told him that I was ready and would be present at V.T. Railway Station on the morning of 17.1.48.' Godse also told him that Gopal would join them with a revolver. 'He then gave me a small pistol and asked me to see if I could exchange it for a bigger one. This pistol he took out from his shirt pocket, and handed it over to me. He told me that in case I was not able to exchange it for a bigger one, I should bring it along with me to Bombay,' Badge added.[29]

Gladdened by the way things were shaping up and after having talked to Badge and Gopal, Godse caught the afternoon train, reaching Bombay's Sea Green Hotel by 9 p.m. Soon, Apte joined him. Till late that night, they discussed Godse's Poona tour and their plans, while Manorama waited for Apte in another room in the hotel. For that night, Apte had booked two rooms, one for Godse and the other for Manorama and himself. She had been with Apte right since Godse left for Poona in the evening on 15 January. Apte had not told her anything about their plan to kill Gandhi except that he and Godse would be leaving for Delhi for some urgent work.

Around 7 a.m., Saturday, 17 January 1948, Godse and Apte reached V.T., where Badge and Shankar were already waiting for them. For a few hours, they visited a few people in Bombay to collect some money. 'Then Godse said that we all should go out and take a last darshan of Tatyarao,' Badge said later.[30] The four then left for Savarkar Sadan. While Shankar waited outside, the rest entered the building where Badge was asked to stay on the ground floor and Godse and Apte went upstairs to meet Savarkar. 'After 5 or 10 minutes, they both came down and as they were getting down the stairs, Savarkar followed them down the stairs and said to them "be successful and return",' Badge recounted. 'On the way Apte stated that Tatyarao had predicted that Gandhiji's hundred years were over. Therefore, there was no doubt that we were bound to be successful in our mission. This statement of Apte coupled with what I heard from Tatyarao confirmed my belief that what was being done had the approval and blessings of Savarkar.'[31]

Around 1.30 p.m., Godse and Apte boarded a plane bound for Delhi via Ahmedabad. As they stepped inside, they saw Dada Maharaj seated comfortably on one of the blue leather chairs of the plane. They greeted each other but didn't talk. After some time, the plane landed in Ahmedabad. Dada Maharaj got up to alight from the plane. It was then that he broached the issue of their failed plans to attack Hyderabad and Pakistan. Godse remained quiet, but Apte said: 'Now you will see what we are going to do.'[32]

12

Reconnaissance

No other city in India as Delhi had been so shaken by the events and emotions that followed the creation of Pakistan and the subsequent flight of minorities from the two countries. The influx of an unimaginable number of Hindu and Sikh refugees crying out their hatred of Muslims, mixed with the conspiratorial activities of Hindu extremists, resulted in a massive communal explosion in the city. For weeks since September 1947, Delhi, the site of seven fallen cities in the past, experienced innumerable blood-chilling incidents of the massacre of Muslims and forcible occupation of their houses, shops and mosques. Panic-stricken Muslims had in thousands clustered in any part of Delhi that offered a safe cover: the Jama Masjid, Purana Quila, Humayun's Tomb, Muslim graveyards, Mughal ruins, the Pakistan High Commission, and the homes and gardens of well-known Muslims, including Jawaharlal Nehru's two Muslim cabinet ministers, Maulana Abul Kalam Azad and Rafi Ahmed Kidwai.[1]

Gandhi was in Calcutta when Delhi detonated. On 9 September 1947, when he arrived back, the city was still a hotbed of violence and misery. Week after week he laboured to bring the Hindu and Sikh minds back to sanity, often putting himself in danger, as he knew that on his victory in this battle against Hindu militants rested the fate of his lifetime's struggle for an independent, secular and democratic India. The weapon that Gandhi used contained all virtues of the human spirit: moral strength, confidence, sagacity and forbearance. Evolved by Gandhi, the weapon had driven the British out of the country. Now he was to deploy it against a section of his own countrymen, those who saw in the human misery an opportunity to cleanse India of Muslims and set up a Hindu rashtra.

From his room in Birla House, Gandhi made public his support for Nehru's unpopular policies to protect Muslims and maintain religious tolerance. Since the time of his arrival, Gandhi acted virtually as the principal adviser to the Indian government on all major political issues. Scarcely was any important decision taken without his prior advice.[2] 'All the time his old friends and colleagues now heading the government, especially Nehru and Sardar Patel, came to him with their problems,' noted Horace Alexander, a close associate of Gandhi, 'and, even if he could not always give the answer, at least he would send them away with fresh strength in their ability to win the battle of decency and good government'.[3]

Boosted by the efforts of the government and the ministrations of Gandhi, Delhi witnessed a spectacular improvement in the situation by January 1948. Violence largely ended and attendance at Gandhi's prayer meetings in the lawns of Birla House started to grow. 'His audience at Birla House in the early days after his arrival were extremely small; perhaps not more than 40 or 50 attended,' read a report on Gandhi's prayer meetings sent to London by the British High Commission during these crucial months:

> And when he held a prayer meeting one evening in Old Delhi—the only one held outside Birla House during all these months—he was forced to abandon it because of Sikh opposition to his habitual practice of including recitations from the Koran in addition to other religious books. [. . .] As the weeks went by his congregations began to increase in size and included a number of Muslims who previously had not dared to leave their homes. There were prospects, very slight admittedly, that people were beginning to heed his exhortations.[4]

Yet, the situation in Delhi remained volatile and Gandhi disconsolate. For weeks at a time, the city seemed to be peaceful, and then fresh trouble would break out. It was painfully apparent that the city had not returned to normality in the real sense and that it was shamefully ill-equipped to tackle another massive explosion. On Tuesday, 13 January 1948—five days before Godse and Apte arrived in Delhi with a plan to kill him—Gandhi set out to stun the city, his friends and his foes. At 11.55 a.m., the aged Mahatma stretched out on a cot in the garden of Birla House, vowing not to eat till the time all seized Muslim establishments and mosques were returned to their rightful owners and total harmony among Hindus, Muslims and Sikhs was restored in Delhi.[5]

'Delhi is on trial,' Gandhi warned during the prayer meeting that evening. 'What I demand is that no amount of slaughter in India or Pakistan should deflect the people of Delhi from the path of duty.'[6] He also declared that he would break his fast only when conditions in Delhi permitted the withdrawal of the military and the police without any danger to peace. 'The police might remain but only to cope with anti-social elements, not for enforcing communal peace,' Gandhi, according to his aide Pyarelal, said.[7]

The fast unto death immediately transported Gandhi from the emotional turmoil he'd been experiencing because of the communal disharmony to a sense of peace, but it evoked in his countrymen a mixture of confusion, consternation and even outright hostility. Rajkumari Amrit Kaur, the health minister in Nehru's cabinet, confided to a staff member of the British High Commission that she thought it would really be a fast unto death at last.[8] All skin and bones, seventy-eight-year-old Gandhi would not survive for more than five or six days without sustenance.

There were many who could not hold back tears, but there were those who responded with extreme hostility. When Nehru heard a crowd of demonstrators outside Birla House chant 'Let Gandhi die', he ran at them and shouted: 'How dare you say that! Come and kill me first.' At this, the demonstrators dispersed.[9] At Connaught Circus, about 4 km away from Birla House, a group of RSS men in their khaki shorts, white shirts and black caps exercised vigorously, shouting at the top of their voices: '*Buddhe ko marne do* [Let the old man die].'[10]

Gandhi, however, had given Delhi the shock it needed. By 17 January, as his health deteriorated, Gandhi's fast started bringing results. Hindu militants vanished from the streets, replaced by massive crowds of all faiths taking out processions and turning up at Birla House as repentant masses, begging Gandhi to give up his fast and save his own life. Representatives from across the city sent assurances that they would respect Muslim life, property and religion. That evening, Gandhi somehow summoned the strength to speak at the time of his prayer meeting. With the help of a microphone that had been brought into his room and placed next to his cot, he addressed the crowd directly from where he lay. He thanked all those who had sent their good wishes.

The next day, shortly after noon, after the high commissioner of Pakistan reiterated the appeal, followed by representatives of the Hindu Mahasabha, the RSS, Delhi Muslims, the Sikhs and the Delhi administration, Gandhi gave up his fast and accepted a glass of lime juice.

By evening, thousands of people gathered at Birla House despite the rain. Speaking into the microphone from his bed at 5.30 p.m., Gandhi said he had earlier dictated his message for the prayer audience, which would be read out to them. 'The letter of my vow has been fulfilled early beyond expectation through the great goodwill of all the citizens of Delhi, including the leaders of the Hindu Mahasabha and the R.S.S,' read the message. 'But beyond the letter of fulfillment of my solemn vow lies its spirit without which the letter killeth. The spirit of the vow is sincere friendship between the Hindus, Muslims and Sikhs of the Union and a similar friendship in Pakistan.'[11]

Moments later, the British High Commission, which was located close to Birla House, sent a telegram to London: 'Time alone will show whether the R.S.S.S's association with other parties in getting these assurances represents a real change of heart by this organization or whether it is only a temporary change brought about by moral pressure from Congress and other leaders.'[12]

~

An hour before Gandhi's written speech was to be read on 18 January, Godse marched into Birla House along with Apte and Karkare for a preliminary survey of the prayer ground where the Mahatma was to be killed.[13] The skies were murky and it was drizzling intermittently. The trio walked across the immaculately trimmed lawn at the edge of which, adjacent to the back of a row of servant quarters, a wooden platform, 6 inches high, had been installed. It was on this platform that Gandhi used to sit and address his countrymen during the evening prayer meetings. A small flight of stairs made of red sandstone on the side of the corridor emerging from Gandhi's quarters led up to the raised lawn. The lawn also had another entrance at the opposite end, constructed recently for visitors to the prayer meetings.

Godse and his colleagues focused primarily on 'the exact place where Gandhiji used to sit and conduct his prayers and the route from his room to the prayer meeting'.[14] There were obvious advantages associated with these spots—both had possible escape routes for the assailants. 'I could see that the window [of the servant quarter] behind the place where Gandhiji used to sit was a suitable place for shooting at him,' Apte later recounted:

> But the number of the persons attending the prayer [meeting] was so low that a necessary disturbance which ought to precede the next act was not possible. My idea was to cause confusion by creating disturbance and then taking advantage of this, have the resort to shooting from behind. This would have given a facility for the culprit to run away from the scene without being detected.[15]

Assassination entailed problems of its own. There were several loose ends which were yet to be tied up. Presumably, Godse and his colleagues had hoped to acquire a particular room in the servant quarters for the operation. Equally important was to locate Gopal, who was to bring the revolver required for the operation. Prompted by their acute sense of anxiety, the three men left the place and went back to Marina Hotel in

Connaught Place, where Godse and Apte had taken a room since their arrival in Delhi the previous day. 'We were still anxious about Gopal's arrival, accordingly left the hotel in a taxi to the Rly. Stn. [railway station]' to locate Godse's brother. Before returning to the hotel, they checked every possible point at the station, on the platforms and in the waiting rooms, but could not find him.[16]

At 10 a.m. on Monday, 19 January 1948, they hired a tonga and set off for Birla House for a clearer, more comprehensive view of the prayer ground. While Godse and Apte got down at the front gate, Karkare took the tonga to the entrance on the opposite side of the lawn. 'I had noticed elaborate police arrangements in front of Birla House,' noted Apte. 'The gateman of the Birla House stopped me and Nathuram at the entrance and asked me to write our names in the chit to the secretary and he would return soon with the permission. As he left the place with the chit we took the advantage and entered the prayer-ground.' Karkare joined them from the other end of the ground. 'We had full survey of the prayer-ground and observed certain points particularly positions where we should remain at the time of action. This took about 10 to 15 minutes and we all the three came out of the Birla House from the rear door,' Apte said later.[17]

Not knowing where Gopal was frightened Godse. Unsure whether the police had arrested him since he was to carry a revolver, Godse, along with his accomplices, boarded the same tonga and went straight to the Hindu Mahasabha office, where his brother had promised to meet them. Then, at last, shortly before noon, he met Gopal, who was waiting for them outside the Hindu Mahasabha office. He had come late the previous night and slept on the platform. He told Godse that he had brought the revolver with him.[18] Godse, Apte and Gopal immediately went into a huddle at Marina Hotel, discussing the plan in detail. During the meeting, Gopal was informed that '20th of January 1948 was selected as the day to carry out the plot'.[19]

After Karkare joined them at 4 p.m., they set out for Birla House for a final survey. 'This was a prayer time and everybody had access to Birla House. We got ourselves mixed up in prayer gathering,' said Apte. 'Both Karkare and Gopal concentrated [on] the route followed by Mahatmaji [. . .]. They also had a full look at the place where Mahatmaji seated.'[20] Gandhi was still too weak to address the prayer meeting, and so his written speech was read out to the audience. For about twenty minutes, Godse and his associates surveyed the prayer ground and then they came out from the rear gate.

All the while, Godse was ponderous, seemingly lost in thought. While Apte was spirited, Godse moved in an elephantine manner, each step appearing as if it required a lot of effort. In a mere couple of days, he seemed to have aged and become exhausted. He had suddenly lost most of his tireless energy and mercurial temperament. 'Wouldn't the entire family be ruined if two of its members took part in such a plot?' he asked himself.[21] Haunted by questions such as this, he seemed paralysed with confusion. His concern was valid but time had run out. The operation was now in progress.

As Godse struggled with himself, Apte asked Karkare to secure the identified room in the servant quarters the following evening by talking to its residents. Karkare promised that he would finish the job well before time. As they moved back to the Hindu Mahasabha office, where Godse had arranged accommodation for Gopal, Karkare and Pahwa, they had no reason to assume that everything was not going according to plan.

The time had come to carry out their plan. And so, the focus shifted on Pahwa, the man chosen to assassinate Gandhi.

~

Shewanti's dreams of a dignified life rested on her pure and unqualified feelings for Pahwa. The swift and overwhelming love she had experienced in such a short span of time infused her with pride and confidence. In less than a fortnight, Pahwa had become the focal point in her life. Although there were moments when she became anxious about Pahwa's association with Karkare, not for a second did she doubt the man in her life. The last time she met him was on 11 January, when Pahwa had visited Ahmednagar briefly, primarily to collect Karkare's luggage. While leaving, he had told her that he would be back soon. But he seemed to have forgotten his promise. Time passed slowly in his absence.

On 15 January, therefore, she sent a letter to Pahwa. 'My heart yearns for you very much,' she wrote:

> I do not feel at home here. Kindly treat this letter as a telegram and reach Ahmednagar City at once. Please do try to come. Moreover, write to me beforehand as to on what date you are coming. You are wise enough. There is no need to write to you anything more in this letter. Please give a reply treating this letter as a telegram and let me know on what date you will come. Please consider these few words as meaning much.[22]

Again, on 16 January, she wrote a letter to Pahwa, this time expressing her feelings more explicitly. 'Please reply [to] this letter soon so that we may not remain in anxiety,' she wrote. 'I am quite happy here, but your remembrance troubles me very much. Please come to Ahmednagar soon. When you come, please bring a pair of sandals and a saree six yards in length for me. Please do bring these articles. Do not forget. Come soon because my heart remains sad.' Shewanti closed her second letter with a few verses:

My flower garden looks desolate without you.
O, come my simple-minded hunter.

Nights are passing, days are going and my heart is sinking.
Spring has come but the flowerbed is being looted.
O, come my simple-minded hunter.

My life companion, your love troubles me and says something else
which I cannot dare tell.
How shall I live alone without you?
O, come my simple-minded hunter.[23]

Shewanti posted these letters to the address Pahwa had given to her during one of their last meetings—Prof. Jain's Bombay residence. He received the first letter on 17 January and the second on 19 January, days after Pahwa had left for Delhi. Pahwa would know about these letters only when the prosecution made available the copies of these documents during the trial following Gandhi's assassination.[24]

It is difficult to discern what impact these letters might have had on Pahwa if he had received them in time. What seems certain is that all his protestations of love towards Shewanti were insincere. Once he met his maternal uncle in Delhi, he seemed content to drift along with his family's choice for as crucial a decision as marriage. There is no specific evidence available on what led Pahwa to discard his feelings towards Shewanti so suddenly.

Pahwa met his uncle hours after he, along with Karkare, reached Delhi and booked a room in a hotel at Fatehpuri, close to Chandni Chowk, on 17 January. For two consecutive days before shifting to the Hindu Mahasabha office in the afternoon of 19 January, while Karkare remained mostly occupied with Godse and Apte, Pahwa spent time with his uncle and the family members of the girl his father wanted him to marry. 'I [. . .] went alone on foot to the house of my uncle named Dr Bal Mukund Ahuja, who resides at Chandni Chowk, Old Delhi, which is very close to the Hotel,' Pahwa said subsequently.

> I met him and had a talk with him on domestic affairs. My aunt was also at home. They both advised me to go to my father at Jullunder and also requested me to make up my mind for marriage. I did not tell him anything about our mission at Delhi but only informed them that I had come there with my "Seth" for business. During the conversation, I found that the girl whose name I was not given was residing with her brother named Babu Satpal Arora at Kesar Building, Sabji Mandi, Old Delhi. I had not seen the girl before but this was only settled by my father and her relatives.[25]

The next day, Sunday, 18 January, Pahwa got Karkare to purchase him a pair of Pathani sandals and then went 'in search of the house of my fiancée'. He succeeded and met the mother of the girl. 'As we were having tea, Babu Bijenderlal, who is the uncle of my fiancée, came there and he told me that there was a meeting of Jawaharlal Nehru at Sabji Mandi,' Pahwa said. Hours earlier, Gandhi had broken his fast. Along with the family members of his 'fiancée', he attended the public meeting of Nehru that evening.[26]

By now, Pahwa clearly seemed to have had a sense that he was his father's heir. He planned another meeting with the family members of the girl the next evening and even a visit to his father in Jalandhar. But he had to put his plans on hold as Karkare came the following afternoon, on 19 January, and asked him to pack and shift to a room reserved for them at the Hindu Mahasabha office.[27] Pahwa couldn't refuse him.

Shewanti, of course, remained unaware of the path Pahwa had taken. Weeks later, after Gandhi's assassination, when she learnt that Pahwa would never return, she froze. 'It was like a body blow,' said Sumanbai. 'Shewanti saw all her dreams suddenly evaporating. When her mother asked, she said nothing, just turned her face away, humiliated by her pathetic helplessness. Tears rolled down her cheeks. Soon thereafter she joined her mother's profession, the sex trade, and quickly became the most sought-after prostitute of the town. Over the years we remained close, but she never fell in love again.'[28]

13

Simple-minded Hunter

Shortly after 9 p.m. on 19 January 1948, less than a day before Gandhi was to be attacked, Pahwa was made privy to the plan. Throughout the weeks of planning, he had been kept out of the discussions. Although he had never been a committed member of the conspiracy and had even vacillated abjectly, his role had been deemed central to the success of the plot. In fact, so critical was his cooperation that scarcely could anything happen without it.

At the time, he was in bed trying to sleep. He was so engrossed in his own thoughts, perhaps of the marriage proposal, that he hardly paid any attention as Apte entered the room quietly, said something to Karkare in a low voice and both went out into the cold night. 'Before I could get a sleep in the room at Mahasabha Bhawan, Karkare returned to the room within about five or ten minutes and whispered to me whether I would be in a position to kill Gandhiji,' Pahwa recounted. 'I stealthily said that I would not be able to do such an act.'[1]

Karkare listened to the reply attentively and left the room without saying anything. Pahwa was surprised. He had not expected this. He seemed to have thought that someone else in the group would take the responsibility to kill Gandhi and that his own role would be limited to assisting Karkare. Moreover, Pahwa never seemed to believe that the enterprise was much more than just a symbolic gesture. If their intention was simply to demonstrate the 'anger' of Hindus, it would have been easy enough. He had conducted such operations several times in Ahmednagar and had escaped unscathed each time. But the actual killing of Gandhi would ruin his life, while other members of the group would go scot-free.

It was not that he had developed any respect for Gandhi. Pahwa, like many refugees, still held Gandhi personally responsible for most of his sufferings. In fact, there had been a time when such an instruction from Karkare might not have shocked him at all and he might even have considered the option. But his priorities had changed drastically. Hatred for Gandhi was no longer the sole driving factor for him; Shewanti had smoothed much of his rough edges, and now he was getting mentally ready to marry the girl his father had chosen for him.

Pahwa pulled the blanket over his face and tried to sleep again but in vain. He was thinking with more clarity. It had been almost a month since he had been taking orders from Karkare. Pahwa had always obeyed him. This was the first time when he had said no to him. He seemed to feel uncomfortable but not enough to leave Karkare, on whom he depended heavily for all his needs. None of the other occupants of the room—Badge and Shankar, who had arrived only a few hours back, as well as Karkare and Gopal—returned before Pahwa fell into a deep slumber. 'I do not know what time the rest returned,' he said later.[2]

~

Things began to go wrong the moment Pahwa refused to take on the responsibility of killing Gandhi. The question of who would spearhead the assassination was revived once again. Godse was still not ready to do it. To Apte's horror, Godse declared on the morning of 20 January, the day Gandhi was to be attacked, that he had had a severe attack of migraine.[3] There is no way to know whether the attack was real or he simply made it up to stay away from all the action after Pahwa's refusal to kill Gandhi blew the plot to smithereens. It is safe to assume Godse believed by now that the plot was doomed.

However, Apte did not give up and tried desperately to engineer the assassination. He seemed determined to go ahead with the plan despite the unexpected development. Leaving Godse at the Marina Hotel room, Apte made an early dash to the Hindu Mahasabha Bhawan and took Badge and Shankar—the two latecomers who had never been to Birla House and not seen the positions earmarked for the attack on Gandhi—for a fresh survey of the ground. Once in the lawn of Birla House, Apte showed them the elevated platform on which Gandhi sat and conducted the prayer meetings. 'At this spot there was chawl [servant quarters] alongside the wall of Birla Bhavan,' said Badge later.

> I was shown a window with trellice [sic] work of bricks and masonry. From the holes which comprised the trellice [sic] work, we made certain that a hand grenade could be thrown on to the prayer ground as also a shot fired from a revolver. Apte then took us round the wall, pointed out to us two spots near the wall where guncotton slabs were to be placed and exploded and during the confusion caused thus Gandhiji was to be assassinated.[4]

Apte also showed them the front side of the room which had the window with the trellis. According to Badge, 'Apte stated that the plan should be to pose as a photographer and enter into the room on the pretext of taking photograph of Gandhiji and shoot and throw grenades through the trellice [sic] work.'[5] They returned to the Hindu Mahasabha Bhawan shortly before noon. 'He [Apte] then asked Gopal Godse, Shankar and myself to accompany him to the jungle behind the Sabha office to try out [the] two revolvers which our party had got. Shankar carried the small revolver and Gopal Godse carried the bigger revolver,' Badge said.[6]

At a seemingly safe location in the jungle, they proceeded to test the revolvers. 'We first tried the revolver which Gopal Godse had with him, but it was not functioning well, in that the chamber was not revolving,' said Badge, 'Apte then decided to try the other revolver which was with Shankar. Shankar was asked to aim at a tree in front and fire one round. He did so but the bullet just fell a few feet away from him and did not reach its mark. Apte then said that this weapon was ineffective.'[7] They set out to repair the bigger revolver. Gopal dismantled the device and started oiling and cleaning its parts. Around that time three forest guards wandered into that part of the forest. Though the group concealed their ammunitions and the guards moved away, Apte considered it risky to stay in the jungle for long. He, therefore, asked them all to shift to his room at Marina Hotel. Before leaving, Apte also instructed Karkare to reach the hotel along with Pahwa and the bag of explosives they had brought from Bombay.

For the next two hours, Godse's room at Marina Hotel was a maelstrom of frenzied activity. Under Apte's auspices, preparations for the attack on Gandhi proceeded in the lavatory attached to the room. 'Nathuram was lying in bed,' Badge recounted later. 'In Nathuram's room behind closed doors, Gopal Godse then reassembled the revolver and we inserted the detonators in the hand grenades and the guncotton slabs.'[8] All members of the group were given aliases and a revised plan was drawn in which Badge—whose alias was Bandopant—was assigned the key role to shoot Gandhi. It was decided that 'I [Badge] should pose as the photographer and take my position in the room of the chawl just behind the spot where Mahatma Gandhi [. . .] sat for the prayer meeting' with a revolver and a hand grenade in his hand.[9]

It must have occurred to Apte that before anything of this ambitious project could be implemented some means had to be devised to ensure that Pahwa remained part and parcel of the plot. He knew too much, and it would be a great risk to let him stay away from the action. The only way to neutralize him and eliminate the chances of Pahwa ever spilling the beans was to make him take part in the implementation of the conspiracy. As Pahwa had declined to take up the lead role, he was asked to perform the seemingly least risky part of the plot—to ignite a guncotton slab at a spot almost outside the prayer ground and far removed from Gandhi and his audience. He was also asked to keep a hand grenade and lob it in a similar manner. The blast he was entrusted with was not meant to hurt anybody but to create a distraction.[10] Karkare and Pahwa agreed to this.

It was also decided that the igniting of the guncotton slab by Pahwa would be followed by other members of the group throwing hand grenades from different directions, thus creating total chaos, which would then be used by Badge to shoot Gandhi.

So far as Godse was concerned, there was no point whatsoever in pursuing a plot that had lost its cohesion. For the whole day he had remained inactive, mostly watching from the sidelines, often from his bed, the hectic efforts of the other members of the group. Although it contravened with his allegiance to the plot, he seemed to have lost his drive. Apte was particularly irritated by the apparent cold feet Godse seemed to have developed. Just when they were setting out for Birla House, with Godse preferring to stay back in the hotel room, Apte took a swipe at him. 'Apte told me that since you are not well we cannot depend upon you. All of them then left the room,' Godse recounted later.[11]

~

Around 5 p.m. on 20 January 1948, Gandhi was carried on a chair to the prayer ground. He looked ill and drawn. Even two days after his fast the doctors had decided that he must continue to be on a liquid diet, as a result of which he was unable to build up his strength. Yet the bleak despair that had shrouded his entourage since the outbreak of the communal frenzy and had accentuated during the last days of his fast had now vanished, replaced by a kind of euphoria.

From the foremost leader of the anti-colonial movement, Gandhi had, after the successful conclusion of the fast, graduated to becoming the icon of communal harmony. Newspapers around the world hailed the courageous display of idealism by Gandhi. Never had his prestige at home and abroad stood higher. Though Hindu communalists despised him even more bitterly now, in the eyes of most Indians he had become a man with miraculous powers, if not a living god. There was no doubt, however, that this fast had damaged some of his vital organs. His kidneys and liver were particularly affected. 'Once more the battleship had gone into action and come out with the colours unlowered and unsoiled,' noted Gandhi's aide Pyarelal, 'but with the hull this time badly damaged.'[12]

However, primarily due to his austere living and self-discipline, his body was extremely well-preserved, its system still retaining ample recuperative powers. His command over sleep was amazing. 'When I lose command over sleep,' he used to say, as recorded by Pyarelal, 'I shall be finished. It will be a sign not merely of physical decay but of the deterioration of the spirit as well. All deterioration begins with the spirit, next affects the body and finally one's environment.'[13]

By the time Gandhi ended his fast, he was already contemplating the launch of what he thought would be the last and the greatest of his campaigns—a march to Pakistan in the hope of bringing the two nations together, leading the Muslim refugees back into India and Hindu refugees to the new country.[14] He seemed to believe that only a campaign of this magnitude would heal the wounds of the people and secure independence for the two dominions permanently.[15] 'Even in the evening of his life,' observed Pyarelal, 'he was quite capable of launching upon one more struggle.'[16]

The idea was one of the most extraordinary ones Gandhi had ever conceived, and it required greater physical strength than what he had after the fast. He, therefore, planned to go to his ashram in Wardha for a few days to regain his strength before putting it into practice. Perhaps it was because of this new spirit bubbling in Gandhi that on the day after the end of his fast he broke one of his unbreakable rules. For ages, he had observed Monday as a day of silence and rest. But on Monday, 19 January 1948, there were too many things on his mind to remain silent. That morning he told two of his visitors, who had come in with terrible stories about what had happened to Hindus and Sikhs in Karachi, that he intended to go to Pakistan. 'Give me in writing what you have told me. I will take the necessary steps to set things right,' Gandhi demanded.[17]

Though Jinnah's distrust made his extraordinary plan appear uncertain, Gandhi was radiant with new fervour. Unlike the past couple of days, when his written speeches had been read out, on the evening of 20 January, he would address the audience directly. He displayed, despite looking haggard, a characteristic self-confidence as he sat on the wooden podium gazing searchingly at the audience. Around 300 people had gathered on the lawns. They seemed more eager to receive his darshan than to listen to his speech. It was the usual crowd, but it also included some people who were interested neither in a darshan nor in his speech.

~

Godse was the last among this set of people to enter the prayer ground. He had excused himself the whole day from all preparatory activities ahead of the planned attack. As they assembled their weapons in his washroom, he mostly remained in bed, hardly even taking part in conversations. While leaving for Birla House, Apte had tried to goad Godse into action. He still did not respond. But the moment his room was empty, he felt isolated from the group. Shortly thereafter, his headache vanished and he rushed after them. 'Around four o'clock in the afternoon, I felt some relief from headache. I boarded a tonga and left for Birla House simply to make a visit to the prayer ground,' Godse said later.[18]

Once at the prayer ground, he wandered among the crowd, searching intently for Apte. 'Five minutes later I met Apte. He told me that he had kept a taxi waiting,' said Godse, 'I asked

Apte what I was supposed to do. He told me that he would let me know about that soon.'[19] Apte then hurried to talk to Badge, who stood with Shankar near the rear gate of the lawn, apparently awaiting instructions.

But things didn't go according to plan. Though Karkare had persuaded the occupants of the identified room to allow a 'photographer' to go inside and take a photograph of Gandhi from behind, Badge developed cold feet at the last minute. 'Apte told me to go into the room,' Badge said later. 'At that time I thought that if I went in the room I would be easily detected and arrested. Thereupon I declined.'[20] He was unscrupulous but by no means a fool. A shrewd businessman, personal safety was always his prime concern. He told Apte that he and Shankar, who carried the smaller revolver and a hand grenade, would prefer to do the job in the open and facing Gandhi.

Both Godse and Apte tried to persuade Badge, assuring him that his escape route had already been planned, but he did not budge. As soon as they left, he took the second revolver from Shankar. Wrapping the two revolvers in a towel he had picked from Marina Hotel, he quietly put them under the backseat of the taxi which was kept waiting nearby.[21] The taxi driver failed to notice this as he was slightly away from his vehicle.

Badge seemed to have realized that he could not trust the men he had accompanied. Carrying revolvers inside the prayer ground in such a situation would be extremely risky. At that point, the plot to murder Gandhi was a lost cause—the revised plan, too, lacked conviction. The nucleus of the plot abdicated once again, although Godse and Apte remained unaware of this development. Having secured himself, Badge walked inside the ground along with Shankar and stood close to the wooden platform from which Gandhi was conducting the prayer meeting.

Just like Badge, Pahwa too suspected the intentions of Apte and the others. Though Pahwa was told that his job would be the least risky, he was not certain whether the others too had to do something or he alone was being pressed into action. He, therefore, walked down to Apte after planting the guncotton slab at the designated place and asked him 'whether I was only doing the work or others were also doing something'. Apte assured him about the roles of the other members of the group. 'He said that all were doing their bit and I should not get frightened. He then opened the plot and told me that I should explode the guncotton slab by the side of the compound wall on the right side of the servant quarters,' Pahwa recounted:

> As soon as this explosion takes place, Shankar would explode another guncotton slab outside the prayer ground on the right side of Gandhiji. After this, Badge would throw a hand grenade outside the prayer meeting ground on the left side of Gandhiji and as soon as this grenade was thrown and I heard the report I was to throw the hand grenade outside the compound wall on the road side. After I had thrown the hand grenade, Shankar was to throw another grenade which would be followed by another grenade to be thrown by Badge. Apte said that he would be sitting on one side of Gandhiji and Gopal Godse would take his place on the other side, both armed with revolvers. Apte then said that after these loud explosions all round the prayer ground there would be terrible commotion amongst the audience and it was at this time that both or either of them [would] shoot Gandhiji.[22]

There was no way Pahwa could verify what Apte had told him. Moreover, since their conversation took place at a distance from

Badge and Shankar, Apte's claim that he and Gopal would be carrying the revolvers and shooting at Gandhi after a spate of blasts could not be contradicted. Thus, despite his misgivings, Pahwa walked to back his designated spot to carry out the instructions, assured that the others would do their bit too.

When the guncotton slab exploded, Gandhi thought it was a military drill. At the time, Dr Sushila Nayar, Pyarelal's sister and one of Gandhi's aides, was repeating the post-prayer speech he had made in a feeble voice.[23] Though the explosion was loud and shook the whole building, it didn't cause much commotion in the gathering. No one jumped and ran but everyone craned their necks to see where the explosion had come from. Gandhi immediately took the microphone: 'If we get panicked like this over nothing, what shall be our plight if something really happens? . . . Listen! Listen! Listen everybody . . . nothing has happened.'[24] Quickly, order was restored and Dr Nayar's speech progressed.

But Pahwa was horrified—there was no follow-up blast, nor was there any sound of firing. Badge ran away. So did Godse and the other conspirators. 'Immediately, after the explosion several persons came out of the compound and I looked towards the place where the car [taxi] was parked and found the same missing. I was also waiting to hear another explosion before throwing the bomb but did not hear any noise except the commotion amongst the persons gathered for prayers,' he recounted.

He was in a fix. Another blast in some other part of the lawn might have deflected attention from him. But in the absence of any follow-up blast, Pahwa was caught off guard and overpowered quickly by the police. 'I thought,' he said later, 'that I was cheated.'[25]

~

When the explosion happened, Godse was in the taxi along with Apte and Gopal. They had occupied their seats in a hurry, the moment after Apte signalled Pahwa to ignite the guncotton slab. Godse grew frantic as he heard the explosion. 'Start the car, start the car,' he shouted, swept apparently by a sense of panic.[26] The driver immediately put the car in gear. 'I did hear some noise of the explosion but cannot exactly recollect whether I heard the noise just before I started the car or just after,' taxi driver Surjit Singh said later.[27]

Godse and his associates could not confirm Gandhi's death, of course. There was no means of doing that. Nevertheless, they were confident. Badge had himself assured them he would see that the job would be done, and so they 'felt that following the explosion the whole plan would be carried through'.[28] It seemed inconceivable that Gandhi could have survived the attack. However, to their horror, as they drove away, they noticed under the back seat the two revolvers which Badge and Shankar were supposed to use to shoot Gandhi.[29] Doubts regarding the success of their plot started to creep in.

When they got down from the taxi at Connaught Circus, Gopal kept the revolvers with him. It was then decided that each should find his way to Bombay individually. Gopal left in a tonga while Godse and Apte hired another taxi and set out for the Hindu Mahasabha office, apparently to find out the outcome of the plot.

Badge, who had already reached the Hindu Mahasabha office, was in despair. After the explosion he and Shankar had rushed to the rear gate of Birla House, hoping that the taxi would be waiting for them. But it was missing. So were all their fellow conspirators. With the getaway vehicle no longer available, the assassination conspiracy seemed like a plot against him. He kept fuming all the way as a tonga carried him and

Shankar to the Hindu Mahasabha office. 'As soon as we got to the office I asked Shankar to take the two hand grenades which he had with him and to dump them in the jungle behind the office,' Badge said later.[30]

As Shankar left, Badge hurriedly packed up, still fuming. 'At this time, Apte and Nathuram both came up to the office and began enquiring as to what had happened,' Badge recounted. 'I swore at them and abused them by their mother and asked them to get away.'[31]

Quietly, almost meekly, they left. With a heavy heart, Godse and Apte went to Marina Hotel, cleared the bill and came out with their luggage. As darkness fell, they escaped by the night train to Kanpur. After spending the whole of 21 January at the railway station, they caught another train around noon the next day for Bombay.

14

Godse Finds His Gun

The idea that Godse would assassinate Gandhi was conceived during the sleepless night of 23 January 1948.

It is, however, not entirely understood whether Godse came up with the idea or Apte made him express his readiness to do the job. After they arrived in Bombay from Kanpur late that evening, they booked a room at Arya Pathik Ashram. They put their luggage in the room and went out. Till late that night the pair stayed out on the streets of Bombay, discussing and agonizing over the prospects and implications as they groped in the dark for a new sense of direction. Even when they returned to their room, the discussion continued and they hardly found time to sleep.

Their agony did not go unnoticed. Gaya Prasad, the manager of the lodge, observed their restlessness with curiosity. 'On 23-1-48, Apte came at 9 p.m. with another man,' he said later. 'They went out and returned at 1 a.m. and spoke until 3 a.m. They kept the light [of the room] on till then.'[1] Early the next morning, they walked out again; Gaya Prasad remained clueless about the identity of the man who accompanied Apte. According to him, 'On 24-1-48 Apte and another man left the hotel at 6.30 a.m. I asked Apte to give me his companion's name. He failed to do so.'[2]

By then, their lengthy conversations were over, and they had come out of their paralysed state and taken a fresh decision: they would no longer depend on a 'third person' to shoot Gandhi. 'Instead of looking for a third person, I decided to go personally in front of Gandhi and empty the pistol in him,' Godse said later. 'It was also decided that Apte and Karkare would come along only to provide support to me.'[3]

How long had Godse harboured this thought has remained a mystery. Since he started hating Gandhi for obstructing the Hindu rashtra project and seeing Gandhi's assassination as an act of, in his mind, masculine valour?[4] Or since his return from Delhi, when the failure of an elaborate assassination plan pushed him to act himself? No one can say with confidence because in public Godse never said anything more than the political rhetoric of a typical tenor.

Godse's change of heart seems to have been given impetus during his day-long stay at Kanpur railway station following the failed assassination attempt. 'There we heard so many people expressing disappointment over the failure of the attempt to kill Gandhi,' he said later. 'Most of them held Gandhi responsible for the killing of Hindus in Pakistan and wished that he should have been killed in the bomb attack. This kind of response made me believe that we were on the right track.'[5]

The responses he heard in Kanpur might well have prompted him to take the risk. There was an obvious danger to his performing that role; the chances of it being a suicide mission were high. Yet Godse opted for it, hoping perhaps that he would be hailed by the larger public, especially Hindu and Sikh refugees. In fact, he seemed to believe that popular reaction aroused by the murder of Gandhi would make him a hero and shield him from the gallows. As always, when he recounted the decisive situations in his life, Godse spoke of the strain of the decision and emphasized the 'hard' mental effort it cost him. 'For three days I had lengthy and reflective conversations with Apte before I came to the conclusion that I had to take this step. There was no option but to kill Gandhiji,' he said.[6]

In any case, once the decision was taken, Godse and Apte moved fast. Haunted by fear of the police, they had to, therefore, remain virtually invisible until the job was done. The fear was real, for Pahwa, during the interrogation, had named 'Karkara Seth' of Ahmednagar and talked about the 'editor and publisher of *Hindu Rashtra*' of Poona and the 'editor's younger brother' as his accomplices. He had also told the interrogators about the involvement of 'a bearded weapons supplier' and his servant.[7] Though he had not specifically mentioned the names of anyone other than Karkare, the leads he had provided were enough to immediately identify all the conspirators.

As the threat of the police loomed large, Apte, once again assuming charge, showed great presence of mind. First, he shifted Godse to a new hotel—Elphinstone Hotel at Carnac Bunder—during the early hours of 24 January. 'Nathuram engaged a room in the Elphinstone hotel and resided there,' Apte revealed later.[8] Then, apparently to remove the suspicion of the manager of Arya Pathik Ashram about Godse and to give him the impression that he remained the same old self, Apte returned with Manorama at 11 a.m. and remained locked up with her in his room for more than two hours.[9]

Having managed the affairs in Bombay, Apte set out to prepare the ground for a fresh attack on Gandhi, while still retaining the room in Arya Pathik Ashram for the day. The most important issue at this stage was to arrange a weapon. Apte accordingly turned to Gopal, who had returned to Kirkee from Delhi with two revolvers and a hand grenade. 'At 9 p.m. on 24-1-48 Apte came to my residence at Kirkee,' recounted Gopal. 'He questioned me whether I was still in possession of the revolvers and the hand grenade. I told him that the stuff was with me. He then asked me to accompany him to Bombay by the night train and to bring along with me the hand grenade and the small revolver. I agreed as the next day was a Sunday.'[10]

Shortly before noon on 25 January, the three met at Elphinstone Hotel, where Gopal handed over the weapons to Godse. Gopal then departed but he was apparently not informed that Godse would personally assassinate Gandhi this time. Around 10 p.m., Godse and Apte revealed their plan to Karkare. 'Godse was in a supreme mood,' Karkare recounted. 'He [. . .] suggested that we should not have nine or ten persons in our clique as history showed that such revolutionary plots where several persons were concerned had turned futile and it was only the individual effort that would succeed. He gave me several examples from the history and told us that acts of individual persons as by Madanlal Dhingra and Vasudevrao Gogate [Vasudev Balwant Gogate] had proved successful because they were individual efforts and therefore he individually had decided to assassinate Gandhiji.'[11]

The conversation, which took place at a relatively quiet corner of a moonlit railway station platform in Thane, shows that Godse conceived his decision to kill Gandhi as an echo of 'revolutionary acts' of two Savarkar loyalists. 'I was stunned and I found Apte was keeping quiet. I thought that Godse and Apte might have already discussed about this and Apte was aware of Godse's decision,' Karkare said. 'I told Godse that I was prepared for the worst and would join them in this mission.'[12]

~

Godse had set an ambitious goal for himself and was feeding on the excitement. However, Godse knew that the revolver in his possession was unfit for the operation and he needed to replace it with a dependable weapon. Apte concurred with him. But they could not depend on Dixit Maharaj, who had failed to help them out the last time. Therefore, they approached his brother Dada Maharaj on 26 January. The latter heard them out but remained unenthusiastic. Perhaps it was because Dada Maharaj saw in their demand a communal thriller concocted with the intension to fleece him. 'They demanded from me the revolver which I had promised to them or the equivalent in money,' he recounted. 'As they did not disclose why they wanted the money I declined to give it to them.'[13] That was certainly a plausible reaction given his experience with Godse and Apte.

Without a dependable firearm or enough money to purchase it, the plan would be a bust. Sensing a fiasco in the making, they embarked on raising money and borrowed Rs 10,000 from their banker in Bombay. The amount was borrowed against a promissory note signed by both Godse and Apte and was purportedly meant to repay the debts piled up in the normal running of their newspaper in Poona. 'We decided to keep Rs. 1,000 out of the sum to meet our expenses and to credit the other Rs. 9,000 to our account in Poona,' recounted Apte. 'Accordingly, that very evening I left Bombay by the Deccan Queen for Poona and after contacting my brother Madhav [who ran the newspaper in their absence] gave him the necessary instruction and without moving about in Poona left for Bombay by the night train.'[14]

On Tuesday, 27 January 1948, Godse and Apte flew to Delhi and then took an afternoon train to Gwalior, a Hindu princely state and one of the remnants of the Peshwa confederacy of the eighteenth and nineteenth centuries, to obtain a reliable pistol with the help of a long-time Mahasabha friend, Dattatreya Sadashiv Parchure. A skilled wrestler and a doctor, Parchure was a zealot whose devotion to the Hindu extremist ideology sometimes surpassed even that of Godse and Apte. Parchure considered himself a disciple of Savarkar and was the leader of the Hindu Mahasabha in Gwalior. He had also formed his own local outfit, the Hindu Rashtra Sena, which he ran on the lines of the HRD. For the last several years they had all acted as friends. On many occasions, Godse and Apte had visited the Parchure family home in Gwalior and the latter had visited them in Poona. At one point, Parchure, while on a political lecture tour in Poona, had even approached Godse with the aim of merging the Sena and the Dal, but the deliberations failed and the two agreed to work independently, though for the same objective.[15]

Like Godse and Apte, Parchure was fervently anti-Gandhi. As per an account recorded by M.A. Sreenivasan, the Dewan of Gwalior state then, Parchure expressed his visceral hatred for Gandhi when he, along with Apte, visited Sreenivasan to register his protest on being left out of the expanded state cabinet that was reconstituted after Independence. 'I offered tea, which they both [Parchure and Apte] drank in silence. Parchure was tense and excited. The cup trembled and rattled on the saucer as he held it,' recorded Sreenivasan.

He added:

> 'Why have you excluded us from the Cabinet?' he [Parchure] asked. 'You have betrayed us.'
> 'It is the ballot box,' I said. 'You get a majority and you will be invited.'
> 'You have betrayed Gwalior. You should go.'

'That is for our Maharaja to say. I am here at his pleasure.'

[. . .]

Parchure's eyes were red. His lips quivered.

'You are no Hindu. You are an enemy of Hinduism.'

'I was born a Hindu and I am still one. [. . .]'

'No,' he cried. 'You are a betrayer of Hinduism, you and your Gandhi.'[16]

So, when Godse and Apte started off for Gwalior in the afternoon of 27 January, they had grown familiar with their ideological brother. They now seemed to consider him as the last hope in their desperate quest for a dependable pistol. The train reached Gwalior railway station at 11.30 p.m. Within half an hour, they were knocking at Parchure's doors. 'We slept in his house,' recounted Godse. 'In the morning [of 28 January] we told him that we needed a pistol in good condition. We told him that the revolver that we possessed was not effective and so we wanted him to get my revolver replaced by a pistol in good condition.'[17]

Parchure then introduced them to one Gangadhar Dandwate, an office-bearer of the Hindu Rashtra Sena. Dandwate virtually combed the city and returned in the evening, along with a companion, carrying a fully loaded automatic pistol. 'In the presence of Dr. Parchure, Dandwate handed over the pistol to Nathuram with about 10 or 12 rounds of ammunition,' said Apte later. 'Nathuram in turn handed over the revolver which he had with him to Dandwate, and paid Rs. 300 in addition for the pistol. He then decided to try the pistol and in the rear courtyard of Dr. Parchure's residence, Nathuram tried the automatic on an improvised target in the presence of Dandwate, his companion and myself. He fired only one shot and the weapon was found to be very effective.'[18]

With a fully loaded automatic pistol in his hand, Godse would now have to move swiftly and stealthily till the plan reached its inevitable conclusion. Hours later, when Godse and Apte stepped into a late-night train for Delhi, there seemed no way for the plan to be miscarried this time.

~

Shortly after noon on 29 January 1948, Godse, Apte and Karkare reassembled at the gate of Birla Mandir, a massive Hindu temple next to the Mahasabha office in Delhi. This was the location Godse and Apte had identified as the meeting place before the fresh murder plan was to be set into motion. Karkare, who had arrived from Bombay the previous night, was the first to arrive. He put his luggage in the temple and came out on to the street, where he hung around till he met Godse and Apte. Around 1 p.m., he saw Apte walking in, followed at some distance by Godse. The latter was in his usual attire—a white shirt and dhoti—while Apte looked totally different as he was not in his usual attire of trousers and shirt. Like Godse, Apte too wore traditional clothes: white dhoti, white shirt and a chequered woollen coat.[19]

Karkare felt that Apte was deliberately attempting to disguise himself while Godse made no such effort. They told Karkare that the assassination plan was under way and that an effective pistol had been procured with the help of Parchure. Godse then explained to Karkare as to why he, and not Apte, would commit the murder of Gandhi. 'He said that Apte was a family person having a wife and a child while he had no family,' Karkare recounted. 'He further said that he was an orator and writer and he would be in a position to impress upon the Government and the Court as to why he had killed Gandhiji.

On the contrary Apte was a man of the world and he could contact people and carry on the business of the Hindu Rashtra paper.'[20] As he talked to Karkare, Godse seemed proud of his red-blooded approach, particularly in comparison to the softer approach of his friends.

Later that evening, Godse and Apte waited in a garden by the side of Old Delhi railway station, while Karkare left to assess the situation at Gandhi's prayer meeting. 'At about 5 p.m., Gandhiji came for the prayer meeting which was attended by about 400 persons,' he recounted. 'My attention was at places where the police were posted and I was not much interested in the prayers or in the speech of Gandhiji. At about 5.30 p.m. or so the prayers concluded and I left the place.'[21]

What Godse and Apte discussed among themselves while Karkare was away at Birla House is still unclear. But it is likely that during the last hours of the day before the assassination, Godse required some persuasion by Apte. For instance, it would have been natural for Godse to visit the prayer site on 29 January to examine the spot himself; he was, after all, slated to kill Gandhi the very next day. But Godse did no such thing. Instead, he kept talking with Apte and let Karkare do the final survey of the prayer ground alone. When Karkare returned late that evening, he found the duo in the garden, with Godse in a meditative mood, apparently trying to conceal his agitation. Some of his agitation may have been caused by the insecurity of his situation. There is, however, no way to ascertain this.

After dinner that night, when Karkare suggested that all three should go to watch a movie, Apte instantly agreed but Godse preferred to stay back in the retiring room of the railway station and rest. 'Apte, however, tried to cheer up Godse but he would [still] not agree and he started reading a book,' Karkare recounted. 'Apte then suggested that we both should go for the picture and hence we started from the room.'[22] On their return about an hour after midnight, they found Godse fast asleep. Karkare then asked Apte whether Godse was nervous. 'Apte said that he did not think that Godse was nervous,' Karkare recounted.[23]

On Friday, 30 January 1948, Godse wanted to go straight from the retiring room to Birla House to complete the job. He, however, was supposed to vacate the room by noon. Therefore, in the morning, Godse, who had booked the room under the alias Vinayak Rao, approached the booking clerk, Sundari Lal, for an extension. But Godse's request was rejected as rules did not permit a visitor to stay in the retiring room for more than twenty-four hours. 'As the occupants did not vacate the room even at 1 p.m., I went to their room,' recalled Sundari Lal. 'I found the two occupants sitting and a third person [Karkare] standing in the room. [. . .] I asked "Vinayak Rao" to vacate the room. He asked the third person to tie up the bedding. I stayed there for fifteen minutes within which time their belongings were taken out of the room.'[24]

By now Godse's frame of mind seemed to have altered dramatically. He calmly put his belongings in the waiting room of the railway station. Apte separated his luggage and kept it at a different location along with Karkare's luggage. Around 3 p.m., they went to Birla Mandir in a tonga. Godse remained mostly silent and aloof. 'Images of Chhatrapati Shivaji Maharaj and [the] first Peshwa Baji Rao were engraved in a pillar in the garden of Birla Mandir,' recounted Godse. 'I bowed before them and then hired a tonga and proceeded alone towards Birla House.'[25]

Taken aback, Apte and Karkare ran through the temple and followed him in another tonga, but Godse was oblivious to them now. 'I reached the prayer ground ten minutes before Gandhi was to come and start the prayer meeting,' Godse said later. 'My entire focus was on Gandhi's arrival. So I did not pay any attention to those who had gathered for the prayer meeting.'[26]

To Apte, such turbulence in Godse was commonplace. To Godse, this was the most defining moment of his life.

~

If anyone in Gandhi's entourage had hoped that the threat to the Mahatma's life had passed with Pahwa's arrest on 20 January, they were soon to be shocked. Gandhi himself seemed oblivious to the threat to his life. He was apparently content with his efforts and raring to carry out his next plan of action. His work in Delhi was almost done. When he had arrived four months ago from Calcutta, Delhi looked like a city of the dead, panic and fear were rampant and governance was in disarray. Now, order was restored and the city was mostly calm.

It was time for Gandhi to leave. He was nurturing the idea to launch a march across the border into Pakistan but understood that he wouldn't be able to do it unless Jinnah showed interest in it. He had waited all these days for a positive signal from him but none came. Gandhi, however, did not give up on the idea; he only put it on hold. He planned to visit his ashram in Wardha and come back a fortnight later to start his march to Punjab and then on to Pakistan. Though the date for his journey to Wardha had not yet been finalized, he had decided tentatively to reach there by 2 February 1948.[27]

All the same, he made plain his desire to see Delhi remain as peaceful as it had been for the last couple of days. He, therefore, took serious note of even small incidents that threatened to disrupt the city's communal harmony. On 29 January, he sent Pyarelal to Dr Rajendra Prasad with a message to get Hindu

Mahasabha leader Mukherjee to rein in party workers who had been delivering inflammatory speeches containing an incitement to kill some Congress leaders.[28] The response from Mukherjee, who was a minister in the central cabinet at that time, was unsatisfactory and he seemed to underestimate the seriousness of the danger such speeches represented. 'Gandhi's brow darkened as I repeated to him Dr. Mukherjee's reply,' Pyarelal noted.[29]

Ever since the aborted attempt to kill him, Gandhi must have had a presentiment of a fresh bid on his life. Early on 30 January, Gandhi asked for his correspondence file. The previous day, he had written to Kishorlal Mashruwala, one of his followers, about his tentative plan to leave Delhi and go to Sevagram in Wardha. As he gave the letter to be posted, his grand-niece Manu asked whether a line should be added saying that they would go to Wardha on 2 February. To this, Gandhi said: 'Who knows what will happen tomorrow? If my going there is finally settled, I will announce it at the prayer-meeting.'[30]

There was something striking in this entire exchange—perhaps it was the absence of Gandhi's here-and-now approach and the absence too of the kind of determination which had seen him through for so long. Such scruples were visible on several occasions as his exchange with Manu continued through the rest of the day.

Because of his fast, Gandhi had a bad cough. He used to take palm-jaggery lozenges along with powdered cloves to treat it. But the clove powder had run out that morning and Manu, instead of joining him in his walk up and down the room, sat preparing some clove powder for the night when he would need it. 'Who knows, what is going to happen before nightfall or even whether I shall be alive?' Gandhi said to Manu and then added: 'If at night I am still alive you can easily prepare some then.'[31]

Then again, just before the prayer meeting, as he was speaking with Sardar Patel, two leaders of Kathiawar in Gujarat came and told Manu they wished to see Gandhi. When Manu inquired with Gandhi whether he would see them, he said in the presence of Patel: 'Tell them that if I remain alive, they can talk to me after the prayer on my walk.'[32] Manu went back to the Kathiawar leaders and asked them to wait till prayer time. They decided to wait and took their seats in Gandhi's room.[33] No one took Gandhi's remark seriously; they seemed to take it as an indication that he was getting exhausted by a series of meetings and discussions.

Gandhi's meeting with Patel had begun at 4.30 p.m. The two remained so engrossed in the conversation that Gandhi got late for the prayer meeting that day. When he got up, it was about ten past five. Manu quickly picked up a pen, Gandhi's rosary, his spectacle case, spittoon and the notebook in which she wrote his discourses.

The scheduled starting time for prayers was 5 p.m. Gandhi disliked being late, especially for prayer meetings. When he stepped out, he was already about fifteen minutes late. With his hands around the shoulders of his grand-nieces Manu and Abha, Gandhi hurried down the corridor—apparently to make up for lost time—that led to the stepped entrance to the raised lawn. The winter sun had dipped low, but the evening air was clear. The flowerbeds were glowing and there was an air of expectancy in the lawn, where a large crowd had gathered.

Everything seemed normal except that Godse, with a fully loaded pistol in the pocket of his trousers, was a part of the assemblage.

15

A Shot Shatters the Winter Evening

Apte seemed to feel calmer when he entered the prayer ground in the evening on 30 January. It was about ten minutes to five.[1] Just as he might have expected, Godse had already positioned himself about 8–10 feet away from the main entrance, right along the path in the lawn Gandhi would take to reach the podium.

All the while, until Gandhi emerged in the prayer ground, Apte kept a watch on Godse from a distance. Godse looked 'unconcerned' and seemed mentally settled to complete the task.[2] He showed no sign of panic, totally unlike the franticness he had displayed on 20 January, ahead of the abortive assassination attempt. Karkare, who had reached the prayer ground along with Apte, stood away from both of his friends.

When Gandhi entered the lawn, it was around 5.15 p.m. Most of the nearly 200 people assembled for the prayer meeting were clustered along the path Gandhi would take to reach the wooden podium. The crowd parted as he hurriedly moved forward. Apte noticed Godse edging his way closer to Gandhi, who walked ahead of his entourage, his palms folded in a namaskar. 'Then with his left hand, he [Godse] pressed aside the girl that was on Mahatmaji's right and fired three or four shots in quick succession at point-blank range,' Apte said later.[3]

As the shots rang, what Apte sought most was to avoid attention. He stood still, confident that the plan had finally been carried out. With his own eyes he had seen Gandhi falling on the ground and Godse being taken into custody. There was chaos in the lawn. No one seemed to know what to do. People were milling about, shouting and weeping and running in all directions.

Karkare, who stood farther away, did not see Godse shooting Gandhi. But he heard the shots, which ruptured the somnolence of the winter evening, followed by chaotic disorder, like a nest of wasps disturbed. 'There was a hue and cry and I saw Godse being arrested,' Karkare said later. 'I was about 15 to 20 paces away from Godse where he was in custody. I had not seen him actually shooting Gandhiji. Apte was also somewhere close by. I went up to Apte and told him that we should leave now. [. . .] Within two or three minutes after the shots were fired, I think, Apte and myself left Birla House by the front gate.'[4]

~

Outside, millions were stunned. Gandhi was not just a leader; he was an object of popular adulation. His assassination by a Hindu communalist had an overnight effect on public opinion. Prior to the murder, the RSS and the Hindu Mahasabha had been riding a tide of anti-Partition, anti-Pakistan and anti-Muslim feeling. The tide had been considerably weakened by Gandhi's last fast as it mostly joined the hearts left divided in the wake of Partition and largely extinguished the fires of mistrust in the glare of which Hindus and Muslims had started viewing each other as strangers. But it did not vanish; sections of Indians—mostly Hindu and Sikh refugees and those under the spell of the RSS and the Hindu Mahasabha—still carried in their heart hatred against Muslims.

The assassination shook post-Partition India to normality. It finished the goal set forth by Gandhi's last fast. Rapidly, almost instantaneously, public opinion took a great swing away from Hindu communalists. Coming soon after Gandhi's painful fast, the murder appeared to be an act by reactionary conspirators desperate to set India in new ideological directions.

The multitude that spent the night of 30 January in grief and anguish was suddenly seized by a blind fury against the ideological proponents of a Hindu rashtra—the RSS, the Hindu Mahasabha as well as the Brahmin community in Maharashtra. 'Bapu's assassination had created violent storm against Brahmins in Maharashtra as Godse was a Konkanastha [another name for Chitpawan] Brahmin,' noted Morarji Desai. 'Tension between Brahmins and non-Brahmins in Maharashtra, and the violent anger against the Brahmins in general was a result of this terrible incident. In several places like Poona, Satara and Sangli, several Brahmins were attacked, and their property destroyed,' he added. [5]

In Bombay, a large mob of about 1000 people stormed Savarkar Sadan and tried to set it on fire. Only because of the timely arrival of the police could Savarkar's residence be saved.[6] Mobs also attacked offices of the RSS and the Hindu Mahasabha across the province and in many other parts of the country. For several days the life and property of every member of the RSS and the Mahasabha was in peril. Many RSS members were stabbed in the streets of Bombay.[7]

Limaye, Godse's patron in the RSS who still headed the organization in Maharashtra, fled when his house was attacked by a mob of non-Brahmins in Sangli. The princely state recorded a prolonged period of anti-Brahmin riots and arson, forcing the king to set up a camp for many homeless people inside the palace compound.[8] 'Along with other people [of the RSS], the house of Limaye Kaka was also set on fire. It was a revenge attack against the assassination,' noted Kirkire in his reminiscences.[9]

Poona was the worst hit. 'Everywhere people started getting mobilized against Brahmins,' noted Dixit, who was an active member of the Hindu Mahasabha in Poona at that time. 'Announcements were being made that Brahmins should be ostracized. Stone pelting on their houses and properties began. Mobs started roaming around in the streets of the city shouting anti-Brahmin slogans. Rumours were deliberately spread that Brahmins had celebrated the murder of Gandhiji by distributing sweets.'[10]

The news that Godse had killed Gandhi pulsed through the city like a crackling current. 'When the name of the murderer reached Poona, feelings ran very high,' said a report published in the 1 February edition of *National Standard*, 'Crowds swarmed round Godse's home and office of his newspaper on Saturday morning [31 January]. Strong police patrols were posted in the area. Throughout the day the crowds swelled. Stones were thrown at the press.'[11] The police succeeded in protecting the whitewashed shed that sheltered the press of the *Hindu Rashtra*.

But the attack on Udyam Engineering Works, the workshop owned by Godse's younger brother Dattatreya, was swift. Dattatreya had steered his business professionally in the last couple of years. Just before Gandhi's assassination, he had registered his firm as a private limited company and was working on plans for its expansion. On 31 January, before the police could arrive, a rioting mob set Udyam Engineering Works on fire. 'The blaze was put out by the fire brigade and the Works was surrounded by police,' said the *National Standard* report.[12]

Especially wretched was the condition of those who carried the Godse surname but were in no way related to the family. When the attack on Chitpawan Brahmins, the Godses in particular, increased, a trader in Poona with the Godse surname came out with an innovative idea to save himself and his establishment. In front of his house, he put up a notice in bold, saying: 'My surname is Godse, and I am not a Brahmin but a Maratha [a non-Brahmin caste]'.[13] As the idea worked, the other unrelated Godses, terrified by the worsening law and order situation, quickly followed his example until the army moved in and a thirty-six-hour curfew was imposed on the night of 31 January.

The situation was no better outside Maharashtra. In Nagpur, the capital of the Central Provinces, a mob attacked the RSS headquarters and stoned Golwalkar's residence.[14] Attacks were also reported on RSS men and their establishments in other parts of the province, including Wardha, Jubbulpore and Chhindwara.

In Delhi, the police had to open fire to quell a vast crowd that had forced its way into the house of Hansraj Gupta, a local RSS leader, and set his car and furniture on fire.[15] Reports of this kind were noted in other parts of the country as well.

The emotional outburst was widespread and it affected even those who had so far tried to look at the communal frenzy with a communal mind. For instance, Hindi newspapers and some other sections of the Indian press that had been conspicuously silent about attacks on Muslims on the Indian side of the border, especially in Punjab, Delhi and Rajputana, now began to report the incidence of such violence faithfully.[16]

~

The assassination of Gandhi accentuated the complexity of the Godse family's position: had they brought shame and disrepute upon the society or had they nurtured a Chitpawan hero who had gone to the extent of killing Gandhi for the sake of a Hindu rashtra? It did not require professional expertise to see the contours of this dilemma as riots flared up in Poona—to please the rioters, the family would have to seek forgiveness and denounce Godse but to Hindu supremacists and a section of Chitpawan Brahmins, such a posture would be seen as craven.

Godse's parents and younger brother Govind, who lived in a rented tenement in Shukrawar Peth in Poona, were unprepared for this dilemma—it was too sudden and the feelings were too raw. When news of Gandhi's assassination broke in the evening of 30 January, they were joined by Gopal, who lived in Kirkee. 'So long as Nathuram's name was not disclosed people were making wild guesses,' Gopal noted in his reminiscence. 'Discussion round the incident was constantly going on till about ten to half past ten at night. Then people in the house started going to sleep. I was lying down in the front room. Because of the restlessness I felt in my mind, I got up and went out. I tried to listen attentively at certain places and heard people saying Nathuram's name was announced as Gandhiji's assassin. There was no room left now for any guess-work whatsoever.'[17]

Gopal quietly came back. His parents were fast asleep. He went to bed and tried to sleep but could not. At 4.30 a.m. on 31 January, he heard footsteps near the door. 'I got out of my bed and opened the door,' he noted. 'Not the police, but two of our acquaintances had come. Stepping in they told that Nathuram's name had been announced as the assassin on the radio at 10 pm [last night]. Before they could finish my parents had already got up. They had overheard the two.'[18]

Godse's parents froze, never having gone through such a tribulation in their life. The two acquaintances consoled them and left. Now it was Gopal's turn to help them deal with the shock. He cleared his throat as his parents looked at him. But before he could say anything, a team of policemen came in and began to search their house. 'They turned everything in the house upside down; but it must be said to their credit that they did not at all resort to any manhandling, any rudeness, high-handedness or the use of any bad words. God knows why, but they seemed to feel sympathy for our house,' Gopal noted.[19]

Later that morning, after the search was over, a mob attacked the house. 'My mother assumed a somewhat fierce posture which helped her in checking the misbehavior of the mob,' Gopal recorded. 'Govind, however, was caught in the crowd and beaten up.'[20] The police acted promptly, and Poona District Magistrate S.G. Barve immediately took Godse's parents into protective custody. Over the next two days, they were kept in a police station to protect them from more attacks.[21] Thereafter, they were shifted to the parental home of Gopal's wife Sindhu. Along with her two daughters, Sindhu had also shifted to her parental place in Shaniwar Peth in Poona.

About a month later, Shantabai Gokhale provided accommodation to Godse's parents in her own building.[22] Govind accompanied them, while Sindhu preferred to stay back with their daughters at her parents' home. Dattatreya's family, which lived in the residential apartment constructed inside Udyam Engineering Works' campus, continued to live there even after suffering a mob attack on 31 January.

It was obviously a messy situation for the whole Godse family. Not all of them, however, looked at Godse's act in the same way. Mathura's husband was visibly upset by the act of assassination and lacked any sympathy for Godse, unlike the rest of the family. Marathe declared that he was estranged from Godse and hadn't seen him in a very long time. For good measure, Marathe added that he thought Godse was a loudmouth and a public nuisance. 'He [Godse] was not on thick terms with me,' Marathe, who worked as sub-assistant station master at Nagpur railway station, said in statement recorded on 5 February 1948. He claimed that he met Godse only thrice in the past ten years, and each time for a very brief period. 'Whenever he came to me, he talked to me for about 10 minutes or so. In Poona, when I had been on leave in 1947, he had talked about [our] welfare for about 10 minutes and went away.'[23] That was the last time Marathe had seen Godse.

According to Marathe, he had not had 'peace of mind' since the time he got the 'shocking' news that the man who killed Gandhi was none other than his own relative. 'On Tuesday [3 February], I reported the matter to the Station Master and told him that I was to be protected as my life was in danger,' he said. 'Then in the end I could succeed getting hold of the Rly. Sub-Inspector, Mr. Ghatpande. Accordingly he asked me to come and live at Rly. Station under his protection with his family.'[24]

Marathe's statement shows that he was oblivious to the possibility that his attitude towards Godse might be seen as offensive by the rest of the family.

~

What the events would mean ultimately for the RSS and the Hindu Mahasabha was difficult to predict, but within twenty-four hours of the assassination they were looking for ways that might save them from ruin and salvage some of their standing. The grief of the multitude was unmistakable, and people seemed to have lost their minds. At the heart of the violent reaction lay the sense of grievance nurtured by many people belonging to the depressed castes towards Maharashtrian Brahmins. It was through the RSS and the Hindu Mahasabha that a section of Maharashtrian Brahmins had dreamt of achieving the goal of a Hindu rashtra. The antipathies that emerged after the assassination intensified the popular distrust of the RSS and the Mahasabha. The retaliation on 31 January was intense, beyond what anyone had imagined.

The next morning, Golwalkar issued a written statement from Nagpur: 'In the presence of this appalling tragedy I hope people will learn the lesson and practice the doctrine of love and service. Believing in this doctrine, I direct all my brother swayamsevaks to maintain a loving attitude towards all, even if there be any sort of provocation born out of misunderstanding and to remember that even this misplaced frenzy is an expression of unbounded love and reverence, in which the whole country held the great Mahatma, the man who made the name of our motherland great in the world. Our salutation to the revered departed one.'[25]

This was not the usual language the RSS used for Gandhi when he was alive. All through, it had spewed venom against him and had even wished his death when he sat on fast a fortnight ago. Rattled by the people's fury, the RSS now did a one-eighty and Golwalkar quickly claimed that his organization believed in the 'doctrine' of Gandhi. Even the reaction to the attacks on RSS workers and offices was infused with utmost caution. The statement also placed the responsibility for the assassination in a generalized context and made no reference to Godse—perhaps the assassin's parent organization lacked the courage to own up to the fact that he was its member.

In fact, another statement, also issued on 1 February, by the 'Sangha Chalak of Rashtriya Swayam Sevak Sangh,

Bombay' totally abandoned Godse. It said 'the alleged assassin of Mahatma Gandhi was never connected in any way' with the RSS. 'We have already condemned the dastardly and cowardly attack on Mahatma Gandhi's life and we mourn this national calamity. We are observing national mourning by closing our centres for 13 days,' the statement said.[26]

Savarkar's attitude was no different. Like Golwalkar, he too grew frantic as soon as the fallout of the assassination became visible. Known for being protective of his reputation, the Mahasabha leader, now in his mid-sixties, was equally prompt in deserting Godse the moment mobs attacked his residence in the morning of 31 January. By evening, Savarkar issued a brief statement expressing strong denunciation and condemnation of the murder. Stating that 'the news of the assassination of Mahatma Gandhi was too shocking and sudden', he appealed to the 'people to stand by the Central Government of Free India and maintain order in the country'.[27] Like Golwalkar, he too made no specific reference to his protégé and ardent follower.

Savarkar's fear and vulnerability were recorded by Jamshed Dorab Nagarwala, deputy commissioner of police, Criminal Investigation Department (CID), Bombay, in his crime report filed based on a search of Savarkar Sadan in the afternoon of 31 January, hours after the police quelled a mob attack. 'When the police party under me arrived for searching Sawarkar's house, Mr. V.D. Sawarkar met the party in the front room and asked me whether I had come to arrest him in connection with Gandhiji's murder,' noted Nagarwala. 'However, on being told that I had come to search his house in connection with Gandhiji's case, Sawarkar pretended to be ill and went into the inside room to lie down. During the course of the search, from time to time, he came out to see the search being conducted by the police.'[28]

For Godse, the shift in the attitude of the RSS and Savarkar might have been the gravest blow. Since the time he met Savarkar and joined the RSS, he had been nothing but loyal. The shift showed, if at all it was needed, how deceptive and distorted was the image of his mentors that Godse had kept in his heart. Abandonment by those he had prided himself on being associated with was to worsen his miseries in the days to come.

16

The Interrogations

In Delhi, Godse sat through two lengthy interrogations during the night after he murdered Gandhi. A preliminary question-and-answer session was held at Tughlak Road police station, followed by an exhaustive cross-examination at Parliament Street police station. He was moved to Parliament Street police station late in the evening, since it was considered a safer place to detain him in case an attempt was made to rescue him. By the time Godse arrived at Parliament Street police station, the temperature had dipped. He had started to shiver feverishly in the van that took him there. It was a speedy journey and he was given a woollen blanket as soon as he reached the destination.

The cell in which he was kept was small and dimly lit. Curtains of blankets on the iron-barred gate in the front prevented a view to the outside.[1] Just before 8 p.m., Dr Gurbakhsh Rai, the medical officer attached to the Police Hospital, entered his cell and examined him thoroughly.[2] The head wound Godse had sustained while being overpowered was cleaned and bandaged. Soon, a meal was also served.

By now, he had recovered some of his spirit, as if he had once again found confidence in the idea of being a martyr in the name of the Hindu rashtra. He, however, remained mostly quiet, speaking only when specifically asked something. Sometimes he looked worried, but he no longer seemed frightened, as if he was unconcerned about his fate.

Around midnight, Lala Hrishikesh, a top officer of the Delhi Police, took charge of Godse.[3] A group of police officers under Hrishikesh's charge ushered Godse into another room, where he was asked to sit on a wooden chair, and his interrogation began. The questions pertained mainly to the actual incident and the chain of events that led to the assassination.[4] As his replies were not always forthcoming, the officers subjected him to physical torture.[5] Thereafter he talked freely, pouring out lists of names, which were to send police squads raiding homes in various cities, including Delhi, Bombay and Poona.[6]

Talking made his mouth dry, and he asked for some water. He was given a glass of water and then a cup of coffee, his favourite drink. He drank eagerly and answered all the questions thrown at him. About an hour later, he seemed completely exhausted and asked if he could go to bed. For a few minutes they denied him permission and kept asking questions. In later months, Godse told Gopal that the interrogation that night ended when he told the cops: 'If you want to know the details of various links of this story, now at least I am not in the state of mind suitable to recollect them coherently and tell you. At present I am badly in need of sleep. However, if you think you are likely to elicit more from me merely by beating me, go right ahead and have your own way.'[7]

Whether Godse said this to the police officers or the quote was an afterthought concocted to match his idea of a masculine self-image remains unclear. Gopal's reminiscence is generally reliable, but in this case, his first-hand knowledge was limited. It seems clear that Godse was physically tortured that night but the interrogation may have ended because of his readiness to speak freely and not due to his alleged audacity. In any case, that was the only occasion during the entire investigation when Godse faced physical torture. Perhaps the torment he was subjected to that night left a deep impact on him and he never ran the risk of doing anything that might entail a repeat of the ordeal.

For their part, the interrogators did accept Godse's request later that night. Perhaps their attitude changed once Godse started cooperating. He was allowed to go back to his cell and sleep peacefully. 'Lala Hrishikesh ordered his subordinates, indeed with a very noble mind, not to subject Nathuram to any physical torture, and also paid his personal attention to see if his orders were faithfully obeyed or not,' Gopal noted. 'Except for the preliminary bodily affliction that he had to undergo, Nathuram was no more subjected to any physical torture. Even the Bombay police did not inflict on Nathuram any sort of physical or mental pain, such as not allowing him any sleep, making him stand for hours together, or hanging him aloft with his hands tied to an upper beam, later when he was in their charge.'[8]

On the morning of 31 January, Godse was taken in a high-security van and produced before a judicial magistrate, who remanded him in police custody.[9] The rest of the day was routine: meals were served on time, interrogation sessions continued and he was given enough time to relax.

Towards the evening, when he might have heard of public outrage over the assassination, Godse started experiencing a faint sense of unease. He had apparently assumed that a significant section of Hindus and Sikhs, particularly refugees, would rise in his support after he killed Gandhi, just like in 1945–46, when the British government had to bow down to intense public pressure during the trial of the captured soldiers of the Netaji Subhash Chandra Bose-led Indian National Army

(INA), which had fought against the British Army during the Second World War. There was, however, no trace of any popular uprising in favour of Godse. If he imagined himself as the triumphant leader of those who held Gandhi responsible for all their sufferings, he now confronted the scary prospect of being left in the lurch and the serious possibility that he would be fighting a lone battle in the days to come.

From what he could make out—and he could not get to know much because he was largely cut off from the outside world—the much-anticipated upsurge that might have turned Godse into a hero was nowhere in sight. Gandhi's murder had swung the public mood but not in the manner Godse had expected. Instead of Godse being hailed as a hero, Gandhi became an even bigger icon. Instead of triggering a wave of sympathy for Godse, the assassination had caused a massive and violent storm of revulsion against him, members of his caste as well as the RSS and the Hindu Mahasabha.

A little later, while discussing the antipathy towards him and Maharashtrian Brahmins with P.L. Inamdar, one of the defence lawyers who had become very close to him during the trial, Godse could not control his emotions. 'With tears streaming down his cheeks he said to me that if he had had an idea of what his community would have to suffer for his deed, he would have thought ten times more before he decided to do it!' Inamdar noted.[10]

Twenty-four hours after the assassination of Gandhi, Godse was depressed to the point of despair.

~

Nagarwala, the young officer who investigated the conspiracy behind Gandhi's murder, was known for his famed powers of perception which, it was said, had never failed him. At thirty-two, he was one of the youngest heads of Bombay CID Special Branch's Sections One and Two and was responsible for gathering political intelligence and surveillance of foreigners. His unit was the glamour division of the Bombay CID. A man of sterling character and practical imagination, Nagarwala—called 'Jimmy' by friends—had been asked to nab the co-conspirators hours after Pahwa blasted the guncotton slab on 20 January. Accordingly, Nagarwala had set the intelligence machinery in motion, quickly identified some of Pahwa's accomplices and then asked Morarji Desai for permission to arrest Savarkar. To his surprise, Nagarwala was denied permission to arrest Savarkar.[11] Roadblocks of this nature considerably decelerated the progress of the investigation.

Still, when Gandhi was killed ten days later and Nagarwala entrusted with the investigation, his colleagues and he moved with promptitude and precision. At 5.30 a.m. on 31 January, just twelve hours after the assassination, Badge was apprehended. That very same afternoon, Savarkar's house was searched. Though he was not arrested at the time, all the documents at his residence were seized and their scrutiny began. Now follow-up plans were devised by Nagarwala and his colleagues. Gopal was picked up from the family's ancestral village of Uksan on 5 February, while Shankar was arrested in Bombay on 6 February. But Apte and Karkare were still at large. All raids in different parts of the province failed to turn up any clue about their hideout.

Godse was then brought into the picture, and the information extracted from him became critical for the investigators. 'Immediately on arrival in Bombay from Delhi, i.e., at about 2.15 a.m. on 12-2-48, the interrogation of accused N.V. Godse, a close associate of the absconding accused Apte and Karkare, was vigorously started as it was quite likely that he may be able to furnish information about them,' noted Nagarwala, 'It was also quite possible that Nathuram Godse may be able to throw more light on his associates Apte and Karkare.'[12]

Godse told the investigators about Manorama. He described her as 'a student of Wilson College' who was 'very intimate' with Apte. Godse also revealed that Apte was in the habit of meeting her in hotels whenever he was in Bombay. 'Without any loss of time enquiries were set afoot,' noted Nagarwala in his daily crime report. 'But as the 12th February was the public mourning day in connection with the immersion of Gandhiji's ashes, Wilson College was closed. Therefore, enquiries were made from the lady students in Pandita Ramabai Hostel for Women, [. . .] and it was learnt that Miss Manorama Salvi was Senior B.A. student and her father was doctor in the Police Hospital.'[13]

Nagarwala rushed one of his colleagues to trace Manorama and bring her to the CID office. By afternoon she was in the interrogation room, her father by her side.[14] She had left the hostel and had been living with her parents after her father was transferred to Northcote Police Hospital, Bombay. Her interrogation that day lasted for almost four hours. After giving evidence to the police team, Manorama slumped in her chair. She was as stunned as her father. The interrogators had given her a tough time and she had not expected that. Until then, she had always felt uncomfortable speaking about her secret relationship with Apte in public. She had met Godse a few times and knew that he had killed Gandhi but she had no idea that Apte too was involved in the crime.

She was caught in a nightmare. Apte had not said a word about his involvement in this horrific murder though he had spent hours with her on 2 February at Sea Green Hotel and then again on 5 February at Arya Pathik Ashram.[15] On both occasions, she had been surprised at how much he had changed. His appearance had been similar: the lean physique, the black hair thrown back to make the face even more defined and his penetrating eyes which had lost none of their sensitive intelligence. It was his attire that had changed: from shirt and trousers, he had suddenly shifted to traditional Maharashtrian clothes. He seemed less passionate somehow—his gait less confident—and he always seemed to be on high alert, as if the hunter she had once known had now become the hunted.

They had been lovers. But now, as she answered the policemen's questions, she found herself hating him. For a few moments she sat there, uncertain what to do. Suddenly, she told her interrogators that she was sure he would contact her again in a day or two. This was the assessment of the interrogators too. 'I, therefore, deputed two police constables to receive every telephone call that came to Miss Salvi on telephone No. 305 at the Police Hospital,' noted Nagarwala.[16] Her residence was also watched.

The wait didn't last long. At 8.30 a.m. on 14 February, the constable deputed at the Police Hospital telephone informed Nagarwala that a phone call had been received from a person who said he was speaking from Apollo Hotel and that it was for Manorama.[17] Nagarwala immediately rushed two of his trusted lieutenants to the hotel. For a whole day, they waited in the hotel in plain clothes. 'At 5.30 p.m., one person answering to the description of Apte walked into the Apollo Hotel. D.I. Sawant [one of the cops] accosted him and patted him saying, "Well, Apte, when did you come to Bombay?" He answered, "Two days ago.". This confirmed his identity with Apte and he was arrested [sic],' noted Nagarwala in his daily crime report.[18]

Three hours later, Karkare too emerged at the entrance of the hotel. As had become his routine since he had returned from Delhi, he sometimes took one route and at other times he took another to shake off anyone tailing him. He looked over his shoulder before getting into the hotel lobby just to be sure that no one was following him. Before he could move another step, the policemen in plain clothes grabbed him.[19]

~

Nagarwala's questioning of Manorama had at least one virtue, from her point of view—that it took place almost entirely in private. Far more painful was the condemnation of her relatives and friends. In the emotional climate that prevailed in the aftermath of Gandhi's murder, they felt they had no choice but to end all relations with Manorama. No one explicitly asked her to leave the family or keep her distance from the community but this could be freely interpreted from their decision to cut ties with her.[20]

Manorama belonged to a traditional Christian family of Ahmednagar. In the post-Partition turmoil, which was filled with rampant Hindu majoritarian onslaught, Gandhi's murder held great political interest for minorities, especially Muslims and Christians. Upholding equal rights for minorities, Gandhi had stood not just against the death dance of those days but had looked down on the idea of a theocratic state. The worst fears of the minorities came true when Gandhi was murdered. A relative of Manorama's, who preferred to remain anonymous, said: 'To them, Manorama's sin was not just that she was in relationship with a criminal but also that this criminal was part of the conspiracy to murder a Christ-like figure. It was because of this that the family and the community backed away from her, and she was left alone.'[21]

A devout Christian, Manorama had been associated in many important respects with the local church. Her voice was melodious and she could sing extempore the Marathi hymns by Narayan Waman Tilak, a renowned poet and a famous convert to Christianity from the Chitpawan Brahmin community. Manorama was also proficient in playing the pipe organ and contributed regularly to social activities organized by the Christian mission. She had not been quite comfortable with Apte's Hindutva ideology, but she seemed to believe that she would ultimately rid him of it.

There was a time when Manorama used to think that Apte hated Gandhi and Muslims because he had misread the situation and that good sense would prevail once the distrust between Hindus and Muslims faded. Like a true Christian, she believed that she would bring about a change in Apte by taking him to church one day. Apte had given her enough reason to feel like that. For all his demerits, he had one quality that she admired: he always gave her the impression that he was ready to change. In her naïve way, she always believed in him.[22]

The realization that she was in love with a man who had taken part in the assassination of Gandhi left her devastated. She now started to think that the trust she had placed in him had never been anything but her foolish assumption. And just like that, the smokescreen of her assumptions regarding Apte vanished. Her new way of thinking told her that the man she loved did not have any mistaken visions of the situation. In fact, he had no vision of any kind. What he had done was not just a crime, it was sacrilege.[23]

Perhaps Manorama also understood what her relationship with Apte would mean for her family. Everything seems to indicate that her inner voice demanded she must remove herself from the scene so that the others could live in peace. But she endured the pain, not just of the abyss that separated her from Apte but also of denunciations by loved ones for having been associated with him.

After the trial ended and Apte was hanged along with Godse, Manorama made a tough decision: she decided that she preferred quiet anonymity to societal hell. She was never seen or heard of again by her family and friends.[24]

~

The Bombay CID's Special Branch office also served as the prison for Godse and most other accused—Apte, Karkare, Gopal, Pahwa, Badge and Shankar. Ordinarily, the accused in cases pursued by the Special Branch were kept in the city's Arthur Road jail. But there was a threat of Godse getting lynched or attacked by other prisoners in that jail. So, it was decided that he and his accomplices should be kept in a makeshift lock-up prepared especially for them in the Special Branch office. Only Savarkar, who was arrested much later, was kept in the Arthur Road jail.

'Instead of locking us up in the custody they kept us in different rooms of that office,' recounted Gopal. 'During the day office work used to be carried on in those very rooms. Only we were not allowed to have any contact with any outsider.'[25] They were also not allowed to see or talk to each other. 'We were never brought together, so that we might not get a chance to verify what the other accused had told the Police. Sometimes we were brought face to face with each other only to cross-question us if what the other said was correct and if not what the correct position was,' Gopal noted.[26] It was from here that

Godse was taken to locations like Thane and Poona to assist with the investigation.

Though Godse was kept in isolation, like his accomplices, arrangements had been made to get him coffee whenever he desired. 'Nathuram was provided with an electric kettle and coffee, sugar and milk. He used to prepare coffee and sometimes used to send it to some of us,' Gopal recounted.[27] Facilities for tea and cigarettes were provided to the other accused.

Godse's interrogation, which began soon after he was brought from Delhi and lodged at the Special Branch office in Bombay on 12 February, continued for twenty-two days. It was completed on 4 March 1948.[28] It was often obstructed by bizarre rumours that started flying around about Godse and became a commodity in the media marketplace. The absurdity of these rumours was articulated by Gopal in his reminiscences. 'Reports stating Nathuram being present at a certain place and, at a certain time were consolidated in the C.I.D. office, wherefrom it appeared that he was present at several towns on the same day and at the same time. This was obviously absurd,' Gopal noted.[29] Nevertheless, some of these rumours often delayed the progress of the interrogation as they led the investigators to probe them before returning to the question-and-answer session with Godse.

One of the features noted by the investigators was that despite the RSS disowning Godse, his popularity had shot up among ordinary swayamsevaks. One of them, for example, even sent a telegram to Nehru, requesting the release of Godse on grounds that such a step would be in accordance with Gandhi's principle of ahimsa. The swayamsevak, Ramchandra Singh Rambhau of Chhindwara in the Central Provinces, was quickly arrested by the police. In his statement, he said he knew Godse as one of the 'instructors' of the RSS in Poona, where he had stayed for five years to complete his college education.[30]

N.P. Thakur, deputy superintendent of police on special duty in Nagpur, focused specifically on checking the antecedents of Godse and exploring the many rumours that reached Delhi and Bombay after Gandhi's assassination. For Thakur, a scrutiny of the papers seized from the RSS headquarters at Nagpur removed much of the confusion, which was apparently sought to be created by the Sangh leadership when it declared that Godse had never been associated with it. Thakur came out with specific information, through the scrutiny of these papers as well as his own independent investigations, to nail the lie being spread by the RSS in this regard and unearth the truth about Godse's past.[31]

Parallel investigations of this kind were conducted at other places as well. In Jubbulpore, for instance, the probe focused on reports of Godse's so-called visit to the place on 21 January, a day after the failed attack on Gandhi, and his secret meetings with RSS men. Jubbulpore was a prominent area of RSS activities and the centre of operations for Eknath Ranade, one of the most famous leaders of the Sangh. As in many other cases, this too turned out to be a rumour.[32]

These formal disclosures and analysis of different centres of RSS activities helped in the overall investigation led by Nagarwala in Bombay. As the probe came to an end in May 1948, Nagarwala relaxed many of the restrictions imposed on Godse. He could now mix with the other accused and meet his family members, who visited the Special Branch office. 'As the investigation drew to its end the restrictions imposed on us were gradually slackened,' wrote Gopal afterward. 'Even then we dared not talk about the matters connected with the investigation because the constable was always within the hearing distance. I was allowed to see Nathuram and we used to talk. We also came together whenever some eatables were brought for us from our home.'[33]

On Thursday, 24 May 1948, Godse and the other accused were flown to Delhi to face trial.[34]

17

The Assassin Is Tried

An hour before the murder trial of Godse and the other accused was to begin on 27 May 1948, the courtroom in Delhi's Red Fort was overflowing with spectators. The room, a large rectangular hall, was on the first floor of an enormous Victorian building erected in the grounds of the fort. The corridors outside the room were jam-packed and police in khaki uniform were stationed at all entrances to control the crowd. Newspaper photographers and reporters were everywhere. For weeks, members of the judiciary had been besieged with requests from friends and relatives to obtain passes to the trial. Those who were able to secure them thronged the room well ahead of time, creating a mad rush much before the proceedings began.

The actual setting of the murder trial was commonplace. The courtroom was old and musty, the arena of two high-profile legal battles that had taken place in the past. Here, exactly nine decades earlier, Bahadur Shah Zafar, the last Mughal emperor, had been tried by the British and banished for life. In 1945, the trial of INA prisoners, which created such a furore that the British were forced to release them, was held here too. The room was 23-feet wide and 100-feet long. At the front of the courtroom was a raised dais with a single chair for the special judge, Justice Atma Charan. The dock for the accused was to the left of the dais and the stand for the witnesses to its right, with tables and chairs for the counsels of both sides in front. 'Leaving an alley after the block for the counsels, there were some seven or eight rows of chairs for spectators, police officers and others,' noted Inamdar.[1]

The accused were brought into a barracks on the ground floor of the courthouse from their specially prepared cells in the Red Fort at 9 a.m. and taken into the courtroom, with Godse leading the band, at 9.50 a.m., ten minutes before the trial was to begin. Godse sat in the first row of the dock, withdrawn and silent, an invisible wall around him. Savarkar, who sat alone on the wooden bench in the third row of the dock, was later, at the request of his counsel and senior Mahasabha leader L.B. Bhopatkar, provided a chair with a backrest so he could sit separately from the other accused in the front row.[2] The accused were, by and large, the focus of attention for the excited spectators of the sensational murder trial.

The trial, among the longest on record, lasted well into the following year. On the first day, however, the court worked only for two hours—the presentation by the prosecution of the chargesheet against Godse and the other accused being the highlight of the proceedings.[3] Godse had already been tried in the newspapers and the minds of the populace, and had been found guilty. No one doubted his guilt for a moment. To the trial, then, was lent the excitement of watching how he and his accomplices would defend themselves against the enormous odds.

That he would be seen as guilty even by his own accomplices would become, to Godse, only too bitterly apparent as soon as all the accused returned to their cells after the first day's proceedings. The cells for the accused stood in a row constructed along the thick walls of the Red Fort and formed part of the prison enclosure. Godse shared a cell with Gopal, while the rest were occupied by the other accused.[4] Godse was berated by his accomplices for carrying on his person a notebook at the time of the murder. The entries in it were being considered as evidence of the coming together of all the accused with the intent to kill Gandhi, thus strengthening the conspiracy angle in the case. 'In the notebook were the entries of the names of the persons and places, of the appointments to be kept, the travelling expenditure and the sundry jottings of the transactions of money,' recorded Gopal.[5]

The chargesheet revealed that the prosecution had relied heavily on the notebook entries and this became even more apparent as the trial progressed. Godse's accomplices knew that the only way they could save themselves was by disproving the charge of conspiracy, for the murder would then be seen as the act of a single man. 'There was one entry to the effect that some money was given to some "Bandopant". Now Badge [who had turned approver] had already made it clear in [his] deposition that "Bandopant" meant "Badge". There were other entries to the effect that some money was given to Nana Apte, some to Gopal, and some was kept with him,' noted Gopal. 'It was obvious that the prosecution attached great importance to these entries as they seemed to help their attempt at providing the existence of a conspiracy immensely.'[6]

In private parleys outside the courtroom, Godse became the target of attack for the serious 'mistake' he had committed. His co-accused seemed to have ganged up on him. Apte was seemingly livid and reproached Godse for his habit of maintaining a notebook with such entries. Gopal recorded

Apte's angry outburst and the plea that Godse offered to justify his action:

> "We collect money for Hindurashtra Ltd.," he [Godse] said, "of which some definite amount we spend for ourselves. If we have no jotting of the untoward expenditure on extraordinary items, we shall not be able to explain anything if some donar [sic] asks any time for our accounts."
>
> "What will they say?" asked Nana [Apte] by way of a sally. "At the worst they might charge us with the misappropriation of funds. Let them! We know our own level!"
>
> "If this expenditure is incurred without our achieving anything concretely," protested Nathuram, "how can we face them unabashed?"[7]

Even Gopal seemed to blame Godse for putting the others in serious trouble by carrying the notebook with him at the time of murder. 'The act of carrying that notebook on his own person by Nathuram, especially at that critical time, was definitely harmful in every way,' he wrote, 'because on the one hand those who were not even remotely concerned with the assassination were likely to be harassed for the simple reason that their names appeared in the notebook, while on the other hand all those who were really involved were likely to be easily rounded up and brought to book with the help of this one clue. [. . .] Nathuram's carrying the said notebook on his person was such a mistake, for which there was no justification.'[8]

In practical terms, the 'mistake' seemed to have pushed Godse into a very difficult emotional situation. There was no denying the fact that his notebook entries, by helping the prosecution build up the conspiracy charge, had made his accomplices extremely vulnerable.

As Godse's sense of guilt increased, his ability to endure it may have weakened. Apte and Savarkar were men who mattered the most in his life. It is through these relationships that Godse had developed his exalted self-image. To that extent, his sentiment towards them was intensely personal. Their indignation probably struck at his very core, sapping the inspiration and sense of mission that sustained him. And though he might not have been threatened by them, he perhaps felt that his only option was rectification—dictated not by self-preservation but by an overwhelming disgust for what he was being blamed for.

In the given situation, there was only one way that Godse could have rectified his 'mistake': by vehemently refuting the existence of a conspiracy. In actual terms, this would involve Godse telling the court that the idea to kill Gandhi was solely his own and he never shared it with any of the co-accused. Such a line of argument would help protect not just Apte and Savarkar, but also Gopal. This line of argument also suited Godse's self-image—by doing so, he could carry the glory all on his own. There is no certainty whether Godse himself came up with this method of rectification or the plan was offered to him by lawyers loyal to Savarkar. It is also unclear when exactly the final decision was taken in this regard. Whatever the inner tensions, they never showed.

In any case, the rectification was to be a mammoth exercise, involving a serious perusal of questions of law. It is unrealistic to expect that Godse, with his limited legal knowledge and command over the English language, managed these questions on his own. There is evidence that the statement he would read out in court was not entirely of his preparation. Inamdar subsequently noted that Mehta, a prominent member of the group of lawyers defending the accused and a staunch

Savarkarite, helped him draw up a calculated written statement. 'In Nathuram's case, it was primarily Jamnadas Mehta, Barrister-at-Law from Bombay, who assisted him in preparing the statement,' Inamdar wrote.[9]

Mehta had been responsible for Savarkar's release from his Ratnagiri confinement in 1937. Mehta's role was to be even more significant this time.

~

It was on 8 November 1948, more than nine months after Gandhi's assassination, that Godse set out to rectify his 'mistake'. The ponderous statement that ran into 150 paragraphs took Godse five hours to read in the courtroom. Speaking quietly in English, he attempted at the very beginning to remove all traces of guilt from Apte, Savarkar and the other accomplices. 'I say that there was no conspiracy of any kind whatsoever amongst the accused to commit any of the offences mentioned in the charge-sheet [sic],' Godse read. 'I may also state here that I have not abetted any of the other accused in the commission of the alleged offences.'[10]

He rejected the prosecution's charge that he was acting under the guidance of Savarkar. 'I take the strongest exception to this untrue and unjust charge and I further regard it as an insult to my intelligence and judgment [sic],' he said.[11] While giving an account of his past life, Godse also claimed that he had broken with the RSS long before he killed Gandhi.[12] The claim ran contrary to what he had told the interrogators and what the documents seized from the RSS Nagpur headquarters had revealed. Years later, Gopal, on seeing the RSS brazenly forsake Godse, sought to set the record straight. 'He [Godse] said it because Golwalkar and the RSS were in a lot of trouble after the murder of Gandhi,' Gopal declared. 'But he [Godse] did not leave the RSS.'[13]

In all, the explanation Godse offered for his conduct was flimsy. In a Marathi accent, possibly believing that his words would create a wave of sympathy for him, he sought to present himself as the saviour of Hindus. He attempted to negate most facts of the case to justify the murder on grounds of the political circumstances of the time. He asserted that he found no other way to end the 'destruction of the Hindus' which, he claimed, was taking place largely due to the politics of Gandhi. 'I deny emphatically and with all the emphasis at my command that Mr. Apte and myself had been to Gwalior to secure a revolver or a pistol, as number of such revolvers were being offered for sale clandestinely,' he asserted. 'Having reached in Delhi in great despair,' he continued,

> I visited the refugee camps at Delhi. While moving in the camps my thought took a definite and final turn. Chancely I came across a refugee who was dealing in arms and he showed me the pistol. I was tempted to have it and I bought it from him. It is the same pistol which I later used in the shots I fired. On coming to the Delhi Railway Station I spent the night of the 29th thinking and re-thinking about my resolve to end the present chaos and further destruction of the Hindus.[14]

Most of the memories and emotions Godse expressed through the statement, some even fabricated, had a single purpose: to showcase himself as the hero of Hindus. 'My confidence about the moral side of my action has not been shaken even by the criticism leveled against it on all sides,' he said, reading out the concluding paragraph of the statement. 'I have no doubt honest writers of history will weigh my act and find the true value thereof on some day in future.'[15]

Godse's statement in the court showed his impeccable command over English, a language he supposedly did not know well. Those who had known him since his pre-assassination days were genuinely surprised by his competence. V.G. Deshpande said in an interview to writer Tapan Ghosh that he was spellbound to read that Gandhi's assassin speaking in English. V.G. Deshpande recalled an incident that took place at a Hindu Mahasabha conference held in Bombay under the chairmanship of Mukherjee. 'Representatives of the two groups [of the Mahasabha] met under his [Mukherjee's] chairmanship,' V.G. Deshpande told Ghosh. 'Nathuram represented the dissident group and in fact was its spearhead. Deliberations were being held in English. When Nathuram was called upon to present his views, he stood up, faltered for about a minute in broken, unintelligible English and resumed his seat in confusion. He simply could not speak English.'[16]

On 10 February 1949, when the judgment was delivered, it was clear that the court was not convinced by most of Godse's arguments and the defence put up by his accomplices and found clear evidence of a conspiracy. 'It has already been held established that there was a "conspiracy" to commit the murder of Mahatma Gandhi, that the conspiracy was definitely in existence in the beginning of January 1948 and continued till 30-1-1948,' the judgment said. 'The "conspiracy" took place at Poona, Bombay, Delhi, Gwalior and other places and that among the conspirators were at least Nathuram V. Godse, Narayan D. Apte, Vishnu R. Karkare, Madanlal K. Pahwa, Shankar Kistayya, Gopal V. Godse and Dattatreya S. Parchure along with Digambar R. Badge. These accused joined the "conspiracy" at different places and at different times.'[17]

Godse and Apte were sentenced to death. All other accused, except Savarkar, were given life imprisonment. Savarkar succeeded in convincing the court that no one had seen him actively engaged in planning the murder or in giving his blessing to the conspirators. He was acquitted.

The wave of sympathy that Godse had expected still never materialized. Perhaps he had seen in it his ultimate chance for survival. Nor did he succeed in engineering a change in Savarkar's attitude towards him until, literally, the last hour in the Red Fort's prison enclosure. Godse might have thought that his court statement would restore him to the position he enjoyed in Savarkar's eyes until his notebook 'mistake'. But it never did. Savarkar continued to ignore him. Godse was deeply hurt, perhaps more than the hurt he might have suffered on being disowned by the RSS. He could not hide the pain and revealed it to Inamdar.

In the group of lawyers defending the accused, Inamdar was the odd man out. While the others had been picked by L.B. Bhopatkar, who headed the team of advocates, Inamdar had joined them independently. He had been sent by Parchure's wife from Gwalior as her husband's counsel. He experienced some difficulties in joining the group initially as L.B. Bhopatkar had sought to discourage him. In a way, therefore, both Inamdar and Godse shared the status of an outlier in their respective groups.

At the time the trial began, Inamdar didn't know much about Godse except that, as Parchure told him, he was 'a staunch R.S.S. man'.[18] But soon Inamdar became so close to Godse that they often spent hours together. 'During the whole of the trial, I never saw Savarkar turning his head towards even Nathuram, who used to sit by him, in fact next to him, much less speak with him,' Inamdar noted. 'During the various talks I had with Nathuram, he told me that he was deeply hurt by this—Tatyarao's calculated, demonstrative non-association with him either in court or in the Red Fort Jail during all the days of the Red Fort Trial. How Nathuram yearned for a touch of Tatyarao's hand, a word of sympathy, or at least a look of compassion in the secluded confines of the cells! Nathuram referred to his hurt feelings in this regard even during my last meeting with him at the Simla High Court!'[19]

According to Inamdar, even while Godse was reading out his statement in court and 'deriding Prosecution for implicating Savarkar in this trial', the Hindutva ideologue did not even look at him and just 'sat in his chair, a sphinx sculpted in stone'.[20] This was not the same Savarkar whom Godse had known as his patron. Godse worshipped him as a father figure and perhaps this was why Savarkar's aloofness hurt Godse so deeply. Even when Inamdar met Savarkar separately in September 1948, he seemed concerned only about his own case. 'He repeatedly asked me if he would be acquitted and wanted me to assure him sincerely,' noted Inamdar, who was surprised to see that Savarkar didn't ask a single question about the fate of Godse or the other accused.[21]

With nothing but the pain of abandonment in his heart, Godse frequently began to lapse into that dull brooding which had been characteristic of his formative years.

~

At 2 p.m. on 10 February 1949, after the judgment was handed down, Godse returned to the Red Fort prison enclosure. It had been improvised as he and the others were no longer undertrials; they were now convicts. Godse and Apte, the death convicts, were shifted to the part of the prison enclosure which had two cells, separated from the rest by a thick wall. Until now, these cells had been occupied by Badge and Shankar. Now they were prepared for Godse and Apte. By evening, a new set of clothes, beddings and utensils meant for convicts arrived. The cots and tables were removed from their cells. 'Officers were the same, we were the same and the place was also the same,' noted Gopal, 'Only the rules now applicable to us were different from those before. The accused of yesterday were now the convicts of today.'[22]

Soon afterwards, preparations for filing an appeal began and Godse became busy with that. The trial judge, at the time of announcing his order, had given the convicts a period of fifteen days to file an appeal. Four days later they signed the appeals, which were filed in the East Punjab High Court at Simla on 22 February 1949.[23]

Since Godse had already assumed sole responsibility for the murder, he stuck by the line he had taken in the trial court. His concern seemed to remain unchanged: to try and arouse sympathy for himself and do everything to minimize punishment for Apte and Gopal. Godse, therefore, neither challenged his conviction for the charge of murder nor the death sentence. His appeal was confined to the finding of the trial court that there was a conspiracy behind the murder.

Two months later, weeks before the high court was to take up the appeals, Godse and the others were shifted to the Central Jail in East Punjab's Ambala. 'According to rules, Nathuram and Apte were fettered during the transit. Their fetters were removed when we reached Ambala prison,' noted Gopal, 'Nathuram and Apte were taken to the cell meant for the death convicts, and we were taken to the cells specified for us.'[24]

Godse's solitary cell was an 8-foot by 6-foot enclosure with a paved floor and stone walls. It had an iron-grill ventilator about a foot and a half square in the ceiling. In the front, the cell's iron-barred and wood-panelled door opened into a room of approximately the same size with an iron-barred gate. Outside this room was stationed an armed guard round the clock. In the cell was a cot measuring about 5 feet by 3 feet with a coarse blanket and sheet on it; a stool and a small table in one corner; and toilet seat in the other. Godse was to be holed up in his cell most of the time and taken to the outer enclosure only twice a day for a bath and fresh air.[25]

On 27 April, a week before the appeal hearing was to commence, Inamdar appeared in Godse's cell. Godse reported that the high court had permitted him to appear and argue his appeal himself, and that he had already made notes from the printed records of the case. 'I explained to him the etiquette of the High Court such as addressing the judges as "My Lords" and beginning with "May it please your Lordships, etc.",' Inamdar noted. 'Our review of the case took nearly two and a half hours.'[26]

The hearing commenced on 2 May 1949 and was heard by a three-judge bench. Godse's shift to Simla to argue his case in person offered him much better living conditions than Ambala jail. In the hill town, he was kept in a makeshift jail prepared especially for him. 'It was in fact an enclosure for a Police Station House Officer, and his quarters,' recorded Inamdar, who visited him frequently. 'In this enclosure, Nathuram was lodged in a twelve foot by ten foot room with a bed and clean sheets, a mosquito curtain frame, a small table and chair with an electric lamp, a teapoy and a vase filled with fresh flowers! [. . .] The room was well lighted and airy and the windows had curtains.'[27]

Godse's arguments began within three days after the commencement of the appeal hearing. It started on Thursday, 5 May, and continued uninterrupted for six working days, concluding on 12 May. 'Before us, he reiterated the arguments he had advanced before the trial judge and supplemented them with some fresh points which he had not thought of before,' Justice G.D. Khosla, one of the three judges on the bench, wrote subsequently.[28]

Godse's long monologue might have appealed to the spectators present in the courtroom but Justice Khosla felt that Godse's real motive behind arguing his case in person was nothing but 'to exhibit himself as a fearless patriot and a passionate protagonist of Hindu ideology'.[29] In his argument, Godse deviated from the main issue and talked about the nature of the 'righteous man's duty' as laid down in the Hindu scriptures. Giving references to historical events, he made an impassioned appeal to Hindus to preserve their motherland and fight for it with their very lives.[30]

'It seemed to me that I was taking part in some kind of melodrama or in a scene out of Hollywood feature film,' Justice Khosla noted. 'Once or twice I had interrupted Godse and pointed out the irrelevance of what he was saying, but my colleagues seemed inclined to hear him and the audience most certainly thought that Godse's performance was the only worth-while part of the lengthy proceedings.' Finally, Justice Khosla, like other judges on the bench, decided to abstain from being too conscientious on the matter. Instead, Justice Khosla watched Godse with a writer's curiosity, telling himself: 'The man is going to die soon. He is past doing any harm. He should be allowed to let off steam for the last time.'[31]

~

On 17 May, five days after Godse completed his arguments in the high court, he received a letter from Ramdas Gandhi, Gandhi's third son. In the two-page letter, Ramdas expressed resentment over Godse's court statement denouncing his father and said that one day he would realize his mistake of killing Gandhi. Ramdas also mentioned that he had requested the Governor General of India not to make Godse 'suffer the penalty awarded' by the trial court.[32] The letter came as a surprise. Godse immediately showed it to Inamdar and N.D. Dange, the advocate representing Karkare, and together they drafted a reply.[33]

In the reply, which was sent on 18 May, the thrust was more on a serious and fruitful engagement than a mere exchange of ideas and feelings. 'As a human being I have no words to express my feeling for the wounds that you and your relatives must have received by the tragic end of your revered father, by my hands. But at the same time I state that there is the other side also to look at. I am not in a position to write all my thoughts on paper nor am I in a position to see you personally. But certainly you are in a position to see me in jail before my execution,' wrote Godse. At the end of the reply, he again stressed his desire for a meeting with Ramdas:

> Anyway I must request you to see me and if possible with some prominent disciples of your father, particularly those who are not interested in power politics, and to bring to my notice my most fatal mistake. Otherwise I shall always feel that this show of mercy is nothing but an eyewash.
>
> If you actually see me and have a talk with me either sentimentally or with reason, then who knows? You may be able to change me and make me repent, or I may change you and make you realize my stand. The condition of the talk must be that we stick to the truth alone.[34]

Behind these ostensibly straightforward lines was a complex subtext. The involvement of two senior lawyers in drafting the reply is an indication that the subtext was intentional and meticulously planned. Perhaps the same subtext was used by Gopal when he wrote, 'If changing of heart was a cardinal principle of Gandhism, it could have been tried here only by not implementing the death sentence. Nathuram in fact anxiously waited for some such effort on the part of the accredited followers of Gandhian philosophy.'[35]

Whatever the finer points of the letter, Ramdas perhaps did not see his correspondence with Godse in the same way. There followed a long spell of silence from his side. Around the time Ramdas finally replied to Godse's letter, the high court had upheld the trial court's death sentence in its judgment, which was pronounced on 22 June 1949. Two weeks before that, after the completion of the hearing in Simla on 6 June, Godse had returned to his cell in Ambala jail.

He received a second letter from Ramdas around 22 June. Ramdas considered it irrelevant for Godse to stipulate that in any conversation between them they 'should stick to the truth alone', although he expressed his keenness to meet him, not because of any other reason but to hear from him words of repentance.[36] Godse replied to him on 24 June. He reiterated that he still looked forward to Ramdas's visit to Ambala jail, even if it took place 'one day before my execution'.[37] The correspondence, however, ended abruptly and the meeting Godse so eagerly awaited never took place.[38]

Nor did he hear any positive news from his appeal to the Privy Council of England. As India was still a British dominion, the Privy Council was the final court of appeal for Indians. Godse felt that if he could somehow get permission to argue his own appeal to the Privy Council, his act would receive justifiable appreciation and he would come to be looked upon as a patriot.[39] But his hopes were dashed when the Privy

Council dismissed the appeals of Godse and the others in the preliminary hearing on 12 October 1949.[40]

Up to this point, it seems, Godse had never really considered the possibility of his irrevocable end. The failure of his attempts to present himself as 'a fearless patriot and a passionate protagonist of Hindu ideology', thus seeking to arouse the sympathy of his co-religionists or try to shift the focus from his execution to the Gandhian method of transformation through a serious engagement with Ramdas, marked the beginning of a trivial departure. From this moment, he seemed to give up his efforts to direct the life he had always regarded as a role to be played.

With events slipping from his hands, Godse seemed to be finally bowing to the inevitable.

18

The Gallows

Outside Ambala jail, there seemed to be some confusion about Godse. In the emotional climate still pervaded by the sense of loss created in the wake of Gandhi's murder, some felt the execution of the assassin was not enough; it would end Godse's life but not the philosophy that fuelled him. This feeling had existed since the time his appeal was rejected by the East Punjab High Court on 22 June 1949. Four days later, the *Leader*, a prominent English daily, expressed this in its editorial: 'Nathuram Godse represents a definite school of thought—a thought based on an evil philosophy. At present the followers of this philosophy are demoralized. But it would be a great mistake to assume that Godse's philosophy is dead. It may be dormant but not dead. One of the things on which a cause, however evil, prospers is martyrdom. Our earnest request to the Government of India is do not make a martyr of Godse. Let him live and earn the contempt of humanity for the rest of his life.'[1]

Having originated in earnest among a section of Gandhians, the debate thereafter became a source of confusion as Godse's family and friends seemed to latch on to it, hoping to exploit it to save the condemned from the gallows. After the Privy Council's refusal to deliberate on Godse's appeal, the debate resurfaced. It lingered on for a few weeks until Mashruwala, the foremost Gandhian of the time, wrote on 30 October in *Harijan*, a journal started by Gandhi, about the government's practical difficulties in granting clemency to Godse. 'On grounds of pure principle, I feel that in hanging Mahatma Gandhi's assassin, there is something which positively takes away from the glory of the Mahatma and the dignity of his country,' said Mashruwala in his article, which was quoted in a report published by the *Times of India* the next day. He continued:

> Hence the granting of life to the murderer of its most beloved and most honoured master, even without his asking, would be an act of supreme grace. [. . .] But it is likely to be interpreted by others as an act of imbecility and incapacity to govern [. . .]. In the present case, the logical consequence of commuting the sentence would be abolition of the death penalty altogether. For, if that is not done, it would mean that in India, it is only the murder of a non-violent Mahatma which is not punishable with death. This is an inconsistency, which again only Gandhiji, a Mahatma that he was, could have had the boldness of perpetrating. He was capable of saying that he would allow other murderers to be hanged, but not his own or a non-violent Mahatma. But the Indian Government cannot claim to be a Mahatma-Government. Hence it would be difficult to find fault with the Indian Government if it takes a political and prudential view of Godse's case and refuses to exercise its prerogative.[2]

Mashruwala's write-up practically ended the confusion and put the entire debate to rest. And with that vanished whatever hope it had generated among Godse's associates for securing his escape from the gallows. This did not, however, deter a long-time friend of the assassin from resorting to histrionics, threatening to launch a hunger strike if Godse was not given an opportunity to transform through Gandhian means under the supervision of the Mahatma's followers. Thatte, the man who had actively assisted Godse in establishing the HRD and who was as anti-Gandhi as any other Hindu communalist, issued his threat about a week before 15 November, the date fixed for the hanging of the assassins.

On 7 November, the *Tribune*, a local English daily in Punjab, carried a report saying that Thatte had 'requested the Governor General of India in a letter to keep Godse and Apte under the direct supervision of leaders of the Sarvoday Samaj [a wing of Gandhians], either in Wardha or in Nagpur jail, so that they might be able to bring about a change in the minds of Godse and Apte'. The report also said that Thatte had mentioned in his letter that he would be 'proceeding to Ambala from Nagpur on 12 November to resort to fast in front of the Ambala jail gate' to prevent the hanging of the two convicts.[3]

The announcement seemed too threatening to be ignored. It unnerved the jail administration and spurred frantic activities in Ambala. On 10 November, Jail Superintendent Arjan Dass wrote to the superintendent of police (SP) in Ambala, saying: 'In case Mr. L.G. Thatte mentioned in the newspaper cutting, comes and resorts to fast in front of the jail, it will prove to be a great nuisance and some untoward incident might occur. I would, therefore, request you to kindly put some of your staff on the lookout for him and stop him from the contemplated mischief.'[4] In another letter written on the same day, the district magistrate of Ambala directed the SP to prevent Thatte from carrying out his threat and to 'see that nothing untoward occurs'.[5]

Thatte, however, did not show up. Perhaps he could not muster the resolve to perform the act.

~

On 14 November 1949, Godse wrote and signed his last will and testament. By this time in Ambala jail, he seemed to have lost all hope of a miracle wrought by Gandhi's followers and was now prepared to die. His last will was in the form of a letter addressed to his brother Dattatreya. The one-page letter contained both his personal and political testament. Instead of calling the letter his will, he titled it as *mrityu patra* or the letter of a dying man. 'If my insurance money is released, use it for the purposes of the family,' Godse wrote. 'In my insurance policy, I have mentioned that after my death, Rs 2,000 should be paid to your wife, Rs. 3,000 to Gopal's wife and Rs. 2,000 to you.'[6]

In a thoroughly downhearted tone, evidently bowing to the inevitable, he gave Dattatreya the right to perform his last rites. 'If you are allowed to perform the last rites of my body, you may perform this sacred work in whatever manner you want,' Godse wrote, and then moved on to enumerate his political testament.[7] Whereas the personal testament was considerably brief, the political one comprised a major part of the letter.

'The river Sindhu [or Indus that flows through Pakistan] is the boundary of Bharatvarsh [India]. Ancient sages composed Vedas on the banks of this river,' he wrote, 'My ashes may be immersed in the holy waters of Sindhu when the river once again flows uninterrupted under the aegis of the flag of Bharatvarsh.'[8]

Clearly, in the political testament, he asserted claims on the history as well as the future of his concept of Hindu rashtra. His explicit advice that his ashes be kept safely until Indus once again formed the boundary of India was obviously intended to be understood as an injunction to continue beyond his death the struggle for a Hindu rashtra that incorporated both India and Pakistan. 'It hardly matters if it takes a couple of generations for realizing my wish. Preserve the ashes till then, and if that holy day doesn't arrive in your lifetime, pass on the remains to your descendents [sic] for translating my desire into a reality,' he wrote.[9]

In the postscript to the letter, Godse gave two more instructions to Dattatreya. One of them pertained to what he evidently considered the most important document of his life—the statement he had read out in the trial court. This document, the publication of which had been banned by the government, seemed to satisfy his craving for what he considered was a virile image and gave meaning to a life which otherwise might have appeared to him prosaic. Its wide circulation was, therefore, imperative to establish the masculine conception he had of himself, even if it happened after his death. 'If and when the government lifts ban on my statement made in the court, I authorize you to publish it,' he wrote to Dattatreya, who was also instructed to donate Rs 101 from his savings to Somnath temple, which was under construction at Junagadh in Gujarat.[10]

This was Godse a day before his death: a man who worried, considering the short time left before his execution, about how he might be remembered. It is difficult to imagine a greater contrast than that between a man who desperately sought the intervention of his victim's followers to save him from the gallows and the one who, seeing the failure of all his efforts, reverted to his old desire for what he considered was an intrepid portrayal of him and sought to influence the themes of his posthumous reputation.

~

Before 7.30 a.m. on Tuesday, 15 November 1949, by the account of Gopal, Godse chanted select verses from the Bhagavad Gita and then, like a committed swayamsevak, recited, along with Apte, the first four sentences of the RSS prayer in Sanskrit:

Namaste Sada Vatsale Matrubhume
Twaya Hindubhume Sukham Vardhitoham
Mahanmangale Punyabhume Twadarthe
Patatvesh Kayo Namaste, Namaste![11]

[O affectionate motherland, I eternally bow to you
O land of Hindus, you have reared me in comfort
O sacred and holy land,
May this body of mine be dedicated to you and I bow before you again and again!]

Godse's decision to recite the RSS prayer on the eve of his execution was perhaps not surprising. In fact, it was revealing of the fact that he was still an active member of the controversial organization—a fact that goes against the efforts of the RSS to conceal its links with Gandhi's assassin. That Godse recited the RSS prayer is also corroborated by the news report published in the *Times of India* on 16 November, a day after the execution. 'Godse and Apte, [. . .] after their usual morning duties, recited the 11th and 15th Chapter of the *Bhagwad Gita* and the first four lines of the R.S.S. prayer and took a cup of coffee each before mounting the gallows,' said the news report.[12]

Gopal had requested the jail superintendent for permission to attend the execution but was allowed to spend time with the condemned men in their cell till 7.30 a.m., half an hour before their hanging.[13] By Gopal's account, it was perhaps the first time that Apte recited the RSS prayer. Unlike Godse, Apte had never formally joined the RSS. In the course of time, however, Godse's affinity for the RSS seemed to have changed Apte's attitude towards it. A few days before being hanged, Apte had revealed this transformation in a conversation with Gopal. 'To tell you the truth, it is our experience for the last four years or more that we [Godse and Apte] generally think on the same lines,' Apte had told Gopal, 'And as regards the R.S.S., if you ask me, we two are the only volunteers who actually lived the sacred vow chanted by the Sangh Volunteers, every day, namely, "Patatvesha Kayo Namaste Namaste!"[sic].'[14]

The appearance of confidence displayed by Godse while reciting the RSS prayer, however, was largely deceptive. It seemed like a last manifestation of his lifelong efforts to conceal his real self. For his steps occasionally faltered as he was led to the gallows, prepared behind the cells of the two death convicts. 'His demeanour and general appearance evidenced a state of nervousness and fear,' noted Justice Khosla. 'He [Godse] tried to fight against it and keep up a bold exterior by shouting every few seconds the slogan "Akhand Bharat"(undivided India). But his voice had a slight croak in it [. . .]. The desperate cry was taken up by Apte, who shouted "Amar rahe". His loud and firm tone made an uncanny contrast to Godse's, at times, almost feeble utterance.'[15]

The jail superintendent and the district magistrate of Ambala, who were present to certify the execution order, observed that Apte, unlike Godse, displayed no sign of nervousness. 'Apte died almost at once and his still body swung in a slow oscillating movement, but Godse, though unconscious and unfeeling, continued to wriggle and display signs of life in the shivering of his legs and the convulsing of his body for quite fifteen minutes,' Khosla subsequently wrote.[16]

Within hours, the bodies were cremated inside the jail and their ashes were later secretly scattered at a secluded spot in the Ghaggar in Punjab.[17]

Author's Note

The self-portrait offered by Godse in his court statement on 8 November 1948—nine months after he killed Gandhi—has blithely shaped the narrative concerning his life history all these years. Though everyone who was familiar with Godse knew that neither the impeccable English of his written statement nor its smart juridical phraseology was of his making, themes that it stressed have passed on without basic scrutiny. Even the court found no merit in the statement and rejected most of its claims. Yet, his written statement has continued to be treated as a reliable source of history. The scenes and dialogues Godse invented and the false impressions he contrived to create in the statement have lived through as historical facts, obscuring his real life story.

No less remarkable was the way a section of writers sympathetic to the RSS quietly went about sanitizing the organization's past soon after Godse was hanged on 15 November 1949. In a manner which scarcely aroused any suspicion, they sought to push a false notion aimed at dissociating the RSS from Gandhi's assassin. In time, the fabrication of history they resorted to became a commonly accepted fact, subsuming the voices questioning the veracity of Godse's court statement and obfuscating his real life even more.

Among the many lies the assassin had told in court, the one that endured the most—and virtually overshadowed all other aspects of the story of his life—was his claim that he had left the RSS and joined the Hindu Mahasabha, the political party of Hindu supremacists, long before he killed Gandhi. Though Godse's court statement was fundamentally directed at establishing that he alone was responsible for the murder, in later years his claim regarding the RSS was picked up and trumpeted as the biggest fact of his life. For out of this claim arose a line of argument that willy-nilly served the RSS's desperate desire to cover its tracks.

When Gandhi was assassinated on 30 January 1948, the RSS had asserted that the assassin had never been its member; this was an assertion that no one took seriously. After Godse delivered his court statement, the RSS totally revised its line. It now argued that the assassin did indeed join the RSS, but that he quit the organization a few years later as soon as he became a member of the Hindu Mahasabha. Apparently to give credence to the new line, pro-RSS writers sought to establish that the RSS and the Hindu Mahasabha existed in total separation since the late 1930s—meaning thereby that Godse couldn't have remained a member of the RSS after he joined the Mahasabha.

The write-up that laid the foundation for the fabrication of history appeared barely two and a half months after Godse was hanged. In its 4 February 1950 issue, the *Economic Weekly*, a reputed English journal, published an account of the RSS's past relationship with the Hindu Mahasabha. Titled 'The R.S.S.', the article declared that not only did the two Hindu organizations exist separately but that there was discord between the two after Savarkar became the president of the Hindu Mahasabha in 1937.

At the time of publication, the account was perceived as extremely straightforward, a mere description of past interactions between the supreme leaders of the two Hindu organizations—Hedgewar of the RSS and Savarkar of the Mahasabha. The article explained how Hedgewar, despite holding Savarkar in 'great esteem', refused to make his organization subservient to the Hindu Mahasabha and how the rift widened in the following years. Authored by D.V. Kelkar, it claimed that Hedgewar's stubborn attitude to keep the RSS away from the Mahasabha so frustrated Savarkar that he said: 'The epitaph for the R.S.S. volunteer will be that he was born, he joined the R.S.S. and he died without accomplishing anything.'[1] This quote of Savarkar is the most commonly cited evidence for the purported severing of ties between the two Hindu outfits, thus making Godse's claim in his court statement—that he had exited the RSS while joining the Hindu Mahasabha—look natural.

Strangely, however, the author's failure to cite any references to back his claims in the article did not seem to pique anyone's interest. The question of provenance in this case was even more important because Kelkar confessed in the same article that he had been a close associate of Hedgewar.[2] This fact leaves enough room for suspicion that the author, out of sympathy for the RSS, might deliberately have twisted historical facts to help the Sangh exonerate itself from the charges of Gandhi murder.

The distorted presentation of history, including the Savarkar quote, has since been ceaselessly reiterated by pro-RSS writers and parroted even by many serious researchers. Though available archival documents show that such a split never happened and that the two Hindu organizations always had close connections—and sometimes even overlapping membership—until Gandhi was assassinated, the myth created after the execution of Godse has persisted.

One of the highlights of my research was discovering another statement of Godse's, the one he had given in the first week of March 1948, eight months before he read out his much-publicized statement in the court. This statement, which was recorded before the beginning of the trial in the Gandhi murder case, seems to have been ignored by generations of academics and journalists. And this even though this statement, unlike the one which Godse delivered in court, is in total conformity with the archival records of the time. A unique source of concise information about the life history of the assassin, the pretrial statement never mentions Godse's departure from the RSS after he became a member of the Hindu Mahasabha; instead, it reveals that he was working for both the organizations simultaneously.

The question that is hard to answer then is why no proper study has ever systematically explored the contents of Godse's pretrial statement. Equally hard to explain is the fact that while the English translation of pretrial statements of all other accused are available at the National Archives of India (NAI), Godse's pretrial statement is almost entirely missing—only the first page of the English translation of his statement, which was originally recorded in Marathi, is catalogued. What is available instead is the ninety-two-page-long Marathi version of his pretrial statement. This version is often difficult to read, not only because of the language barrier that it creates for a non-Marathi researcher but also because it was written by hand using a pencil and is at times so faded that it cannot be deciphered without the help of a magnifying glass.

No less exciting was it to discover a set of reports prepared by intelligence agencies after scrutinizing papers seized from the RSS headquarters in Nagpur in the aftermath of Gandhi's assassination. Many of these papers corroborate Godse's revelations in his pretrial statement and contradict several claims he made in the court later. Like his pretrial statement, this source too has remained untapped for the study of the life story of Godse.

These proved a rich find. So did sources such as autobiographies, private papers and reminiscences of some of the Hindu Mahasabha and RSS members who had been active in the 1930s and 1940s, especially in Poona, the locus of Godse's enterprises during the decade preceding Gandhi's assassination. Many of them knew Godse, and their accounts often carry some references to him. Though these references are not in detail, they still provide glimpses of his real life; these are important to understand the private and individual self of Godse as well as his world—India in the first half of the twentieth century.

If these archival records occupy primacy of position in my telling the story of Godse's life, it is because they throw a clear light on the obscured layers of the assassin's past and explain his complex childhood experiences, the pattern of his evolution, his relationship with different organizations and individuals around him, longings and desires, his fateful decisions, the intrigues, the parts played by other actors behind the scenes, the secret acts committed in the name of a Hindu rashtra—all this and more. They also refute the self-portrait which Godse offered in the courtroom and the myths which pro-RSS writers created to suppress the real life that the assassin had lived and influences that had worked on him and led him to murder Gandhi.

Acknowledgements

I must begin with thanks to Hartosh Singh Bal, who first suggested I write a profile of Nathuram Godse for the *Caravan* magazine, and to Basharat Peer, who advised that I should develop the resulting piece into a book. I owe special thanks to Anil Rajimwale, whose remarkable translation from the sometimes indecipherable Marathi documents was essential to the creation of the book. Much that is most interesting within it is the product of his translations, which he made with sensitivity and accuracy. I am extremely grateful to Krishna Jha whose constant, well-aimed questions and insights were crucial during the research and writing of this book.

A large number of friends and strangers—all extremely generous—enabled the research for this book. I will not attempt to make a roll-call of all of them, but I must thank certain persons whose contributions to my work were very specific: Arvind Gokhale, Kumar Ketkar, Anant Bagaitkar, Chand Singh, Abhishek Choudhary, Rahul Thorat, Shekhar Joshi, Anil Vasudev Gogate, Vrinda Godse, Ajinkya Godse, Nitin Shastri, Prof. Raja Dixit, Sharad Khare, Vinayak Kanitkar, Janardan Limaye, Kumar Saptarshi, Narendra K. Bar, Samar Khadas,

Subhash Lande, Girish Kulkarni and Shankar Anand. I am grateful and indebted to every single person at NAI, Ambala Division of the Haryana State Archives, Nehru Memorial Museum and Library, National Gandhi Museum, Mumbai Marathi Grantha Sangrahalaya and Pune's Maharashtra Sahitya Parishad Library.

I am also grateful to many individuals who agreed to share their memories with me. Among them are Sumanbai, Shrinivas D. Acharya, Bapusaheb Pujari and Vishwanath Dattatreya Godse.

My agent, Shruti Debi, made the book immeasurably better than it would have been without her suggestions. And Elizabeth Kuruvilla and Radhika Agarwal were meticulous and unsparing in their editing.

Most of all, I wish to acknowledge the memory of Prof. D.N. Jha. He contributed appreciably to the work's original inspiration and later through critical suggestions during the time I was actively researching and writing, but because of his sudden death he will not see the finished version of this book.

Notes

Preface

1. Jawaharlal Nehru papers (SG), File No. 6, p. 87, Manuscript Section, NMML, New Delhi.
2. Jawaharlal Nehru papers (SG), File No. 26 (II), p. 261, Manuscript Section, NMML, New Delhi.

Chapter 1: Nathu

1. Manuben Gandhi, *Last Glimpses of Bapu*, Shiva Lal Agarwala & Co. (P) Ltd., Agra, 1962, p. 308.
2. Mahatma Gandhi Murder Case, Statement of Accused in Original, File No. 23, p. 90, National Archives of India (NAI), New Delhi.
3. Manuben Gandhi, *Last Glimpses of Bapu*, Shiva Lal Agarwala & Co. (P) Ltd., Agra, 1962, pp. 308–309.
4. Mahatma Gandhi Murder Case, Statement of Accused in Original, File No. 23, pp. 90–91, NAI, New Delhi.
5. Ramachandra Guha, *Gandhi: The Years that Changed the World, 1914–1948*, Penguin Random House India, Gurgaon, 2018, p. 882.
6. D.G. Tendulkar, *Mahatma: Life of Mohandas Karamchand Gandhi*, Volume Eight, The Publications Division, New Delhi, 1963, p. 288.
7. *New York Herald Tribune*, 1 February 1948, Sardar Patel Papers, NAI, New Delhi.

8. Ibid.
9. K.L. Gauba, *The Assassination of Mahatma Gandhi*, Jaico Publishing House, Bombay, 1969, pp. 149–150.
10. 'The Assassin', p. 1, *Hindustan Times*, 31 January 1948.
11. Ibid.
12. Gopal Godse, *Gandhiji's Murder & After*, Surya Prakashan, Delhi, 1989, p. 95.
13. Based on interview with Vishwanath Dattatreya Godse, son of Dattatreya Vinayak Godse, held at Pune on 27 July 2019.
14. Ashis Nandy, *At the Edge of Psychology: Essays in Politics and Culture*, Oxford University Press, Delhi, 1980, p. 79.
15. Gopal Godse, *Gandhiji's Murder & After*, Surya Prakashan, Delhi, 1989, p. 98.
16. Ibid., p. 99.
17. Mahatma Gandhi Murder Case, Statement of Accused in Original, File No. 23, pp. 1–92, NAI, New Delhi.
18. Mahatma Gandhi Murder Case, Statement of Accused in Original, File No. 23, pp. 1–2, NAI, New Delhi.
19. Mahatma Gandhi Murder Case, Statement of Accused in Original, File No. 23, p. 2, NAI, New Delhi.
20. Gopal Godse, *Gandhiji's Murder & After*, Surya Prakashan, Delhi, 1989, p. 100.
21. Mahatma Gandhi Murder Case, Statement of Accused in Original, File No. 23, p. 3, NAI, New Delhi.
22. Louis Fischer, *The Life of Mahatma Gandhi*, Jonathan Cape, London, 1951, p. 220.
23. Jawaharlal Nehru, *An Autobiography*, The Bodley Head, London, 1958, p. 84.
24. Mahatma Gandhi Murder Case, Statement of Accused in Original, File No. 23, p. 4, NAI, New Delhi.
25. Mahatma Gandhi Murder Case, Statement of Accused in Original, File No. 23, p. 5, NAI, New Delhi.
26. Mahatma Gandhi Murder Case, Statement of Accused in Original, File No. 23, p. 7, NAI, New Delhi.
27. Mahatma Gandhi Murder Case, Statement of Accused in Original, File No. 23, p. 6, NAI, New Delhi.
28. Gandhi Murder Trial Papers, File No. 5, Crime Report No. 30, p. 91, NAI, New Delhi.

Chapter 2: Savarkar vs Gandhi

1. See, for example, V.D. Savarkar's self-glorification efforts, extolling his sacrifices as a patriot in pro-Hindu Mahasabha paper, *The Mahratta*, p. 3, 23 May 1947. This was the time when freedom fighters across the country were mostly busy in ensuring smooth transition to independence for India.
2. Ashis Nandy, *Regimes of Narcissism, Regimes of Despair*, Oxford University Press, New Delhi, 2013, p. 26.
3. Ashis Nandy, *Regimes of Narcissism, Regimes of Despair*, Oxford University Press, New Delhi, 2013, p. 35.
4. V.N. Datta, *Madan Lal Dhingra and the Revolutionary Movement*, Vikas Publishing House Pvt Ltd, New Delhi, 1978, p. 51.
5. Dhananjay Keer, *Veer Savarkar*, Popular Prakashan, Bombay, 1966, p. 52.
6. Dhananjay Keer, *Veer Savarkar*, Popular Prakashan, Bombay, 1966, p. 52.
7. Dhananjay Keer, *Veer Savarkar*, Popular Prakashan, Bombay, 1966, p. 71.
8. Dhananjay Keer, *Veer Savarkar*, Popular Prakashan, Bombay, 1966, p. 72.
9. Chitra Gupta, *Life of Barrister Savarkar*, Veer Savarkar Prakashan, Bombay, 1987, pp. 82–86, (first published in December 1926).
10. Vaibhav Purandare, *Savarkar: The True Story of the Father of Hindutva*, Juggernaut Books, New Delhi, 2019, p. 147.
11. *Frontline*, 17 January 2020, Vol. 37, No. 1, p. 97.
12. Trailokya Nath Chakraborty, *Thirty Years in Prison: Sensational Confessions of Revolutionary*, Alpha-Beta Publications, Calcutta, 1963, p. 127.
13. Trailokya Nath Chakraborty, *Thirty Years in Prison: Sensational Confessions of Revolutionary*, Alpha-Beta Publications, Calcutta, 1963, p. 127.
14. Trailokya Nath Chakraborty, *Thirty Years in Prison: Sensational Confessions of Revolutionary*, Alpha-Beta Publications, Calcutta, 1963, p. 139.
15. *Frontline*, 17 January 2020, Vol. 37, No. 1, p. 97.

16. For details see Vaibhav Purandare, *Savarkar: The True Story of the Father of Hindutva*, Juggernaut Books, New Delhi, 2019.
17. Ashis Nandy, *Regimes of Narcissism, Regimes of Despair*, Oxford University Press, New Delhi, 2013, p. 43.
18. Dhananjay Keer, *Veer Savarkar*, Popular Prakashan, Bombay, 1966, p. 4.
19. Ashis Nandy, *Regimes of Narcissism, Regimes of Despair*, Oxford University Press, New Delhi, 2013, p. 45.
20. For details see V.D. Savarkar, *The Story of My Transportation for Life*, Sadbhakti Publications, Bombay, 1950.
21. Dhananjay Keer, *Veer Savarkar*, Popular Prakashan, Bombay, 1966, pp. 140–143.
22. A.G. Noorani, *Savarkar and Hindutva: The Godse Connection*, LeftWord Books, New Delhi, 2015, p. 54.
23. V.D. Savarkar, *Hindutva: Who is a Hindu?*, Hindi Sahitya Sadan, New Delhi, 2005, p. 85.
24. V.D. Savarkar, *Hindutva: Who is a Hindu?*, Hindi Sahitya Sadan, New Delhi, 2005, p. 92.
25. V.D. Savarkar, *Hindutva: Who is a Hindu?*, Hindi Sahitya Sadan, New Delhi, 2005, p. 42.
26. V.D. Savarkar, *Hindutva: Who is a Hindu?*, Hindi Sahitya Sadan, New Delhi, 2005, p. 44.
27. Aakar Patel, *Our Hindu Rashtra*, Westland Publications, Chennai, 2020, p. 6.
28. Gopal Godse, *Gandhiji's Murder & After*, Surya Prakashan, Delhi, 1989, p. 108.
29. Gopal Godse, *Gandhiji's Murder & After*, Surya Prakashan, Delhi, 1989, p. 109.
30. Mahatma Gandhi Murder Case, Statement of Accused in Original, File No. 23, p. 5, NAI, New Delhi.
31. Mahatma Gandhi Murder Case, Statement of Accused in Original, File No. 23, p. 5, NAI, New Delhi.
32. Ashis Nandy, *At the Edge of Psychology: Essays in Politics and Culture*, Oxford University Press, Delhi, 1980, p. 77.
33. Shri Prakash Narhar Godse (editor and publisher), *Godse Kulvritant*, Mumbai, 2006, p. 702.
34. Gopal Godse, *Gandhiji's Murder & After*, Surya Prakashan, Delhi, 1989, pp. 93–94.

35. Mahatma Gandhi Murder Case, Statement of Accused in Original, File No. 23, p. 6, NAI, New Delhi.
36. Mahatma Gandhi Murder Case, Statement of Accused in Original, File No. 23, p. 7, NAI, New Delhi.
37. Ashis Nandy, *At the Edge of Psychology: Essays in Politics and Culture*, Oxford University Press, Delhi, 1980, p. 71.
38. Ramachandra Guha, *Gandhi: The Years that Changed the World, 1914–1948*, Penguin Random House India, Gurgaon, 2018, p. 898.
39. Robert Payne, *The Life and Death of Mahatma Gandhi*, Rupa & Co., Calcutta, 1997, p. 205.
40. *The Collected Works of Mahatma Gandhi*, Vol. IX, The Publications Division, Government of India, Delhi, 1963, p. 499; Dhananjay Keer, *Veer Savarkar*, Popular Prakashan, Bombay, 1966, pp. 62–64.
41. *The Collected Works of Mahatma Gandhi*, Vol. XXXIII, The Publications Division, Government of India, Delhi, 1963, p. 136
42. Ibid.
43. Ibid.
44. Gopal Godse, *Gandhiji's Murder & After*, Surya Prakashan, Delhi, 1989, p. 109.
45. Gopal Godse, *Gandhiji's Murder & After*, Surya Prakashan, Delhi, 1989, p. 109.
46. Mahatma Gandhi Murder Case, Statement of Accused in Original, File No. 23, p. 6, NAI, New Delhi.

Chapter 3: The Brahmins of Bombay

1. Mahatma Gandhi Murder Case, Statement of Accused in Original, File No. 23, p. 10, NAI, New Delhi.
2. Mahatma Gandhi Murder Case, Statement of Accused in Original, File No. 23, p. 10, NAI, New Delhi.
3. Gopal Godse, *Gandhiji's Murder & After*, Surya Prakashan, Delhi, 1989, p. 113.
4. Mahatma Gandhi Murder Case, Statement of Accused in Original, File No. 23, p. 11, NAI, New Delhi.
5. Mahatma Gandhi Murder Case, Statement of Accused in Original, File No. 23, p. 11, NAI, New Delhi.

6. M.J. Akbar, *India: The Siege Within*, Penguin Books India, New Delhi, 1985, p. 306.
7. Chetan Bhatt, *Hindu Nationalism: Origins, Ideologies and Modern Myths*, Berg, Oxford-New York, 2001, p. 121.
8. Ibid.
9. Nilanjan Mukhopadhyay, *The RSS: Icons of the Indian Right*, Tranquebar, Chennai, 2019, p. 40.
10. B.V. Deshpande and S.R. Ramaswamy, *Dr Hedgewar The Epoch-Maker: A Biography*, Sahitya Sindhu, Bengaluru, 1981, p. 118.
11. Delhi Police Record, IX Installment, File No. 72, p. 217, Records Section, Nehru Memorial Museum and Library (NMML), New Delhi.
12. Ibid.
13. Ibid., p. 229.
14. Based on an interview with ninety-three-year-old Bapusaheb Pujari, who joined the RSS in 1933 at the age of seven under the influence of Kashinath Bhaskar Limaye, in Sangli on 14 October 2019.
15. Ibid.
16. D.S. Harshe, *Adarsh Hindu Sanghatak: Ka. Bha. Limaye*, published by Sudha Dattatreya Harshe, Satara, 1981, p. 1.
17. Ibid.
18. Ibid.
19. D.S. Harshe, *Adarsh Hindu Sanghatak: Ka. Bha. Limaye*, published by Sudha Dattatreya Harshe, Satara, 1981, p. 2.
20. Ibid., p. 1.
21. Ibid., p. 4.
22. Ibid., p. 5.
23. Ibid.
24. Ibid.
25. N.H. Palkar (ed.), *Dr. Hedgewar: Patraroop-Vyaktidarshan*, Archana Prakashan, Indore, 1989, p. 30.
26. Ibid., pp. 29–30.
27. D.S. Harshe, *Adarsh Hindu Sanghatak: Ka. Bha. Limaye*, published by Sudha Dattatreya Harshe, Satara, 1981, p. iv.
28. Based on an interview with ninety-three-year-old Bapusaheb Pujari, who joined the RSS in 1933 at the age of seven under

the influence of Kashinath Bhaskar Limaye, in Sangli on 14 October 2019.

29. Mahatma Gandhi Murder Case, Statement of Accused in Original, File No. 23, p. 12, NAI, New Delhi.
30. S.H. Deshpande, *My Days in the RSS*, Quest, July–August 1975, p. 20.
31. Valmiki Choudhary, *Dr. Rajendra Prasad: Correspondence and Select Documents*, Vol. X, Allied Publishers Private Limited, Delhi, 1988, pp. 181–183.
32. Ibid.
33. S.H. Deshpande, *My Days in the RSS*, Quest, July–August 1975, p. 19.
34. Mahatma Gandhi Murder Case, Statement of Accused in Original, File No. 23, p. 12, NAI, New Delhi.
35. Ibid., p. 13.

Chapter 4: Sangh and Sabha

1. Mahatma Gandhi Murder Case, Statement of Accused in Original, File No. 23, p. 14, NAI, New Delhi.
2. Ibid.
3. Ibid.
4. Based on an interview with ninety-three-year-old Shrinivas D. Acharya, who joined the RSS in 1940 at the age of fourteen in Pune, on 11 October 2019. He passed away in 2021.
5. S.H. Deshpande, *My Days in the RSS*, Quest, July–August 1975, p. 21.
6. Mahatma Gandhi Murder Case, Statement of Accused in Original, File No. 23, p. 15, NAI, New Delhi.
7. Dhananjay Keer, *Veer Savarkar*, Popular Prakashan, Bombay, 1966, p. 220.
8. A.G. Noorani, *Savarkar and Hindutva: The Godse Connection*, LeftWord Books, New Delhi, 2015, p. 21.
9. Dhananjay Keer, *Savarkar and His Times*, Published by A.V. Keer, 1950, p. 199.
10. Ibid.
11. Ibid., p. 200.

12. Vaibhav Purandare, *Savarkar: The True Story of the Father of Hindutva*, Juggernaut Books, New Delhi, 2019, p. 241.
13. Indra Prakash, *A Review of the History and Work of the Hindu Mahasabha and the Hindu Sanghatan Movement*, Dharmarajya Press, Delhi, 1952, p. 13.
14. Myron Weiner, *Party Politics in India: The Development of a Multi-Party System*, Princeton University Press, Princeton, 1957, p. 167.
15. Dhananjay Keer, *Savarkar and His Times*, Published by A.V. Keer, 1950, p. 203.
16. Vinayak Damodar Savarkar, *Samagra Savarkar Vangmaya*, Vol. 6, Hindu Mahasabha, Poona, 1963, p. 296.
17. V.D. Savarkar, *Hindutva: Who is a Hindu?*, Hindi Sahitya Sadan, New Delhi, 2005
18. Marzia Casolari, 'Hindutva's Foreign Tie-up in the 1930s: Archival Evidence', *Economic and Political Weekly*, 22 January 2000, p. 223.
19. Ramachandra Guha, *Gandhi: The Years that Changed the World, 1914–1948*, Penguin Random House India, Gurgaon, 2018, p. 525.
20. N.H. Palkar (ed.), *Dr. Hedgewar: Patraroop-Vyaktidarshan*, Archana Prakashan, Indore, 1989, p. 84.
21. Based on an interview with ninety-three-year-old Bapusaheb Pujari, who joined the RSS in 1933 at the age of seven under the influence of Kashinath Bhaskar Limaye, in Sangli on 14 October 2019.
22. Gopal Godse, *Gandhiji's Murder & After*, Surya Prakashan, Delhi, 1989, p. 116.
23. Mahatma Gandhi Murder Case, Statement of Accused in Original, File No. 23, p. 9, NAI, New Delhi.
24. Ibid., p. 14.
25. Ibid., p. 15.
26. Dhirendra K. Jha, 'The Apostle of Hate', The *Caravan*, Volume 12, Issue 1, January 2020, pp. 28–49.
27. Government of India, Home Department (Political), File No. 220-P/42 (Sec), 1942, p. 1, NAI, New Delhi.
28. D.R. Goyal, *Rashtriya Swayamsevak Sangh*, Radhakrishna Prakashan, Delhi, 1979, pp. 82–83.

29. B.V. Deshpande and S.R. Ramaswamy, *Dr Hedgewar The Epoch-Maker: A Biography*, Sahitya Sindhu, Bengaluru, 1981, pp. 14–32.
30. Government of India, Home Department (Political), File No. 88/33, 1933, p. 28, NAI, New Delhi.
31. Marzia Casolari, 'Hindutva's Foreign Tie-up in the 1930s: Archival Evidence', *Economic and Political Weekly*, 22 January 2000, pp. 219–220.
32. Government of India, Home Department (Political), File No. 220-P/42 (Sec), 1942, p. 1, NAI, New Delhi.
33. D.R. Goyal, *Rashtriya Swayamsevak Sangh*, Radhakrishna Prakashan, Delhi, 1979, p. 83.
34. Ibid.
35. N.G. Dixit (ed.), *Dharmaveer Dr. B.S. Moonje Commemoration Volume*, Centenary Celebration Committee, Nagpur, 1973, p. 22.
36. S.H. Deshpande, *My Days in the RSS*, Quest, July–August 1975, p. 21.
37. For details see A.S. Bhide (ed.), *Whirlwind Propaganda: Extracts from President's Diary of His Propagandist Tours, Interviews from December 1937 to October 1941*, All India Hindu Mahasabha, Bombay, 1941.
38. Marzia Casolari, 'Hindutva's Foreign Tie-up in the 1930s: Archival Evidence', *Economic and Political Weekly*, 22 January 2000, p. 228.
39. Government of India, Home Department (Political), File No. 220-P/42 (Sec), 1942, p. 3, NAI, New Delhi.
40. J.A. Curran, Jr., *Militant Hinduism in Indian Politics: A Study of the R.S.S.*, Institute of Pacific Relations, New York, 1951, p. 64.

Chapter 5: Ramachandra Becomes Nathuram

1. N.V. Godse to V.D. Savarkar, cited in K.L. Gauba, *The Assassination of Mahatma Gandhi*, Jaico Publishing House, Bombay, 1969, pp. 81–82.
2. Ibid.
3. Gandhi Murder Trial Papers, File No. 5, p. 224, NAI, New Delhi.

4. Mahatma Gandhi Murder Case, Statement of Accused in Original, File No. 23, p. 15, NAI, New Delhi.
5. Gopal Godse, *Why I Assassinated Mahatma Gandhi?*, Surya Bharti Parkashan, Delhi, 1993, p. 102.
6. J.A. Curran, Jr., *Militant Hinduism in Indian Politics: A Study of the R.S.S.*, Institute of Pacific Relations, New York, 1951, p. 13.
7. Ibid., p. 3.
8. N.V. Godse to V.D. Savarkar, cited in K.L. Gauba, *The Assassination of Mahatma Gandhi*, Jaico Publishing House, Bombay, 1969, p. 82.
9. Ian Copland, *Communalism' in Princely India: The Case of Hyderabad, 1930–1940*, Modern Asian Studies, Vol. 22, No. 4, 1988, p. 803.
10. The *Times of India*, 27 December 1938, p. 14.
11. Ian Copland, *Communalism in Princely India: The Case of Hyderabad, 1930–1940*, Modern Asian Studies, Vol. 22, No. 4, 1988, p. 800.
12. Marzia Casolari, 'Hindutva's Foreign Tie-up in the 1930s: Archival Evidence', *Economic and Political Weekly*, 22 January 2000, pp. 218–219.
13. Ibid., p. 219.
14. Ibid., p. 221.
15. Gandhi Murder Trial Papers, File No. 5, p. 224, NAI, New Delhi.
16. Mahatma Gandhi Murder Case, Statement of Accused in Original, File No. 23, p. 16, NAI, New Delhi.
17. Ibid.
18. Ibid., pp. 16–17.
19. 'More About the Assassin', *Hindustan Times*, 2 February 1948.
20. Mahatma Gandhi Murder Case, Statement of Accused in Original, File No. 23, p. 16, NAI, New Delhi.
21. Ian Copland, *Communalism in Princely India: The Case of Hyderabad, 1930–1940*, Modern Asian Studies, Vol. 22, No. 4, 1988, p. 810.
22. Tapan Ghosh, *The Gandhi Murder Trial*, Asia Publishing House, New Delhi, 1974, p. 24.
23. Ibid., p. 27.

24. Ibid.
25. Laxman Vasudev Paranjpe, 'Dr. Hedgewar Yanche Charitra Va Kaarya', *Kesari*, 5 July 1940.
26. Justice J.L. Kapur, Report of Commission of Inquiry in to Conspiracy to Murder Mahatma Gandhi, Part II, New Delhi, Government of India, 1969, p. 61.
27. Ashis Nandy, *At the Edge of Psychology: Essays in Politics and Culture*, Oxford University Press, Delhi, 1980, p. 81.
28. S.H. Deshpande, *My Days in the RSS*, Quest, July–August 1975, p. 27.
29. Valmiki Choudhary, *Dr. Rajendra Prasad: Correspondence and Select Documents*, Vol. X, Allied Publishers Private Limited, Delhi, 1988, p. 183.
30. Mahatma Gandhi Murder Case, Statement of Accused in Original, File No. 23, p. 17, NAI, New Delhi.
31. Vasudha Ganesh Paranjpe, *Ek Jhunjar Stri: Shantabai Gokhale*, Ram Laxmi Mandal, Pune, 2003, p. 111.
32. D.P. Mishra Papers, I & II Inst., Sub File No. 18, p. 139, Records Section, NMML, New Delhi.
33. In archival sources, the acronym RSSS is occasionally used for this organization whereas nowadays shorter form RSS is more common. However, the meaning in both cases is the same.
34. D.P. Mishra Papers, I & II Inst., Sub File No. 18, p. 137, Records Section, NMML, New Delhi.
35. D.S. Harshe, *Adarsh Hindu Sanghatak: Ka. Bha. Limaye*, published by Sudha Dattatreya Harshe, Satara, 1981, pp. 5–6.
36. Mahatma Gandhi Murder Case, Statement of Accused in Original, File No. 23, p. 18, NAI, New Delhi.
37. Ibid.
38. Ibid., pp. 18–19.
39. Marzia Casolari, 'Hindutva's Foreign Tie-up in the 1930s: Archival Evidence', *Economic and Political Weekly*, 22 January 2000, p. 219.
40. B.S. Moonje Papers, Sub Files No. 59, p. 252, Records Section, NMML, New Delhi.
41. Ibid., p. 257.

42. Laxman Vasudev Paranjpe, 'Dr. Hedgewar Yanche Charitra Va Kaarya', *Kesari*, 5 July 1940.
43. Marzia Casolari, 'Hindutva's Foreign Tie-up in the 1930s: Archival Evidence', *Economic and Political Weekly*, 22 January 2000, p. 226.
44. Ibid.
45. Ibid.
46. Home Department (Political), File No. 190-P (S), 1943, p. 2, NAI, New Delhi.
47. Home Department (Political), File No. 220-P/42 (Sec), 1942, p. 5, NAI, New Delhi.
48. Ibid.
49. S.H. Deshpande, *My Days in the RSS*, Quest, July–August 1975, p. 22.
50. Mahatma Gandhi Murder Case, Statement of Accused in Original, File No. 23, p. 19, NAI, New Delhi.

Chapter 6: An Army

1. Mahatma Gandhi Murder Case, Statement of Accused in Original, File No. 23, p. 135, NAI, New Delhi.
2. Ibid., p. 134.
3. N.D. Apte to V.D. Savarkar, cited in K.L. Gauba, *The Assassination of Mahatma Gandhi*, Jaico Publishing House, Bombay, 1969, pp. 90–91.
4. Ibid.
5. Ibid., pp. 86–88 and 94–95.
6. Ibid., pp. 86–87.
7. Ibid., p. 87.
8. Ibid., p. 88.
9. Ibid.
10. Ibid.
11. Ibid., p. 94.
12. Ibid., pp. 94–95.
13. Tapan Ghosh, *The Gandhi Murder Trial*, Asia Publishing House, New Delhi, 1974, p. 38.
14. Ibid.

15. Mahatma Gandhi Murder Case, Statement of Accused in Original, File No. 23, p. 20, NAI, New Delhi.
16. Mahatma Gandhi Murder Trial Papers, Special Branch, CID, Bombay, File No. 5, Crime Report No. 2, pp. 9–10, NAI, New Delhi.
17. Mahatma Gandhi Murder Case, Statement of Accused in Original, File No. 23, p. 20, NAI, New Delhi.
18. Ibid.
19. Mahatma Gandhi Murder Trial Papers, Special Branch, CID, Bombay, File No. 5, p. 228, NAI, New Delhi.
20. Vasudev Balwant Gogate, *Hotson-Gogate: Atmavritta*, published by Anil Vasudev Gogate, Pune, 2006, p. 94.
21. Ibid.
22. Ibid., p. 95.
23. Jawaharlal Nehru, *The Discovery of India*, Penguin Books India, New Delhi, 2008, p. 454.
24. Ibid., pp. 460–464.
25. Ramachandra Guha, *Gandhi: The Years that Changed the World, 1914—1948*, Penguin Random House India, Gurgaon, 2018, p. 684.
26. S.H. Deshpande, *My Days in the RSS*, Quest, July–August 1975, p. 23.
27. Ibid.
28. Interview with ninety-three-year-old RSS member Shrinivas D. Acharya, who lived in Pune since 1941, was done on 11 October 2019. He passed away in 2021.
29. N.C. Chatterjee to B.S. Moonje, 14 August 1942, cited in Ramachandra Guha, *Gandhi: The Years that Changed the World, 1914–1948*, Penguin Random House India, Gurgaon, 2018, pp. 684–685.
30. File No. F-3-53, Home Political–I, 1942, Repository II, pp. 7–8, NAI, New Delhi.
31. Ibid.
32. Ibid.
33. Ibid.
34. Interview with ninety-three-year-old RSS member Shrinivas D. Acharya, who lived in Pune since 1941, was done on 11 October 2019. He passed away in 2021.

Chapter 7: And a Newspaper

1. B.S. Moonje Papers, Sub File No. 75, p. 68, Records Section, NMML, New Delhi.
2. Mahatma Gandhi Murder Case, Statement of Accused in Original, File No. 23, p. 21, NAI, New Delhi.
3. B.S. Moonje Papers, Sub File No. 75, p. 68, Records Section, NMML, New Delhi.
4. Ibid.
5. Ibid., p. 67.
6. Ibid.
7. Interview with ninety-three-year-old RSS member Shrinivas D. Acharya, who lived in Pune since 1941, was done on 11 October 2019. He passed away in 2021.
8. Ibid.
9. B.S. Moonje Papers, Sub File No. 75, p. 67, Records Section, NMML, New Delhi.
10. Neela Vasant Upadhye (ed.), *D.V. Gokhale: Vyaktitva Va Krititva*, Navachaitanya Prakashan, Mumbai, 2013, p. x.
11. B.S. Moonje Papers, Sub File No. 75, p. 67, Records Section, NMML, New Delhi.
12. S.H. Deshpande, *My Days in the RSS*, Quest, July–August 1975, p. 28.
13. D.R. Goyal, *Rashtriya Swayamsevak Sangh*, Radhakrishna Prakashan, New Delhi, 2000, p. 17.
14. Home Pol (I), File No. 220-P/42 (Sec), 'Summery of a report on the Officers' Training Camp of the Rashtriya Swayam Sevak Sangh held in April/May 1942 at Poona' p. 83, NAI, New Delhi.
15. S.H. Deshpande, *My Days in the RSS*, Quest, July–August 1975, p. 21.
16. B.S. Moonje Papers, Sub File No. 75, p. 67, Records Section, NMML, New Delhi.
17. Walter K. Andersen and Shridhar D. Damle, *The Brotherhood in Saffron: The Rashtriya Swayamsevak Sangh and Hindu Revivalism*, Westerview Press, Boulder and London, 1987, pp. 43, 65.

18. D.P. Mishra Papers, I & II Inst., Sub File No. 18, p. 122, Records Section, NMML, New Delhi.
19. Narhari N. Kirkire, *Sangliche Diwas* (1937–1945), N.N. Kirkire (publisher), Satara, 2008, p. 62.
20. Based on an interview with ninety-three-year-old Bapusaheb Pujari, who joined the RSS in 1933 at the age of seven under the influence of Kashinath Bhaskar Limaye, in Sangli on 14 October 2019.
21. File No. 190-P (S), 1943, p. 51, Home Department (Political), Government of India, NAI, New Delhi.
22. File No. 28/5/46–Pol (I): Home Department, Government of India, P. 15, NAI, New Delhi.
23. File No. 28/5/46–Pol (I): Home Department, Government of India, P. 15, NAI, New Delhi.
24. File No. 190-P (S), 1943, Home Department (Political), Government of India: Extract from Daily Report No. 36 of 1943, received from Central Intelligence Officer, the Central Provinces and Berar, NAI, New Delhi.
25. Mahatma Gandhi Murder Case, Statement of Accused in Original, File No. 23, p. 20, NAI, New Delhi.
26. Godse's letter to Savarkar, cited in K.L. Gauba, *The Assassination of Mahatma Gandhi*, Jaico Publishing House, Bombay, 1969, p. 83.
27. Gandhi Murder Trial Papers, File No. 5, p. 232, NAI, New Delhi.
28. Mahatma Gandhi Murder Case, Statement of Accused in Original, File No. 23, p. 21, NAI, New Delhi.
29. Gandhi Murder Trial Papers, File No. 5, P. Crime Report No. – 38, p. 101, NAI, New Delhi.
30. Mahatma Gandhi Murder Case, Statement of Accused in Original, File No. 23, p. 21, NAI, New Delhi.
31. Ibid., p. 135.
32. Ibid.
33. J. Natarajan, *History of Indian Journalism*, Publications Division, New Delhi, 1955, p. 236.
34. Mahatma Gandhi Murder Case, Statement of Accused in Original, File No. 23, pp. 23–25, NAI, New Delhi.
35. Ibid., pp. 24–25.

36. Ibid., p. 23.
37. Interview with ninety-three-year-old RSS member Shrinivas D. Acharya, who lived in Pune since 1941, was done on 11 October 2019. He passed away in 2021.
38. J. Natarajan, *History of Indian Journalism*, Publications Division, New Delhi, 1955, p. 236.
39. Based on an interview with ninety-three-year-old Bapusaheb Pujari, who joined the RSS in 1933 at the age of seven under the influence of Kashinath Bhaskar Limaye, in Sangli on 14 October 2019.
40. Interview with ninety-three-year-old RSS member Shrinivas D. Acharya, who lived in Pune since 1941, was done on 11 October 2019. He passed away in 2021.
41. Mahatma Gandhi Murder Case, Statement of Accused in Original, File No. 23, pp. 25–26, NAI, New Delhi.
42. Ibid., p. 26.
43. Sumit Sarkar, *Modern India: 1885–1947*, Macmillan India Limited, New Delhi, 1983, p. 415.
44. Mahatma Gandhi Murder Case, Statement of Accused in Original, File No. 23, p. 27, NAI, New Delhi.
45. Ibid.
46. Ibid., p. 29.
47. Ramachandra Guha, *Gandhi: The Years that Changed the World, 1914–1948*, Penguin Random House India, Gurgaon, 2018, p. 732.
48. Ibid.
49. The *Times of India*, 23 July 1944, cited in Justice J.L. Kapur, Report of Commission of Inquiry in to Conspiracy to Murder Mahatma Gandhi, Part–I, 1969, pp. 116–117.
50. Mahatma Gandhi Murder Case, Statement of Accused in Original, File No. 23, pp. 30, 136, NAI, New Delhi.

Chapter 8: Psychosexual Pangs

1. Larry Collins and Dominique Lapierre, *Freedom at Midnight*, Vikas Publishing House Pvt Ltd, Delhi, 1976, p. 366.
2. D.P. Mishra Papers, I & II Inst., Sub. File No. 18, Statement of Narain Vithal Paranjpe, p. 17, NMML, New Delhi.

3. Dhananjay Keer, *Veer Savarkar*, Popular Prakashan, Bombay, 1988, p. 230.
4. Ibid., pp. 210, 213.
5. Ibid., p. 213.
6. Ibid.
7. Ibid., p. 214.
8. Vasudha Ganesh Paranjpe, *Ek Jhunjar Stri: Shantabai Gokhale*, Ram Laxmi Mandal, Pune 2003, p. 101.
9. Statement of Manorama Salvi, cited in K.L. Gauba, *The Assassination of Mahatma Gandhi*, Jaico Publishing House, Bombay, 1969, pp. 225–226.
10. Ibid., p. 226.
11. Ibid., p. 226.
12. Ibid.
13. Ibid.
14. Ibid.
15. Ibid.
16. Ibid.
17. Ibid., p. 228.
18. Based on interview with a close relative of Manorama Salvi conducted on 17 October 2019 at Ahmadnagar. As the interviewee preferred anonymity, the name has not been disclosed.
19. Ibid.
20. Interview with ninety-three-year-old RSS member Shrinivas D. Acharya, who lived in Pune since 1941, was done on 11 October 2019. He passed away in 2021.
21. M.S. Dixit, *Mi, Ma. Shri*, Utkarsh Prakashan, Pune, 2004, pp. 44–45.
22. Interview with ninety-three-year-old RSS member Shrinivas D. Acharya, who lived in Pune since 1941, was done on 11 October 2019. He passed away in 2021.
23. Ibid.
24. *Sunday Standard*, 15 February 1948: Story of 'Brooding Little Fanatic'.
25. Mahatma Gandhi Murder Trial Papers, File No. 5, 'History of the Hindu Mahasabha', p. 32, NAI, New Delhi.

26. N.D. Apte to V.D. Savarkar, cited in K.L. Gauba, *The Assassination of Mahatma Gandhi*, Jaico Publishing House, Bombay, 1969, p. 90.
27. Delhi Police Record, V Inst., File No. 137, p. 43, Records Room, NMML, New Delhi.
28. Mahatma Gandhi Murder Case, Statement of Accused in Original, File No. 23, p. 44, NAI, New Delhi.
29. Morarji Desai, *The Story of My Life*, Vol. I, Macmillan India, Delhi, 1974, p. 248.
30. Ibid., p. 250.
31. Mahatma Gandhi Murder Trial Papers, File No. 5, 'History of the Hindu Mahasabha', p. 26, NAI, New Delhi.
32. Ibid.
33. Mahatma Gandhi Murder Case, Statement of Accused in Original, File No. 23, p. 43, NAI, New Delhi.
34. Mahatma Gandhi Murder Trial Papers, File No. 5, 'History of the Hindu Mahasabha', p. 40, NAI, New Delhi.
35. Ibid.
36. Ibid., p. 41.
37. 'Godse and Apte Threatened to Stab Mr. Bhopatkar', The *Times of India*, 24 July 1948, p. 8.
38. Tapan Ghosh, *The Gandhi Murder Trial*, Asia Publishing House, New Delhi, 1974, p. 59.
39. Mahatma Gandhi Murder Case, Statement of Accused in Original, File No. 23, p. 95, NAI, New Delhi.

Chapter 9: 'Gandhi, Commit Suicide'

1. Mahatma Gandhi Murder Trial Papers, File No. 5, 'History of the Hindu Mahasabha', p. 41, NAI, New Delhi
2. Mahatma Gandhi Murder Trial Papers, File No. 5, 'History of the Hindu Mahasabha', pp. 41–42, NAI, New Delhi.
3. Ibid.
4. Ibid., pp. 42–43.
5. Mahatma Gandhi Murder Case, Statement of Accused in Original, File No. 23, p. 137, NAI, New Delhi.
6. Mahatma Gandhi Murder Trial Papers, File No. 5, 'History of the Hindu Mahasabha', p. 43, NAI, New Delhi.

7. Mahatma Gandhi Murder Case, Statement of Accused in Original, File No. 23, p. 45, NAI, New Delhi.
8. Justice J.L. Kapur, Report of Commission of Inquiry in to Conspiracy to Murder Mahatma Gandhi, Part II, Government of India, New Delhi, 1969, p. 61.
9. Mahatma Gandhi Murder Trial Papers, File No. 5, 'History of the Hindu Mahasabha', p. 44, NAI, New Delhi.
10. Mahatma Gandhi Murder Trial Papers, Special Branch, CID, Bombay, File No. 5, Crime Report No. 62, pp. 170–171.
11. Mahatma Gandhi Murder Case, Statement of Accused in Original, File No. 23, p. 169, NAI, New Delhi.
12. Ibid., p. 172.
13. G.D. Khosla, *The Murder of the Mahatma: And Other Cases from a Judge's Note-book*, Chatto & Windus, London, 1963, p. 222.
14. Mahatma Gandhi Murder Case, Statement of Accused in Original, File No. 23, p. 176, NAI, New Delhi.
15. Ibid.
16. Ibid.
17. Ibid., pp. 176–177.
18. Ibid., p. 177–178.
19. Ibid., p. 177.
20. Ibid., p. 137.
21. Ibid., p. 177.
22. Tapan Ghosh, *The Gandhi Murder Trial*, Asia Publishing House, New Delhi, 1974, p. 87.
23. Ibid.
24. Statement of Dada Maharaj, cited in K.L. Gauba, *The Assassination of Mahatma Gandhi*, Jaico Publishing House, Bombay, 1969, p. 330.
25. Tapan Ghosh, *The Gandhi Murder Trial*, Asia Publishing House, New Delhi, 1974, pp. 87–88.
26. Larry Collins and Dominique Lapierre, *Freedom at Midnight*, Vikas Publishing House Pvt Ltd, Delhi, 1976, p. 365
27. Tapan Ghosh, *The Gandhi Murder Trial*, Asia Publishing House, New Delhi, 1974, p. 88.
28. Ibid.

29. Statement of Dada Maharaj, cited in K.L. Gauba, *The Assassination of Mahatma Gandhi*, Jaico Publishing House, Bombay, 1969, p. 331.
30. Ibid.
31. Statement of Manorama Salvi, cited in K.L. Gauba, *The Assassination of Mahatma Gandhi*, Jaico Publishing House, Bombay, 1969, p. 229.
32. Ibid., p. 228.
33. Ibid.
34. Ibid.
35. Ibid., pp. 228–229.
36. Ibid., p. 228.
37. Based on interview with a close relative of Manorama Salvi conducted on 17 October 2019 at Ahmadnagar. As the interviewee preferred anonymity, the name has not been disclosed.
38. M.S. Dixit, Mi Ma Shri, Utkarsh Prakashan, Pune, 2004, p. 45.
39. Ibid., p. 46.
40. Ibid.

Chapter 10: The Plan

1. Mahatma Gandhi Murder Case, Statement of Accused in Original, File No. 23, p. 66, NAI, New Delhi.
2. Mahatma Gandhi Murder Trial Papers, File No. 5, Crime Report No. 82, pp. 205–206, NAI, New Delhi.
3. Ibid., p. 206.
4. Mahatma Gandhi Murder Case, Statement of Accused in Original, File No. 23, p. 138, NAI, New Delhi.
5. Ibid., p. 185.
6. Ibid.
7. Mahatma Gandhi Murder Case, Statement of Accused, File No. 47, pp. 23–24, NAI, New Delhi.
8. Ibid., pp. 30–45.
9. Ashis Nandy, *Regimes of Narcissism, Regimes of Despair*, Oxford University Press, New Delhi, 2013, p. 75.
10. Mahatma Gandhi Murder Case, Statement of Accused, File No. 47, p. 48, NAI, New Delhi

11. Ibid.
12. Based on interview with Sumanbai, an acquaintance of Shewanti till the time she died in 1988, conducted on 17 October 2019 at Ahmednagar.
13. Ibid.
14. Ibid.
15. Ibid.
16. Mahatma Gandhi Murder Case, Statement of Accused, File No. 47, pp. 49–50, NAI, New Delhi.
17. Ibid., p. 50.
18. Ibid., pp. 50–51.
19. Ibid., p. 55.
20. Ibid.
21. Ibid., pp. 56–58.
22. Ibid., p. 72.
23. Ibid.
24. Mahatma Gandhi Murder Case, Statement of Accused in Original, File No. 23, p. 66, NAI, New Delhi.
25. Gopal Godse, *Why I Assassinated Mahatma Gandhi?,* Surya Bharti Parkashan, Delhi, 1993, pp. 110–111.
26. M.S. Golwalkar, *We or Our Nationhood Defined*, Bharat Prakashan, Nagpur, Fourth Edition, 1947 (First published in 1939)
27. M.S. Golwalkar, *We or Our Nationhood Defined*, Bharat Prakashan, Nagpur, 1947, p. 43.
28. Ibid., pp. 55–56.
29. Rashtriya Swayam Sewak Sangh—Source Report, Delhi Police Records, V Instalment, File No. 138, p. 82, Records Section, NMML, New Delhi.
30. Ibid.
31. Mahatma Gandhi Murder Case, Statement of Accused in Original, File No. 23, pp. 68–69, NAI, New Delhi.
32. Mahatma Gandhi Murder Case, Statement of Accused, File No. 47, pp. 58–60, NAI, New Delhi.
33. Ibid., p. 60.
34. Mahatma Gandhi Murder Case, Statement of Accused in Original, File No. 23, p. 189, NAI, New Delhi.
35. Ibid.
36. Ibid.

Chapter 11: Alibi

1. Mahatma Gandhi Murder Case, Statement of Accused in Original, File No. 23, p. 71, NAI, New Delhi.
2. D.P. Mishra Papers, I & II Inst., Sub. File No. 18, Statement of P.T. Marathe, p. 61, NMML, New Delhi.
3. Ibid., p. 82.
4. Ibid., p. 17.
5. Ibid., p. 104.
6. Mahatma Gandhi Murder Trial Papers, File No. 5, Crime Report No. 12, p. 43, NAI, New Delhi.
7. Mahatma Gandhi Murder Case, Statement of Accused in Original, File No. 23, p. 72, NAI, New Delhi.
8. Statement of Shanta Modak, cited in K.L. Gauba, *The Assassination of Mahatma Gandhi*, Jaico Publishing House, Bombay, 1969, p. 69.
9. Ibid., p. 70.
10. Mahatma Gandhi Murder Case, Statement of Accused in Original, File No. 23, p. 140, NAI, New Delhi.
11. Ibid.
12. Ibid.
13. Ibid., p. 101.
14. Ibid., pp. 101–102.
15. Ibid., p. 141.
16. Ibid.
17. Ibid.
18. Ibid.
19. Mahatma Gandhi Murder Case, Statement of Accused, File No. 47, pp. 71–72, NAI, New Delhi.
20. Ibid., p. 72.
21. Ibid., p. 73.
22. Prof. J.C. Jain, *The Murder of Mahatma Gandhi: Prelude and Aftermath*, Chetana Limited, Bombay, 1961, p. 17.
23. Ibid., p. 18.
24. Mahatma Gandhi Murder Case, Statement of Accused, File No. 47, p. 73, NAI, New Delhi.
25. Mahatma Gandhi Murder Case, Statement of Accused in Original, File No. 23, p. 103, NAI, New Delhi.

26. Ibid.
27. Ibid., p. 73.
28. Ibid., pp. 73–74.
29. Ibid., p. 105.
30. Ibid., p. 107.
31. Ibid.
32. Statement of Dada Maharaj, cited in K.L. Gauba, *The Assassination of Mahatma Gandhi*, Jaico Publishing House, Bombay, 1969, p. 331.

Chapter 12: Reconnaissance

1. Alex Von Tunzelmann, *Indian Summer: The Secret History of the End of an Empire*, Simon & Schuster UK Ltd, London, 2007, pp. 270–271.
2. Foreign Office Files for India, Pakistan and Afghanistan, 1947–1964, Foreign Office, File: FO 371/69729, p. 3, The National Archives, Kew, London.
3. Horace Alexander, *Gandhi through Western Eyes*, Asia Publishing House, New Delhi, 1969, p. 166.
4. Foreign Office Files for India, Pakistan and Afghanistan, 1947–1964, Foreign Office, File: FO 371/69729, p. 4, The National Archives, Kew, London.
5. Pyarelal, *Mahatma Gandhi: The Last Phase, Vol. X*, Navajivan Publishing House, Ahmedabad, 1997, p. 705; Also see Larry Collins and Dominique Lapierre, *Freedom at Midnight*, Vikas Publishing House Pvt Ltd, Delhi, 1975, p. 376.
6. Larry Collins and Dominique Lapierre, *Freedom at Midnight*, Vikas Publishing House Pvt Ltd, Delhi, 1975, pp. 378–379.
7. Pyarelal, *Mahatma Gandhi: The Last Phase, Vol. X*, Navajivan Publishing House, Ahmedabad, 1997, p. 707.
8. Alex Von Tunzelmann, *Indian Summer: The Secret History of the End of an Empire*, Simon & Schuster UK Ltd, London, 2007, pp. 308–309.
9. Ibid., p. 309.
10. Ramachandra Guha, *Gandhi: The Years That Changed the World*, Penguin Random House India, Gurgaon, 2018, p. 869.

11. Pyarelal, *Mahatma Gandhi: The Last Phase, Vol. X*, Navajivan Publishing House, Ahmedabad, 1997, p. 733.
12. Foreign Office Files for India, Pakistan and Afghanistan, 1947–1964, Foreign Office, File: DO 133/93, p. 32, The National Archives, Kew, London.
13. Mahatma Gandhi Murder Case, Statement of Accused in Original, File No. 23, p. 146, NAI, New Delhi.
14. Ibid.
15. Ibid.
16. Ibid., pp. 146–147.
17. Ibid., p. 147.
18. Ibid., p. 148.
19. Ibid., p. 125.
20. Ibid., p. 148.
21. Ibid., p. 70.
22. English translation of Shewanti's letters in Marathi, cited in K.L. Gauba, *The Assassination of Mahatma Gandhi*, Jaico Publishing House, Bombay, 1969, pp. 232–233.
23. Ibid., pp. 233–234.
24. Ibid., p. 234.
25. Mahatma Gandhi Murder Case, Statement of Accused, File No. 47, pp. 74–75, NAI, New Delhi.
26. Ibid., pp. 75–76.
27. Ibid., pp. 76–78.
28. Based on an interview with Sumanbai, an acquaintance of Shewanti till she died in 1988, conducted on 17 October 2019 at Ahmadnagar.

Chapter 13: Simple-minded Hunter

1. Mahatma Gandhi Murder Case, Statements of Accused, File No. 47, p. 79, NAI, New Delhi.
2. Ibid.
3. Mahatma Gandhi Murder Case, Statement of Accused in Original, File No. 23, p. 77, NAI, New Delhi.
4. Ibid., p. 113.
5. Ibid., pp. 113–114.

6. Ibid., p. 114.
7. Ibid.
8. Ibid., p. 115.
9. Ibid., pp. 115–116.
10. Mahatma Gandhi Murder Case, Statements of Accused, File No. 47, p. 82, NAI, New Delhi.
11. Mahatma Gandhi Murder Case, Statement of Accused in Original, File No. 23, p. 78, NAI, New Delhi.
12. Pyarelal, *Mahatma Gandhi: The Last Phase, Vol. X*, Navajivan Publishing House, Ahmedabad, 1997, p. 747.
13. Ibid.
14. Robert Payne, *The Life and Death of Mahatma Gandhi*, Rupa & Co., Calcutta, 1997, pp. 567–568.
15. Ibid., p. 568.
16. Pyarelal, *Mahatma Gandhi: The Last Phase, Vol. X*, Navajivan Publishing House, Ahmedabad, 1997, p. 748.
17. Robert Payne, *The Life and Death of Mahatma Gandhi*, Rupa & Co., Calcutta, 1997, p. 569.
18. Mahatma Gandhi Murder Case, Statement of Accused in Original, File No. 23, p. 78, NAI, New Delhi.
19. Ibid., p. 79.
20. Ibid., p. 118.
21. Ibid.
22. Mahatma Gandhi Murder Case, Statements of Accused, File No. 47, pp. 83–84, NAI, New Delhi.
23. Brijkrishna Chandiwala, *At the Feet of Bapu*, Navajivan Publishing House, Ahmedabad, 1954, p. 244.
24. Pyarelal, *Mahatma Gandhi: The Last Phase, Vol. X*, Navajivan Publishing House, Ahmedabad, 1997, p. 749.
25. Mahatma Gandhi Murder Case, Statements of Accused, File No. 47, p. 85, NAI, New Delhi.
26. Tapan Ghosh, *The Gandhi Murder Trial*, Asia Publishing House, Bombay, 1974, p. 83.
27. Ibid.
28. Mahatma Gandhi Murder Case, Statement of Accused in Original, File No. 23, p. 129, NAI, New Delhi.
29. Ibid.

30. Ibid., p. 119.
31. Ibid.

Chapter 14: Godse Finds His Gun

1. Statement of Gaya Prasad, cited in K.L. Gauba, *The Assassination of Mahatma Gandhi*, Jaico Publishing House, Bombay, 1969, pp. 332–333.
2. Ibid.
3. Mahatma Gandhi Murder Case, Statement of Accused in Original, File No. 23, p. 85, NAI, New Delhi.
4. For details see Ashis Nandy, *At the Edge of Psychology: Essays in Politics and Culture*, Oxford University Press, Delhi, 1980, pp. 70–98.
5. Mahatma Gandhi Murder Case, Statement of Accused in Original, File No. 23, p. 82, NAI, New Delhi.
6. Ibid., p. 85.
7. Tushar A. Gandhi, *'Let's Kill Gandhi': A Chronicle of His Last Days, the Conspiracy, Murder, Investigation and Trial*, Rupa Publications India Pvt. Ltd., New Delhi, 2011, p. 97.
8. Mahatma Gandhi Murder Case, Statement of Accused in Original, File No. 23, p. 154, NAI, New Delhi.
9. Statement of Gaya Prasad, cited in K.L. Gauba, *The Assassination of Mahatma Gandhi*, Jaico Publishing House, Bombay, 1969, pp. 332–333.
10. Mahatma Gandhi Murder Case, Statement of Accused in Original, File No. 23, p. 130, NAI, New Delhi.
11. Ibid., p. 214.
12. Ibid., pp. 214–215.
13. Statement of Dada Maharaj, cited in K.L. Gauba, *The Assassination of Mahatma Gandhi*, Jaico Publishing House, Bombay, 1969, p. 331.
14. Mahatma Gandhi Murder Case, Statement of Accused in Original, File No. 23, p. 155, NAI, New Delhi.
15. Vinayak Chaturvedi, 'Vinayak & Me: Hindutva and the Politics of Naming', *Social History*, Vol. 28, No. 2 (May 2003), p. 163.

16. M.A. Sreenivasan, *Of the Raj, Maharajas and Me*, Ravi Dayal Publisher, Delhi, 1991, pp. 219–220.
17. Mahatma Gandhi Murder Case, Statement of Accused in Original, File No. 23, pp. 86–87, NAI, New Delhi.
18. Ibid., p. 156.
19. Ibid., p. 217.
20. Ibid., p. 218.
21. Ibid., p. 219.
22. Ibid., p. 220.
23. Ibid., p. 221.
24. Tapan Ghosh, *The Gandhi Murder Trial*, Asia Publishing House, Bombay, 1974, pp. 92–93.
25. Mahatma Gandhi Murder Case, Statement of Accused in Original, File No. 23, pp. 89–90, NAI, New Delhi.
26. Ibid., p. 90.
27. Ramchandra Guha, *Gandhi: The Years that Changed the World, 1914–1948*, Penguin Random House India, Gurgaon, 2018, p. 875.
28. Pyarelal, *Mahatma Gandhi: The Last Phase, Vol. X*, Navajivan Publishing House, Ahmedabad, 1997, p. 768.
29. Ibid.
30. Manuben Gandhi, *Last Glimpses of Bapu*, Shiva Lal Agarwala & Co. (P) Ltd., Agra, 1962, p. 301.
31. Pyarelal, *Mahatma Gandhi: The Last Phase, Vol. X,* Navajivan Publishing House, Ahmedabad, 1997, p. 767.
32. Manuben Gandhi, *Last Glimpses of Bapu*, Shiva Lal Agarwala & Co. (P) Ltd., Agra, 1962, pp. 305–306.
33. Ibid., p. 306.

Chapter 15: A Shot Shatters the Winter Evening

1. Mahatma Gandhi Murder Case, Statement of Accused in Original, File No. 23, pp. 157–158, NAI, New Delhi.
2. Ibid., p. 158.
3. Ibid.
4. Ibid., p. 224.
5. Morarji Desai, *The Story of My Life, Vol. One*, Macmillan India, Delhi, 1974, p. 248.

6. Tapan Ghosh, *The Gandhi Murder Trial*, Asia Publishing House, Bombay, 1974, p. 47.
7. Ibid.
8. Based on an interview with ninety-three-year-old Bapusaheb Pujari, who joined the RSS in 1933 at the age of seven under the influence of Kashinath Bhaskar Limaye, in Sangli on 14 October 2019.
9. Narhari N. Kirkire, *Sangliche Diwas (1937–1945)*, N.N. Kirkire (publisher), Satara, 2008, p. 64.
10. M.S. Dixit, *Mi Ma Shri*, Utkarsh Prakashan, Pune, 2004, pp. 63–64.
11. 'Godse Told Friends of Murder Plot', *National Standard*, 1 February 1948.
12. Ibid.
13. Vasudha Ganesh Paranjpe, *Ek Jhunjar Stri: Shantabai Gokhale*, Ram Laxmi Mandal, Pune 2003, p. 122.
14. Craig Baxter, *The Jana Sangh: A Biography of an Indian Political Party*, University of Pennsylvania Press, Philadelphia, 1969, p. 41.
15. Tapan Ghosh, *The Gandhi Murder Trial*, Asia Publishing House, Bombay, 1974, p. 48.
16. Gyanendra Pandey, *Remembering Partition: Violence, Nationalism and History in India*, Cambridge University Press, Cambridge, 2001, p. 145.
17. Gopal Godse, *Gandhiji's Murder & After*, Surya Prakashan, Delhi, 1989, p. 278.
18. Ibid., p. 278.
19. Ibid., p. 279.
20. Ibid., p. 286.
21. Ibid.
22. Vasudha Ganesh Paranjpe, *Ek Jhunjar Stri: Shantabai Gokhale*, Ram Laxmi Mandal, Pune 2003, p. 133.
23. D.P. Mishra Papers, I & II Inst., Sub File No. 18, Statement of Prabhakar Trimbak Marathe, p. 61, NMML, New Delhi.
24. Ibid., p. 63.
25. Craig Baxter, *The Jana Sangh: A Biography of an Indian Political Party*, University of Pennsylvania Press, Philadelphia, 1969, p. 43.

26. 'Assassin not connected with R.S.S.', *Hindustan Times*, 2 February 1948.
27. Dhananjay Keer, *Veer Savarkar*, Popular Prakashan, Bombay, 1988, p. 403.
28. Mahatma Gandhi Murder Trial Papers, File No. 5, Crime Report No. 2, p. 10, NAI, New Delhi.

Chapter 16: The Interrogations

1. 'Story of Brooding Little Fanatic', *Sunday Standard*, 15 February 1948.
2. Medical Examination Report by Dr Gurbakhsh Rai, cited in K.L. Gauba, *The Assassination of Mahatma Gandhi*, Jaico Publishing House, Bombay, 1969, p. 374.
3. Gopal Godse, *Gandhiji's Murder & After*, Surya Prakashan, Delhi, 1989, p. 291.
4. Ibid.
5. Ibid.
6. 'Story of Brooding Little Fanatic', *Sunday Standard*, 15 February 1948.
7. Gopal Godse, *Gandhiji's Murder & After*, Surya Prakashan, Delhi, 1989, p. 291.
8. Ibid.
9. 'Godse Remanded', *National Standard*, 1 February 1948.
10. P.L. Inamdar, *The Story of the Red Fort Trial, 1948–49*, Popular Prakashan, Bombay, 1979, p. 201.
11. Larry Collins and Dominique Lapierre, *Freedom at Midnight*, Vikas Publishing House Pvt Ltd, Delhi, 1976, pp. 416–417.
12. Mahatma Gandhi Murder Trial Papers, File No. 5, Crime Report No. 12, p. 41, NAI, New Delhi.
13. Ibid.
14. Ibid., p. 42.
15. Ibid.; See also Statement of Gaya Prasad, cited in K.L. Gauba, *The Assassination of Mahatma Gandhi*, Jaico Publishing House, Bombay, 1969, p. 333.
16. Mahatma Gandhi Murder Trial Papers, File No. 5, Crime Report No. 13, p. 44, NAI, New Delhi.

17. Mahatma Gandhi Murder Trial Papers, File No. 5, Crime Report No. 14, p. 46.
18. Ibid., p. 47.
19. Ibid., pp. 47–48.
20. Based on interview with a close relative of Manorama Salvi's, conducted on 17 October 2019 at Ahmadnagar. As the interviewee preferred anonymity, the name has not been disclosed.
21. Ibid.
22. Ibid.
23. Ibid.
24. Ibid.
25. Gopal Godse, *Gandhiji's Murder & After*, Surya Prakashan, Delhi, 1989, p. 298.
26. Ibid., p. 299.
27. Ibid., p. 298.
28. Mahatma Gandhi Murder Trial Papers, File No. 5, Crime Report No. 30, p. 90, NAI, New Delhi.
29. Gopal Godse, *Gandhiji's Murder & After*, Surya Prakashan, Delhi, 1989, p. 299.
30. D.P. Mishra Papers, I & II Inst., Sub File No. 18, Progress Report No. 12, pp. 83–84, Records Section, NMML, New Delhi.
31. See for details D.P. Mishra Papers, I & II Inst., Sub File No. 18, Records Section, NMML, New Delhi.
32. Ibid., pp. 15–18.
33. Gopal Godse, *Gandhiji's Murder & After*, Surya Prakashan, Delhi, 1989, p. 299.
34. Tushar A. Gandhi, *'Let's Kill Gandhi': A Chronicle of His Last Days, the Conspiracy, Murder, Investigation and Trial*, Rupa Publications India Pvt. Ltd., New Delhi, 2011, p. 536.

Chapter 17: The Assassin Is Tried

1. P.L. Inamdar, *The Story of the Red Fort Trial, 1948–49*, Popular Prakashan, Bombay, 1979, p. 23.
2. Ibid., p. 141.

3. Tushar A. Gandhi, *'Let's Kill Gandhi': A Chronicle of His Last Days, the Conspiracy, Murder, Investigation and Trial*, Rupa Publications India Pvt. Ltd., New Delhi, 2011, p. 539.
4. Gopal Godse, *Gandhiji's Murder & After*, Surya Prakashan, Delhi, 1989, pp. 125–126.
5. Ibid., p. 142.
6. Ibid., pp. 142–143.
7. Ibid., pp. 143–144.
8. Ibid., p. 143.
9. P.L. Inamdar, *The Story of the Red Fort Trial, 1948–49*, Popular Prakashan, Bombay, 1979, p. 197.
10. Gopal Godse, *Why I Assassinated Mahatma Gandhi?*, Surya Bharti Parkashan, Delhi, 1993, p. 16.
11. Ibid., p. 21.
12. Ibid., p. 102.
13. 'He did not leave the RSS', *Frontline*, 28 January 1994.
14. Ibid., p. 25.
15. Ibid., p. 118.
16. Tapan Ghosh, *The Gandhi Murder Trial*, Asia Publishing House, New Delhi, 1974, pp. 280–281.
17. Tushar A. Gandhi, *'Let's Kill Gandhi': A Chronicle of His Last Days, the Conspiracy, Murder, Investigation and Trial*, Rupa Publications India Pvt. Ltd., New Delhi, 2011, p. 692.
18. P.L. Inamdar, *The Story of the Red Fort Trial, 1948–49*, Popular Prakashan, Bombay, 1979, p. 25.
19. Ibid., p. 141.
20. Ibid., pp. 141–142.
21. Ibid., 143.
22. Gopal Godse, *Why I Assassinated Mahatma Gandhi?*, Surya Bharti Parkashan, Delhi, 1993, p. 338.
23. Ibid.
24. Ibid., pp. 339–340.
25. P.L. Inamdar, *The Story of the Red Fort Trial, 1948–49*, Popular Prakashan, Bombay, 1979, p. 203.
26. Ibid.
27. Ibid., p. 206.

28. G.D. Khosla, *The Murder of the Mahatma And Other Cases from a Judge's Note-book*, Chatto & Windus, London, 1963, p. 243.
29. Ibid., p. 214.
30. Ibid., p. 243.
31. Ibid.
32. Robert Payne, *The Life and Death of Mahatma Gandhi*, Rupa & Co., Calcutta, 1997, p. 643.
33. P.L. Inamdar, *The Story of the Red Fort Trial, 1948–49*, Popular Prakashan, Bombay, 1979, p. 206.
34. Nathuram Godse's letter to Ramdas Gandhi, cited in Robert Payne, *The Life and Death of Mahatma Gandhi*, Rupa & Co., Calcutta, 1997, pp. 643–644.
35. Gopal Godse, *Why I Assassinated Mahatma Gandhi?*, Surya Bharti Parkashan, Delhi, 1993, p. 349.
36. Robert Payne, *The Life and Death of Mahatma Gandhi*, Rupa & Co., Calcutta, 1997, p. 644.
37. Ibid.
38. Ibid., p. 645.
39. Tapan Ghosh, *The Gandhi Murder Trial*, Asia Publishing House, New Delhi, 1974, p. 300.
40. Gopal Godse, *Why I Assassinated Mahatma Gandhi?*, Surya Bharti Parkashan, Delhi, 1993, p. 347.

Chapter 18: The Gallows

1. The *Leader*, 26 June 1949.
2. The *Times of India*, 'Granting Clemency to Godse, 31 October 1949, p. 9.
3. The *Tribune*, 'Thate to Fast in Front of Ambala Jail', 7 November 1949.
4. File No. 119–10 (II), Letter No. 12466–67, Ambala Division of Haryana State Archives, Ambala.
5. File No. 119–10 (II), Letter No. 763–S.T., Ambala Division of Haryana State Archives, Ambala.
6. Nathuram Godse's letter to Dattatreya Vinayak Godse, cited in Gopal Godse, *Why I Assassinated Gandhi?*, Surya Bharti Prakashan, Delhi, 1993, p. 188.

7. Ibid.
8. Ibid.
9. Ibid.
10. Ibid.
11. Gopal Godse, *Gandhiji's Murder & After*, Surya Prakashan, Delhi, 1989, pp. 14–141.
12. The *Times of India*, 'Godse & Apte Executed, 16 November 1949, p. 5.
13. Gopal Godse, *Gandhiji's Murder & After*, op. cit., p. 139.
14. Ibid., p. 160.
15. G.D. Khosla, *The Murder of the Mahatma and Other Cases from a Judge's Note-book*, Chatto & Windus, London, 1963. P. 244.
16. Ibid., p. 245.
17. Ibid.

Author's Note

1. D.V. Kelkar, 'The R.S.S.', *Economic Weekly*, 4 February 1950, p. 133.
2. Ibid., p. 132.

Bibliography

Archival Materials and Reports

B.S. Moonje Papers, Nehru Memorial Museum and Library (NMML), New Delhi.

D.P. Mishra Papers, NMML, New Delhi.

Gandhi Murder Trial Papers, National Archives of India (NAI), New Delhi.

Hindu Mahasabha Papers, NMML, New Delhi

N.B. Khare Papers, NAI, New Delhi.

N.B. Khare: Oral History Transcripts, NMML, New Delhi.

Sardar Patel Papers, NAI, New Delhi.

Delhi Police Record, V & IX Installments, NMML, New Delhi.

File No. F–3–53, Home Political–I, 1942, Repository II, NAI, New Delhi.

File No. 190–P (S), 1943, Home Department (Political), Government of India, NAI, New Delhi.

File No. 28/5/46–Pol (I): Home Department, Government of India, NAI, New Delhi.

Government of India, Home Department (Political), File No. 220–P/42 (Sec), 1942, NAI, New Delhi.

Government of India, Home Department (Political), File No. 88/33, 1933, NAI, New Delhi.

Government of India, Home Department (Political), File No. 28/3/43, NAI, New Delhi.

Foreign Office Files for India, Pakistan and Afghanistan, 1947–1964, Foreign Office, Files: FO 371/69729 & DO 133/93, The National Archives, Kew, London.

Haryana State Archives, Ambala Division, File No. 119–10 (II), Ambala.

Justice J.L. Kapur, Report of Commission of Inquiry in to Conspiracy to Murder Mahatma Gandhi, Part–I & II, New Delhi: Government of India, 1969.

The Collected Works of Mahatma Gandhi, Volumes XXXIII and IX, The Publications Division, Government of India, Delhi.

Newspapers

Kesari, 5 July 1940.

National Standard, 1 February 1948.

New York Herald Tribune, 1 February 1948.

Hindustan Times, 31 January 1948.

Hindustan Times, 2 February 1948.

National Standard, 1 February 1948.

Sunday Standard, 15 February 1948.

The *Leader*, 26 June 1949.

The *Mahratta*, 23 May 1947.

The *Times of India*, 27 December 1938.

The *Times of India*, 23 July 1944.

The *Times of India*, 24 July 1948.

The *Times of India*, 31 October 1949.

The *Times of India*, 16 November 1949.

The *Tribune*, 7 November 1949.

Books and Periodicals

Alex Von Tunzelmann, *Indian Summer: The Secret History of the End of an Empire*, Simon & Schuster UK Ltd., London, 2007.

Antony Copley, *Religions in Conflict: Ideology, Cultural Contact and Conversion in Late Colonial India*, Oxford University Press, Delhi, 1997.

A.S. Bhide (ed.), *Whirlwind Propaganda: Extracts from President's Diary of His Propagandist Tours, Interviews from December 1937 to October 1941*, All India Hindu Mahasabha, Bombay, 1941.

Ashis Nandy, *Regimes of Narcissism, Regimes of Despair*, Oxford University Press, New Delhi, 2013.

Ashis Nandy, *At the Edge of Psychology: Essays in Politics and Culture*, Oxford University Press, Delhi, 1980.

A.G. Noorani, 'Savarkar & the BJP', *Frontline*, 17 January 2020, vol. 37, Number 01.

A.G. Noorani, *Savarkar and Hindutva: The Godse Connection*, LeftWord Books, New Delhi, 2015.

Balraj Madhok, *R.S.S. and Politics*, Hindu World Publications, Delhi, 1980.

Bipin Chandra, *Communalism in Modern India*, Vikas Publishing House, Delhi, 1987.

Brijkrishna Chandiwala, *At the Feet of Bapu*, Navajivan Publishing House, Ahmedabad, 1954.

B.V. Deshpande and S.R. Ramaswamy, *Dr Hedgewar The Epoch-Maker: A Biography*, Sahitya Sindhu, Bangalore, 1981.

Chetan Bhatt, *Hindu Nationalism: Origins, Ideologies and Modern Myths*, Berg, Oxford-New York, 2001.

Chitragupta, *Life of Barrister Savarkar*, Veer Savarkar Prakashan, Bombay, 1987, (first published in December 1926).

C.H. Philips and Mary Doreen Wainwright (ed.), *The Partition of India: Policies and Perspectives 1935–1947*, George Allen and Unwin Ltd, London, 1970.

Colonel L.W. Shakespear, *A Local History of Poona and its Battlefields*, Macmillan and Co. Limited, London, 1916.

C.P. Bhishikar, *Dr. Hedgewar: The Master Man-Maker*, Jagarana Prakashana, Bangalore, 1989.

Craig Baxter, *The Jana Sangh: A Biography of an Indian Political Party*, University of Pennsylvania Press, Philadelphia, 1969.

Christophe Jaffrelot, *The Hindu Nationalist Movement and Indian Politics 1925 to the 1990s: Strategies of Identity-Building, Implantation and Mobilisation*, Viking Penguin India, Delhi, 1996.

C.V. Mathew, *The Saffron Mission: A Historical Analysis of Modern Hindu Missionary Ideologies and Practices*, Indian Society for Promoting Christian Knowledge, Delhi, 1999.

David Ludden (ed.), *Making India Hindu: Religion, Community and the Politics of Democracy in India*, Oxford University Press, Delhi, 1996.

D.E.U. Baker, *Changing Political Leadership in an Indian Province: The Central Provinces and Berar 1919–1939*, Oxford University Press, Delhi, 1979.

D.G. Tendulkar, *Mahatma: Life of Mohandas Karamchand Gandhi, Volume Eight*, The Publications Division, New Delhi, 1963.

Dhananjay Keer, *Veer Savarkar*, Popular Prakashan, Bombay, 1966.

Dhananjay Keer, *Savarkar and His Times*, Published by A.V. Keer, 1950.

Dhirendra K. Jha, 'The Apostle of Hate', The *Caravan*, vol. 12, Issue 1, January 2020.

D.P. Karmarkar, *Bal Gangadhar Tilak: A Study*, Popular Book Depot, Bombay, 1956.

D.R. Goyal, *Rashtriya Swayamsevak Sangh*, Radhakrishna Prakashan, Delhi, 1979.

D.S. Harshe, *Adarsh Hindu Sanghatak: Ka. Bha. Limaye*, published by Sudha Dattatreya Harshe, Satara, 1981.

D.V. Kelkar, 'The R.S.S.', *Economic Weekly*, 4 February 1950

G.D. Khosla, *The Murder of the Mahatma And Other Cases from a Judge's Note-book*, Chatto & Windus, London, 1963.

Gopal Godse, *Why I Assassinated Mahatma Gandhi?*, Surya Bharti Parkashan, Delhi, 1993.

Gopal Godse, *Gandhiji's Murder & After*, Surya Parkashan, Delhi, 1989.

Gyanendra Pandey, *Remembering Partition: Violence, Nationalism and History in India*, Cambridge University Press, Cambridge, 2001.

Horace Alexander, *Gandhi through Western Eyes*, Asia Publishing House, New Delhi, 1969.

Ian Copland, '"Communalism" in Princely India: The Case of Hyderabad, 1930–1940', *Modern Asian Studies*, vol. 22, No. 4, 1988.

Indra Prakash, *A Review of the History and Work of the Hindu Mahasabha and the Hindu Sanghatan Movement*, Dharmarajya Press, Delhi, 1952.

Indulal Yagnik, *Shyamaji Krishnavarma: Life and Times of an Indian Revolutionary*, Lakshmi Publications, Bombay, 1950.

Jagat S. Bright, *Guruji Golwalkar & R.S.S.*, New India Publishing House, Delhi, 1950.

Jawaharlal Nehru, *An Autobiography*, The Bodley Head, London, 1958.

Jawaharlal Nehru, *The Discovery of India*, Penguin Books India, New Delhi, 2008.

J.A. Curran, Jr., *Militant Hinduism in Indian Politics: A Study of the R.S.S.*, Institute of Pacific Relations, New York, 1951.

J.E. Llewellyn, *The Arya Samaj as a Fundamentalist Movement: A Study in Comparative Fundamentalism*, Manohar, Delhi, 1993.

J. Natarajan, *History of Indian Journalism*, Publications Division, New Delhi, 1955.

K.K. Gangadharan, *Sociology of Revivalism: A Study of Indianisation, Sanskritisation and Golwalkarism*, Kalamkar Prakashan, Delhi, 1970.

K.L. Gauba, *The Assassination of Mahatma Gandhi*, Jaico Publishing House, Bombay, 1969.

K.L. Panjabi, *The Indomitable Sardar*, Bharatiya Vidya Bhavan, Bombay, 1964.

K.N. Panikkar, *Communalism in India: History, Politics and Culture*, Manohar, Delhi, 1991.

K.R. Malkani, *The RSS Story*, Impex India, Delhi, 1980.

Larry Collins and Dominique Lapierre, *Freedom at Midnight*, Vikas Publishing House Pvt Ltd, Delhi, 1976.

Louis Fischer, *The Life of Mahatma Gandhi*, Jonathan Cape, London, 1951.

M.A. Sreenivasan, *Of the Raj, Maharajas and Me*, Ravi Dayal Publisher, Delhi, 1991.

Manuben Gandhi, *Last Glimpses of Bapu*, Shiva Lal Agarwala & Co. (P) Ltd., Agra, 1962, p. 308.

Marzia Casolari, 'Hindutva's Foreign Tie-up in the 1930s: Archival Evidence', *Economic and Political Weekly*, 22 January 2000.

Maulana Abul Kalam Azad, *India Wins Freedom*, Orient Longman, Bombay, 1955.

Michael Edwards, *The Last Years of British India*, World Publishing Company, New York, 1965.

M.J. Akbar, *India: The Siege Within*, Penguin Books India, New Delhi, 1985.

Morarji Desai, *The Story of My Life, Volume 1*, Macmillan India, Delhi, 1974.

M.S. Dixit, *Mi, Ma. Shri*, Utkarsh Prakashan, Pune, 2004.

M.S. Golwalkar, *We or Our Nationhood Defined*, Bharat Prakashan, Nagpur, 1947.

Mushirul Hasan, *Nationalism and Communal Politics in India 1885–1930*, Manohar, Delhi, 1991.

Myron Weiner, *Party Politics in India: The Development of a Multi-Party System*, Princeton University Press, Princeton, 1957.

Narhari N. Kirkire, *Sangliche Diwas (1937–1945)*, N.N. Kirkire (publisher), Satara, 2008.

Neela Vasant Upadhye (ed.), *D.V. Gokhale: Vyaktitva Va Krititva*, Navachaitanya Prakashan, Mumbai, 2013.

N.G. Dixit (ed.), *Dharmaveer Dr. B.S. Moonje Commemoration Volume*, Centenary Celebration Committee, Nagpur, 1973.

N.H. Palkar (ed.), *Dr. Hedgewar: Patraroop-Vyaktidarshan*, Archana Prakashan, Indore, 1989.

Nilanjan Mukhopadhyay, *The RSS: Icons of the Indian Right*, Tranquebar, Chennai, 2019.

Papia Chakravarty, *Hindu Response to Nationalist Ferment*, Subarnarekha, Calcutta, 1992.

P.L. Inamdar, *The Story of the Red Fort Trial, 1948–49*, Popular Prakashan, Bombay, 1979.

Prof. J.C. Jain, *The Murder of Mahatma Gandhi: Prelude and Aftermath*, Chetana Limited, Bombay, 1961.

Pyarelal, Mahatma Gandhi: *The Last Phase*, *Volume X*, Navajivan Publishing House, Ahmedabad, 1997.

Rajendra Prasad, *At the Feet of Mahatma Gandhi*, Asia Publishing House, Bombay 1961.

Rajendra Prasad, *Satyagraha in Champaran*, Navajivan Publishing House, Ahmedabad, 1949.

Ramchandra Guha, *Gandhi: The Years that Changed the World, 1914–1948*, Penguin Random House India, Gurgaon, 2018.

Ramnarayan Choudhary, *Bapu as I Saw Him*, Navajivan Publishing House, Ahmedabad, 1959.

Robert Payne, *The Life and Death of Mahatma Gandhi*, Rupa & Co., Calcutta, 1997.

S.H. Deshpande, *My Days in the RSS*, *Quest*, July–August 1975.

Shri Prakash Narhar Godse (editor and publisher), *Godse Kulvritant*, Mumbai, 2006.

S.K. Biswas, *Hindu Raj: Today-Yesterday-Tomorrow*, Orion Books, Bangalore, 1996.

Sumit Sarkar, *Modern India: 1885–1947*, Macmillan India Limited, New Delhi, 1983.

Tapan Ghosh, *The Gandhi Murder Trial*, Asia Publishing House, New Delhi, 1974.

Trailokya Nath Chakraborty, *Thirty Years in Prison: Sensational Confessions of Revolutionary*, Alpha-Beta Publications, Calcutta, 1963.

Tushar A. Gandhi, *'Let's Kill Gandhi': A Chronicle of His Last Days, the Conspiracy, Murder, Investigation and Trial*, Rupa Publications India Pvt. Ltd., New Delhi, 2011.

Vaibhav Purandare, *Savarkar: The True Story of the Father of Hindutva*, Juggernaut Books, New Delhi, 2019.

Valmiki Choudhary, *Dr. Rajendra Prasad: Correspondence and Select Documents, Volume X*, Allied Publishers Private Limited, Delhi, 1988.

Vasudev Balwant Gogate, *Hotson-Gogate: Atmavritta*, published by Anil Vasudev Gogate, Pune, 2006.

Vasudha Ganesh Paranjpe, *Ek Jhunjar Stri: Shantabai Gokhale*, Ram Laxmi Mandal, Pune, 2003.

V.D. Savarkar, *The Story of My Transportation for Life*, Sadbhakti Publications, Bombay, 1950.

V.D. Savarkar, *Hindutva: Who is a Hindu?*, Hindi Sahitya Sadan, New Delhi, 2005.

Vinayak Damodar Savarkar, *Samagra Savarkar Vangmaya, Volume 6*, Hindu Mahasabha, Poona, 1963.

Vinayak Chaturvedi, 'Vinayak & Me: Hindutva and the Politics of Naming', *Social History*, vol. 28, No. 2 (May 2003).

V.N. Datta, *Madan Lal Dhingra and the Revolutionary Movement*, Vikas Publishing House Pvt Ltd, New Delhi, 1978.

Walter K. Andersen and Shridhar D. Damle, *The Brotherhood in Saffron: The Rashtriya Swayamsevak Sangh and Hindu Revivalism*, Westerview Press, Boulder and London, 1987.

Yasmin Khan, *The Great Partition: The Making of India and Pakistan*, Penguin Books India, New Delhi, 2007.

Index